GOING TO WAR?

Going to War?

Trends in Military Interventions

EDITED BY
STÉFANIE VON HLATKY
AND
H. CHRISTIAN BREEDE

McGill-Queen's University Press
Montreal & Kingston · London · Chicago

© McGill-Queen's University Press 2016

ISBN 978-0-7735-4757-5 (cloth)
ISBN 978-0-7735-4758-2 (paper)
ISBN 978-0-7735-9932-1 (ePDF)
ISBN 978-0-7735-9933-8 (ePUB)

Legal deposit second quarter 2016
Bibliothèque nationale du Québec

Printed in Canada on acid-free paper that is 100% ancient forest free
(100% post-consumer recycled), processed chlorine free

This book has been published with the help of a grant from the
Canadian Federation for the Humanities and Social Sciences, through
the Awards to Scholarly Publications Program, using funds provided by
the Social Sciences and Humanities Research Council of Canada.

McGill-Queen's University Press acknowledges the support of the
Canada Council for the Arts for our publishing program. We also
acknowledge the financial support of the Government of Canada
through the Canada Book Fund for our publishing activities.

Library and Archives Canada Cataloguing in Publication

Going to war? : trends in military interventions / edited by Stéfanie
von Hlatky and H. Christian Breede.

Includes bibliographical references and index.
Issued in print and electronic formats.
ISBN 978-0-7735-4757-5 (cloth). – ISBN 978-0-7735-4758-2 (paper). –
ISBN 978-0-7735-9932-1 (PDF). – ISBN 978-0-7735-9933-8 (ePUB)

1. War – Decision making. 2. Intervention (International law). 3.
Canada – Military policy – Decision making. 4. United States – Military
policy – Decision making. I. Von Hlatky, Stéfanie, 1982–, editor II.
Breede, H. Christian author, editor

UA600.G65 2016   355'.033071   C2016-903068-7
                                     C2016-903069-5

Typeset by New Leaf Publication Design in 10.5/13 Baskerville

Contents

Tables and Figures

Acronyms and Abbreviations

AAG	Afghan Assessment Group
ABCA	American, British, Canadian, Australian, and New Zealand allies
AFL	Armed Forces of Liberia
ANSF	Afghan National Security Forces
APSA	African Peace and Security Architecture
ASF	African Standby Force
AU	African Union
AVF	all-volunteer force
AWACS	Airborne Warning and Control System
BRIC	Brazil, Russia, India, and China
BRS	Brown & Root Services
C4ISR	command, control, communications, computers, intelligence, surveillance, and reconnaissance
CAAT	COIN Advisory and Assistance Team
CAF	Canadian Armed Forces
CAG	Commander's Action Group
CDAI	Conference of Defence Associations Institute
CFDS	Canada First Defence Strategy
CGD	civilian government departments
CJ2	Combined Joint Intelligence staff
CJIATF–435	Combined Joint Interagency Task Force–435
CJIATF–Shafafiyat	Combined Joint Interagency Task Force–Shafafiyat
COIN	counter-insurgency
COMISAF	Commander International Security Assistance Force
CREW	counter radio-controlled IED electronic warfare
CRS	Congressional Research Service

CSDP	Common Security and Defence Policy
CT	counterterrorism
CT ratio	casualty troop ratio
DARPA	Defense Advanced Research Projects Agency
DPS	Defence Policy Statement
EOD	explosive ordnance disposal
EU	European Union
EUPOL COPPS	European Union Police Coordinating Office for Palestinian Police Support
GOC	government of Canada
GIROA	government of the Islamic Republic of Afghanistan
HMMWV	high-mobility multi-purpose wheeled vehicle
IED	improvised explosive device
IJC	ISAF Joint Command
IS	Islamic State
ISAF	International Security Assistance Force
ISR	intelligence, surveillance, and reconnaissance
J2	Deputy Chief of Staff Intelligence
JFC	Joint Forces Command
JIEDDO	Joint IED Defeat Organization
JSTARS	Joint Surveillance Target Acquisition Radar System
KBR	Kellogg Brown & Root
LAV	light-armoured vehicles
LOO	lines of operation
MENA	Middle East and North Africa
MESF	Middle East Stabilization Force
MIPS	Military Intervention by Powerful States
MPRI	Military Professional Resources Incorporated
MRAP	mine-resistant ambush-protected
NATO	North Atlantic Treaty Organization
NCO	non-commissioned officer
NGO	non-governmental organization
NORAD	North American Aerospace Defence
NTM-A	NATO Training Mission–Afghanistan
NVA	North Vietnamese Army
OCO	Overseas Contingency Operations
OECD	Organization for Economic Co-operation and Development
OEF	Operation Enduring Freedom
OIF	Operation Iraqi Freedom

OND	Operation New Dawn
OUP	Operation Unified Protector
PASF	Palestinian Authority Security Forces
PSO	peace support operations
R2P	Responsibility to Protect
RAF	Royal Air Force
RCS	Regional Commands
RCAF	Royal Canadian Air Force
RCN	Royal Canadian Navy
RC-S	Regional Command-South
RC-SW	Regional Command-Southwest
RMA	Revolution in Military Affairs
RPG	rocket-propelled grenade
SCR	senior civilian representative
SIGIR	Special Inspector General for Iraqi Reconstruction
SOF	special operations forces
UAS	unmanned aircraft system
UAV	unmanned aerial vehicle
UN	United Nations
USAFRICOM	United States African Command
USCENTCOM	United States Central Command
USAF	United States Air Force
USFOR-A	US Forces-Afghanistan
VC	Viet Cong
WMD	weapons of mass destruction

Preface

Like most contributions to the field of security studies, this book was written in reaction to events. We convened a number of experts to take part in a workshop at the Centre for International and Defence Policy to consider several significant questions. First, Canada's withdrawal from the Afghanistan War prompted us to ask: what's next? Second, under what conditions would Canada commit to another sizable deployment in the future? Based on our assessment, which sought to bridge the civilian–military divide, the answer was unclear and certainly warranted more research. The contributors to this edited volume, a diverse group of university professors, defence scientists, senior military officers from several different countries, and former senior Canadian public servants, rose to the challenge and produced a thought-provoking collection. In answering questions about *Going to War*, the volume reflects a diversity of views and perspectives. Moreover, we have witnessed a number of the authors' predictions play out since the time of writing. One of these predictions is that Canadian interventions post-Afghanistan will be small in size, limited in scope, and far from the minds of everyday Canadians. Gone are the Red Fridays that typified the home front of the last decade or so. Starting in the mid-2000s, local groups started encouraging people to wear red clothing on Fridays as a sign of support for Canadian soldiers. Red Fridays caught on and – particularly in communities close to Canadian military bases – people started wearing red T-shirts on Fridays each week. Moreover, the "Highway of Heroes" – the route from the airforce base in Trenton to the Ontario Coroner's Office in downtown Toronto – is simply a series of signs on an otherwise jam-packed limited-access highway. Canada's new "wars" – efforts against the Islamic State in Iraq and Syria being a case in point – are limited to training, special operations forces, and air strikes. Canada is engaged but keenly aware of the political costs of caskets and perceptions of failure. With the election of a Liberal government under Justin Trudeau's leadership, our expectations remain the same, as political decision makers will continue to address threats through the prism of limited political capabilities and a risk-averse public, when it comes to military engagement.

Throughout this book, we have chosen the term *9/11 Wars* to refer to the conflicts in Afghanistan and Iraq, which started in 2001 and 2003 respectively, rather than the more common term *global war on terror*. The label *9/11 Wars* is one that we find more neutral and descriptive, absent the normative challenges that sometimes are associated with the term *global war on terror*. However, the term is not our own; rather, it comes from a 2011 book by Jason Burke called *The 9/11 Wars*. His title is clear and to the point and we feel it describes the events that characterized the early part of this new century without any normative overtones.

We are deeply grateful to all contributors for their insights, and there are many others who also supported this project. Sincere thanks goes to Maureen Bartram, the administrator of the Centre for International and Defence Policy at Queen's University, as well as several research assistants: Chris Cowan, Sam Kary, Claire Gummo, Meaghan Shoemaker, and most importantly, Jeffrey Rice, who co-organized the workshop. Finally, we would like to thank our families. Our respective partners in life, Michelle Breede and Phillippe Lacoursière, have shown unwavering support and encouragement throughout our careers. Our children continue to be a source of inspiration and energy. Without you all, this book would not have been possible.

Stéfanie von Hlatky and H. Christian Breede
March 2016

GOING TO WAR?

INTRODUCTION

Military Interventions:
Threats, Capabilities, and Responses

STÉFANIE VON HLATKY

In March 2014, Canada withdrew its last troops from Afghanistan, putting an end to its almost thirteen-year-long commitment. After the terrorist attacks of 11 September 2001, Canada joined a coalition of allies with the United States to hunt down al Qaeda in Afghanistan, to overthrow the Taliban regime, and eventually, to pursue more holistic security objectives, including humanitarian goals.[1] Imposing stability throughout the Afghan territory while pushing for economic and social development became the difficult balancing act of the International Security Assistance Force (ISAF), which was created in December 2001 and came under North Atlantic Treaty Organization (NATO) leadership in 2003. US-led combat operations continued under the banner of Operation Enduring Freedom (OEF). From an alliance perspective, the war in Afghanistan embodied a level of sustained interstate coordination that had never been seen before, with strong coordination efforts from NATO's operational headquarters and US Central Command (USCENTCOM).[2] NATO's twenty-eight member states, joined by a significant number of other partner countries, pooled their resources and military personnel, perfecting the skill of working as a coalition.

From both Canadian and allied perspectives, then, the period since 2001 has been characterized by sustained engagement of their military forces abroad. The successes that seemed to have been achieved in Afghanistan, but also in Iraq, where the United States was leading a concurrent intervention, were steadily reversed as the governments in Kabul and Baghdad proved unable to protect civilian populations and provide basic services to the entire territory. These governments were also plagued by corruption that hampered development efforts. Attacks by extremists are endemic to the security preoccupations of both countries, where trillions of dollars have been invested by the US and its allies and thousands of lives lost.

Less than a year after the Canadian withdrawal from Afghanistan in 2014, Prime Minister Stephen Harper announced a new commitment, this time in Iraq, to bomb the strongholds of the Islamic State (IS), a terrorist network that capitalized on the power vacuums in Iraq and Syria. The rise of IS has also led to a troubling trend: the participation of Western citizens to support IS efforts in Iraq and Syria, the so-called war tourists or extremist travellers. The social media campaign launched by IS has also encouraged its followers to perpetrate attacks on Western soil, to punish the states who support the US-led operation, code-named Operation Inherent Resolve (Operation Impact in Canada). Although direct causality is difficult to establish, "lone-wolf" terrorist attacks were perpetrated in Canada and elsewhere, bringing the threat closer to home.

Challenged by these developments, states are coordinating a response at both the domestic and international levels, increasing their counterterrorism efforts but also designing policies meant to curtail individuals from travelling to Syria and Iraq to join the IS fight, or to prevent them from returning home if they participated in terrorist activities abroad.[3] These events remind us that military drawdowns must be managed carefully, because an imperfect transfer of security responsibilities to national authorities can unravel quickly.

The wars in Afghanistan and Iraq, symbolizing a war-intensive decade, seem very different from the operations now being conducted in Iraq and Syria. In all instances, there is no clear model of success on which politicians or military planners can rely. What is vexing is that the United States, Canada, and their allies should be at the top of their game, given the pace of military interventions in the recent past. Why is military intervention, then, so unpredictable and prone to indecisive outcomes? How can we apply the lessons and skills acquired from the 9/11 Wars to direct future military action abroad? This edited volume attempts to offer perspectives on how nations perceive and respond to threats, how they mobilize capabilities in support of their efforts, and how military interventions abroad affect domestic populations and alliance politics. Can lessons be drawn from thirteen years of military co-operation in Afghanistan or is the ISAF model of intervention best understood as a unique occurrence? What about Iraq and Libya? The United States and its allies have certainly gained valuable experience in terms of improving military coordination over this period, but can this be replicated in another context?[4]

This book gathers viewpoints from academics, government, and the military to discuss possible trends in military interventions, considering the post-2014 security environment. The contributors to this volume focused on a common set of questions:

- Is the threshold for military intervention higher in today's war-weary political climate? What are the potential trigger points for Canada and its allies when considering the use of force?
- How will regional security concerns and alliance priorities impact the ranking of international priorities for Canada, the United States, or Europe?
- What are the implications of defence budget cuts for future military capabilities and overall capacity?
- Has the NATO experience in Afghanistan and elsewhere led to changes in how military interventions and allied coordination take place?

The rest of this chapter discusses some of the core themes that were identified by the contributors and offers some policy prescriptions to address the strategic uncertainty that inevitably follows massive military drawdowns.[5] A stated goal of this edited collection is to marry the viewpoints of both academics and practitioners. This attempt to bridge the gap between these two communities is in line with an emerging research trend that favours multi-sector partnerships in order to infuse practical security concerns in the research activities of scholars.[6] The participation of stakeholders in the research process is a fruitful strategy to advance knowledge. *Going to War* represents a test of this framework, with collaborators from Queen's University's Centre for International and Defence Policy, the Royal Military College of Canada, the Canadian Department of National Defence, the Canadian Armed Forces, the German Armed Forces, and the US Army. Given the diversity of views represented in this volume, the discussion on threats, responses, capabilities, and trends produced a rich debate. Before exploring these themes further, an overview of the scholarly literature on alliance politics and military interventions is warranted.

DEBATES IN THE LITERATURE

The 9/11 Wars were decidedly multinational. Appropriately, the wars in Afghanistan and Iraq generated a lot of research questions in the field of alliance theory and international relations, from questions on the sustainability of American hegemony to burden-sharing within coalitions. This volume attempts to integrate insights from the last decade to make predictions about what we can expect in the next decade. In other words, the contributions are focused on a timeframe that goes beyond explanations of current interventions, but that is also more circumscribed than war-gaming or "futures" exercises as conducted in Western militaries. This struck the authors as the missing link in the existing literature on the use of force.

In the scholarly literature on military alliances, recent research has focused on the political constraints faced by governments during military interventions, outlining how domestic factors interacted with alliance politics to produce different patterns of military co-operation.[7] Indeed, as major interstate war appears unlikely in the short to medium term, more scholarly work has been devoted to alliance- and coalition-led military interventions and thus, the two-level negotiation game where states must reconcile the demands of allies with domestic political constraints.[8] This is a theme that is discussed throughout the book, as the public and civil society organizations increasingly scrutinize foreign and defence policy decisions. The democratization of international policy-making on the part of world democracies has received considerable attention in the literature since the end of the Cold War.[9] The need to sustain public consent throughout the war in Afghanistan, for example, was a challenge felt acutely in states with minority governments or coalition governments, where the merits of the mission were most vehemently challenged.[10]

Another theme in the literature on alliance politics deals more directly with the machinery behind the management of multinational military operations. Sarah Kreps, for instance, stresses the importance of qualitative indicators to assess the extent to which multilateralism is participatory and inclusive of coalition partners.[11]

While the US-led Operation Iraqi Freedom (OIF) had an impressive number of participating countries, the dynamics of multilateralism were rather superficial, with the exception of highly interoperable countries such as the United Kingdom and Australia. Smaller but more integrated coalitions that also benefit from institutional backing at the international level, as was the case with Operation Unified Protector in Libya, lend support to Kreps's argument: more is not necessarily better.

Other authors, like Peter W. Singer also acknowledge that certain clusters of countries, primarily those that share similar and high-end military technology, will work more effectively as part of a coalition.[12] Technological interoperability has been a major argument in support of large procurement programs, even controversial ones like the F-35.[13] Technology, however, is just one aspect of interoperability. As Michael Horowitz notes, technological innovation leads to organizational changes with implications for interstate interactions, including allied military co-operation.[14] Organizational culture, then, is as important as technology to understand the coordination of multinational efforts.

Indeed, managing differences in norms, culture, and training can be just as daunting for allied military co-operation as technological gaps.[15] There is a growing interest in research that examines human interoperability as a key determinant of military effectiveness. In other words, it is not just a matter of which states have overwhelming capabilities and superior technology; it is about how that military might translates into force employment.[16] An additional layer of complexity is added when national force-employment strategies coexist as part of allied operations. As Patricia Weitsman notes, while an alliance confers clear benefits by pooling resources from a group of countries, it also adds an institutional layer to operational design.[17] Having more players does not necessarily increase military effectiveness, an argument which echoes Kreps's work.[18]

The contributions included in this book build on the above themes and investigate the foreign and defence policy trade-offs at the heart of allied military operations. Together, the arguments bring nuance to some of the claims made in the literature and by policy-makers about the lopsided nature of US-led military co-operation, showing that American foreign and defence policy is vulnerable to similar domestic political constraints as those faced in allied capitals. Moreover, US allies do indeed pull their weight

by identifying comparative advantages to focus on, meaning there
is a complex logic that explains how coalitions divide the labour
during war.[19] The chapters are discussed in the following sections:
perceived threats and capabilities that are mobilized in response
to those threats, and finally, the debates that animate the public
domain throughout military operations.

THREATS AND CAPABILITIES

Given the last decade's emphasis on irregular conflict and counter-
insurgency, it is interesting to track the challenges faced by the
world's strongest militaries when it came to adapting their tactics
to deceive the enemy. Insurgents and terrorists are often invisible,
leaving booby traps and improvised explosive devices (IEDs) in their
tracks. During the wars in Afghanistan and Iraq, these asymmetric
conflict interactions were extremely difficult to cope with because
they proved highly demoralizing and the responses, ineffective. To
be sure, the response to the IED threat was "massive," to use Christopher Barron's characterization.[20] Yet, these types of asymmetrical
confrontations were hardly new. The puzzle of why conventional
militaries often fail in those contexts is enduring and worthy of
investigation.[21] As was pointed out in the preceding section, technological superiority is not enough to achieve a successful outcome.

In this case, blind trust in superior technology crippled the US
military's ability to adapt quickly to the threat posed by IEDs. One
lesson to draw from this is that the military establishment has grown
too reliant on concepts such as the Revolution in Military Affairs
(RMA), a military *transformation* initiated in the United States and
described at length in Asa McKercher's contribution to this volume. Indeed, the promise of the RMA is well-suited for the casualty-
averse mindsets of Western governments, but is not a concept that
has been proven in asymmetric wars. The RMA, with its heavy reliance on precision airstrikes, has dealt decisive blows in conventional
terms against Saddam Hussein in 1991, Slobodan Milosevic in 1999,
the Taliban in 2001, Hussein (again) in 2003, and Moammar Gadhafi in 2011. However, most of these interventions have shown that
the conventional defeat of an adversary through superior military
capabilities does not guarantee lasting victory.

These experiences should have profound and immediate implications for training and capabilities, yet each time, these hard-
learned lessons are brushed aside as "unique" to the context of the

battlefield. Given the inability of the United States and its allies to fully cope with the IED threat, an obsession with force protection, massively investing in capabilities to reduce troops' vulnerability to IEDs, has been the chosen course of action. While tactics and procedures were continuously revised, as Barron notes, trial and error characterized the pattern of threat response. What are the implications for Canada, the United States, and their allies going into the next irregular or non-conventional conflict?

On the spectrum of non-conventional threats are disasters, both natural and man-made, which require immediate emergency assistance and humanitarian intervention.[22] While natural disasters tend to elicit quick responses from the international community, given that nations typically ask for outside help when confronted with major disasters, the same cannot be said for man-made disasters, such as humanitarian emergencies in the context of intrastate war, where the sovereignty of the state is being contested but is also cause for caution when considering an intervention. Indeed, there are competing norms and international principles involved in those international decisions on the use of force.[23] While the doctrine referred to as the Responsibility to Protect (R2P) has updated the conditions through which an intervention would be warranted, a rebranding of the human security motive of the 1990s, the inconsistent application of R2P is perplexing.[24] Indeed, it appears that the United Nations Security Council, the final arbiter for establishing the legitimacy of R2P interventions, sets limits on R2P-applicable contexts. Perhaps unsurprisingly, these decisions seem highly correlated with the permanent five's (China, France, Russian Federation, United Kingdom, and the United States) geopolitical priorities and alliance networks.

Nevertheless, mapping the types of disasters that require international action, as well as the capabilities needed in each context is a useful exercise and one that has been aptly undertaken in Rachel Lea Heide's chapter. It seems likely that, given that domestic publics rarely oppose their government's participation in emergency assistance operations following natural disasters, these interventions will be on the rise. The same cannot be said for man-made disaster relief, given the thorny issue of sovereignty. These differences matter when justifying military interventions to domestic publics, as will be discussed in a subsequent section. An additional source of domestic constraints, of course, is the suitability and availability of a state's military capabilities.

Despite the technological advances embodied by the Revolution in Military Affairs, the last decade of coalition-supported military interventions remind us that predominant military capabilities are not enough to win wars. As Asa McKercher notes in his chapter, "[A]s the West's experience in Afghanistan, Iraq, and Libya has shown, technology is not a panacea and war remains nasty and difficult." Indeed, certain threats, such as IEDs, seem immune to technologically driven countermeasures. Investing in technology to win conflicts is insufficient. Yet, concerns about casualties and the pressure of keeping a technological edge are strong motives for successive US administrations. That pressure is diffused to allies which, in turn, want to remain technologically interoperable with their most important ally, the United States. These are ambitions that have proven difficult to sustain in a constrained fiscal environment, as made clear in Christian Leuprecht and Joel J. Sokolsky's chaper.

Since the 2008 global economic recession, fiscal constraints are not only putting a downward pressure on defence budgets, they are influencing domestic public's willingness to consider unpredictable and expensive military interventions. Several chapters in this volume highlight that the will to wage war is affected by considerations that go above and beyond the nature of the threat.[25] Whether these considerations are presented and debated in Parliament, Congress, the media, or Twitter the constant is that a variety of motives affect perceptions and, ultimately, final decisions on the use of force. Less perceptible but equally critical for decisions leading to military interventions are alliance dynamics, negotiations, and alignments between close political and military partners, as well as region-specific strategic interests. While allies cannot always agree on which regions to prioritize, Africa and the Middle East remain conflict-prone, and thus, likely to solicit, if not receive, military or economic assistance from Canada, the United States, or Europe.[26] In each case, however, the type and scope of the intervention will be hotly debated, behind closed doors, and in public settings.

DEBATES ON THE USE OF FORCE

Governments bear a great responsibility when deciding on the use of force.[27] As several chapters in this volume emphasize, a mix of international and domestic factors inform the decision-making process leading to war.[28] Political leaders have a duty to inform their citizens about the reasons why military force is being pursued in support of the national interest. These reasons must be sufficiently clear and compelling to justify the risk of casualties and material costs involved.[29] Although this risk has substantially decreased, at least for technologically advanced states, discussions over casualties are still central to the public debate on the use of force.

While the evidence is mixed with regards to the impact of casualties on public support for intervention, casualty aversion has motivated the prioritization of force protection in the development of military capabilities.[30] Indeed, as highlighted in the chapters by Christopher Barron and Peter Tikuisis, technological innovation in support of force protection is a significant trend. To be fair, other factors, including improved training and better medical care, have led to a decrease in the number of casualties during armed conflict. As public expectations of low or no casualties become the norm, the military's reliance on expensive technology will increase. Resorting to autonomous systems and robotics to replace soldiers for the more dangerous tasks appears to be an inevitable outcome. High casualty rates are now considered to be indicators of failure, while few or no casualties are becoming the new norm of the *Western* way of war. This is an important distinction, especially given the finding that failure, rather than casualty numbers, drives public opposition to war.[31]

In addition to these factors, I would argue that the *type* of military intervention also influences the public's predisposition toward supporting the war or opposing it.[32] As Bob Martyn notes in this volume, a return to a peacekeeping role for the Canadian Armed Forces might pre-empt a lot of the domestic public's opposition to expeditionary operations. Even though the CAF have been out of the peacekeeping business for some time and have acquired the reputation of being a flexible, multi-purpose warfighting force, it seems that Canadians' attachment to the country's peacekeeping legacy is not weakening with time, a fact not lost on Prime Minister Justin Trudeau.[33] In addition, Canadian participation in peace support operations might be more realistic given the limited capabilities and stagnant defence budgets that continue to challenge the military.[34] It is perhaps an argument that the Canadian Army might wish to pursue as it too faces daunting cuts in budgets and personnel in the post-Afghanistan period.

Whether future Canadian involvement is geared toward combat or peace support,[35] an important lesson from the war in Afghanistan is the importance of communicating the objectives of the intervention clearly.[36] Here, the suggestion is not to inject this process with cumbersome bureaucratic requirements, as the quarterly reports on Canada's engagement in Afghanistan did. A list of benchmarks, performance indicators, and completed projects is one way to measure progress and dollars spent in a constantly evolving security environment. However, the government could more clearly explain major changes in mission objectives and goals, from combat, to stability operations, to military training.

CONCLUSION

One of the most obvious but perhaps uncomfortable lessons of military intervention since the end of the Cold War is that examples of success are rare. Certainly, one could point to Desert Storm in 1990–91, to repel Saddam Hussein's attack against Kuwait, as one successful example. The military interventions that followed, however, proved more complex operationally but also more politically controversial. Perhaps we would be better served in taking a longer view of history. If one thinks back to the immediate post–Second World War era, one could focus on the incredibly costly and labour-intensive nation-building efforts of the United States and the international community to support Germany and Japan. In those cases, the commitment was total. There was no exit strategy and no appeals for a less ambitious intervention were entertained. The cumulative social and material devastation of two world wars was still fresh enough to remind governments and domestic audiences that such commitments are sometimes warranted.

Even if today's security environment does not present similar levels of global urgency, perhaps the lesson about demonstrating resolve and long-term commitment is nonetheless transferable to contemporary military interventions. In the end, the ability to conduct military interventions abroad to support international peace and security goals is a responsibility that few states can afford to shoulder. Both the political responsibility and financial burdens are great. The justification of war aims must be clear to the population who is bearing the sacrifice. Moreover, public opinion has proven remarkably responsive to cycles of perceived success and failure, so the low odds of immediate triumph must be humbly communicated and hard-won progress on the battlefield must be aptly reported.[37] Understanding the conditions of progress, rather than success, thus emerges as a core lesson of the book. Another lesson, from both a research and practical standpoint, is that any analysis on the likelihood of *Going to War* must absolutely take into account the security imperatives, the alliance politics, as well as the domestic constraints.

This introductory chapter has described the contemporary international security environment, focusing on the military interventions led by Canada, the United States, and their allies. The central puzzle of the book is to reconcile our perceptions of international threats with the political and technological means Western governments have at their disposal. Part 1 focuses on threats and capabilities. Asa McKercher (chapter 1) describes the technological advances that have revolutionized military operations, from a historical perspective. Rachel Heide (chapter 2) provides us with a map of both natural and man-made disasters across different regions of the world, with the aim of understanding how Canada and its allies might be called upon to respond. Christopher Barron (chapter 3) examines the impact of the IED threat and how this has affected the conduct of war in Afghanistan and Iraq.

Part 2 turns to observable trends in military interventions. Peter Tikuisis (chapter 4) tracks casualty rates and draws practical implications from the long-term trend of decreasing deaths from conflict. Bob Martyn (chapter 5) delves deeper into the phenomenon of war-weariness, in order to investigate what types of interventions might be more publically tolerable. Aaron Ettinger (chapter 6) demonstrates how the increasing tendency to integrate private military contractors by the US has impacted interventions, challenging the rationale for their use but recognizing their utility as a hedge force.

In part 3, contributors focus on allied experiences in contemporary military interventions. Heather Hrychuk, Paul Dickson, and Anton Minkov (chapter 7) chronicle their time in Afghanistan observing the inner workings of ISAF. Jan von der Felsen (chapter 8) examines the predispositions toward military interventions, drawing on European country's ties to Africa. Part 4 turns to the Canadian experience, focusing on the possibility of future interventions in the Middle East, as discussed by Ali Dizboni and Peter Gizewski (chapter 9), while Christian Leuprecht and Joel J. Sokolsky (chapter 10) show how diminishing military capabilities are impacting Canadian grand strategy. Finally, H. Christian Breede (chapter 12) summarizes the volume's contributions in the conclusion and provides additional insights on how interventions affect the military and society differently, with long-term implications for civil-military relations.

NOTES

1 Albrecht Schnabel and Marc Krupanski, "Mapping Evolving Internal Roles of the Armed Forces," SSR Paper 7 (Geneva: Geneva Centre for the Democratic Control of the Armed Forces, 2012); Timothy Edmunds, "What Are Armed Forces For? The Changing Nature of Military Roles in Europe," *International Affairs* 82, no. 6 (2006): 1059–75.

2 David Auerswald and Stephen Saideman, *NATO in Afghanistan: Fighting Together, Fighting Alone* (Princeton, NJ: Princeton University Press, 2014).

3 Philip A. Russo and Patrick J. Haney, "Intermestic Politics and Homeland Security," in *The Domestic Sources of American Foreign Policy: Insights and Evidence*, ed. James McCormick (Lanham, MD: Rowman and Littlefield, 2012).

4 On the complexity of alliance coordination, see the chapter by Heather Hrychuk, Paul Dickson, and Anton Minkov in this volume.

5 Alexandre Debs and Nuno P. Monteiro, "Known Unknowns: Power Shifts, Uncertainty, and War," *International Organization* 68, no. 1 (2014): 1–31.

6 Alexander L. George, *Bridging the Gap: Theory and Practice in Foreign Policy* (Washington, DC: United States Institute of Peace Press, 1993); Joseph S. Nye, "Bridging the Gap between Theory and Policy," *Political Psychology* 29, no. 4 (2008): 593–603.

7 Auerswald and Saideman, *NATO in Afghanistan*.

8 Stéfanie von Hlatky, *American Allies in Times of War: The Great Asymmetry* (Oxford: Oxford University Press, 2013).

9 Kim Richard Nossal, "The Democratization of Canadian Foreign Policy?," *Canadian Foreign Policy Journal* 1, no. 3 (1993): 95–105. Furthermore, Dan Reiter and Allan Stam have argued that the necessity to obtain public consent makes democracies' foreign policies more effective. See Dan Reiter and Allan Stam, *Democracies at War* (Princeton, NJ: Princeton University Press, 2002).

10 Auerswald and Saideman, *NATO in Afghanistan*.

11 Sarah Kreps, *Coalitions of Convenience: United States Military Interventions after the Cold War* (New York: Oxford University Press, 2011).

12 Peter W. Singer, *Wired for War: The Robotics Revolution and Conflict in the 21st Century* (New York: Penguin, 2009).

13 Srdjan Vucetic and Atsushi Tago, "Why Buy American? The International Politics of Fighter Jet Transfers," *Canadian Journal of Political Science* 1, no. 4 (2015): 1–24.

14 Michael Horowitz, *The Diffusion of Military Power: Causes and Consequences for International Politics* (Princeton, NJ: Princeton University Press, 2010).

15 Robert A. Rubinstein, Diana M. Keller, and Michael E. Scherger, "Culture and Interoperability in Integrated Missions," *International Peacekeeping* 15, no. 4 (August 2008): 540–55; Risa A. Brooks and Elizabeth A. Stanley, eds., *Creating Military Power: The Sources of Military Effectiveness* (Stanford, CA: Stanford University Press, 2007).

16 Stephen Biddle, *Military Power: Explaining Victory and Defeat in Modern Battle* (Princeton, NJ: Princeton University Press, 2004).

17 Patricia Weitsman, *Waging War: Alliances, Coalitions, and Institutions of Interstate Violence* (Stanford, CA: Stanford University Press, 2013).

18 Daniel Byman, *Going to War with the Allies You Have: Allies, Counterinsurgency, and the War on Terror* (Carlisle, PA: US Army War College, 2014).

19 Mark A. Boyer, *International Cooperation and Public Goods: Opportunities for the Western Alliance* (Baltimore: Johns Hopkins University Press, 1993).

20 See chapter 3 in this volume.

21 Ivan Arreguin-Toft, *How the Weak Win Wars: A Theory of Asymmetric Conflict* (Cambridge, MA: Cambridge University Press, 2006).

22 Arjen Boin, Magnus Ekengren, and Mark Rhinard, *The European Union as Crisis Manager: Patterns and Prospects* (Cambridge, UK: Cambridge University Press, 2013).

23 Martha Finnemore, *The Purpose of Intervention: Changing Beliefs about the Use of Force* (Ithaca, NY: Cornell University Press, 2004).

24 Thomas G. Weiss, "The Sunset of Humanitarian Intervention? The Responsibility to Protect in a Unipolar Era," *Security Dialogue* 35, no. 2 (2004): 135–53; Alex Bellamy, "The Responsibility to Protect and the Problem of Military Intervention," *International Affairs* 84, no. 4 (2008): 615–39; Theresa Reinold, "The Responsibility to Protect – Much Ado about Nothing?," *Review of International Studies* 36, no. S1 (2010): 55–78.

25 See chapters by Bob Martyn, Christian Leuprecht and Joel J. Sokolsky, as well as H. Christian Breede in this volume.

26 See chapters by Jan van der Felsen, Ali Dizboni and Peter Gizewski, as well as H. Christian Breede in this volume.

27 Peter D. Feaver and Christopher Gelpi, *Choosing Your Battles: American Civil-Military Relations and the Use of Force* (Princeton, NJ: Princeton University Press, 2004).

28 See Gideon Rose, "Neoclassical Realism and Theories of Foreign Policy," *World Politics* 51, no. 1 (1998): 144–72.

29 See chapter by Breede in this volume.

30 Michael Tomz, "Domestic Audience Costs in International Relations: An Experimental Approach," *International Organization* 61, no. 4 (2007); Matthew A. Baum and Tim J. Groeling, *War Stories: The Causes and Consequences of Public Views of War* (Princeton, NJ: Princeton University Press, 2010).

31 James A. Nathan and Charles Tien, "Casualties and Threats: Conditions of Support for War," *Defence & Security Analysis* 26, no. 3 (2010), 291–2; Feaver and Gelpi, *Choosing Your Battles*. See also Breede's chapter in this volume.

32 Richard C. Eichenberg, "Victory Has Many Friends: U.S. Public Opinion and the Use of Military Force, 1981–2005," *International Security* 30, no. 1 (2005): 140–77; Adam J. Berinsky, "Assuming the Costs of War: Events, Elites, and American Public Support for Military Conflict," *The Journal of Politics* 69, no. 4 (2007): 975–97.

33 See Martyn's chapter in this volume.

34 Bastian Giegerich, "NATO's Smart Defence: Who's Buying?," *Survival* 54, no. 3 (2012): 69–77; Paul Cornish and Andrew M. Dorman, "Dr Fox and the Philosopher's Stone: The Alchemy of National Defence in the Age of Austerity," *International Affairs* 87, no. 2 (2011): 335–53.

35 A. Walter Dorn, "Canadian Peacekeeping: Proud Tradition, Strong Future?," *Canadian Foreign Policy Journal* 12, no. 2 (2005): 7–32.

36 Heiner Hänggi, "The Use of Force under International Auspices: Parliamentary Accountability and 'Democratic Deficits,'" in *The "Double Democratic Deficit": Parliamentary Accountability and the Use of Force under International Auspices*, eds. Hans Born and Heiner Hänggi (Aldershot, UK: Ashgate, 2004).

37 Robert Keohane, "The Contingent Legitimacy of Multilateralism," in *Multilateralism under Challenge: Power, International Order, and Structural Change*, eds. Edward Newman et al. (Tokyo: United Nations University Press, 2006); Arita Holmberg, "The Changing Role of NATO: Exploring Implications for Security Governance and Legitimacy," *European Security* 20, no. 4 (2011): 529–46.

PART ONE

Threats and Capabilities

1

War Made New? Cycles of Revolutions in Military Affairs and Intervention

ASA MCKERCHER

In the mid-1990s, alongside dial-up Internet and mobile phones, came the Revolution in Military Affairs (RMA). The notion of a military revolution was not new: historians had, for instance, long pointed to the gunpowder revolution of the sixteenth century as kicking off a period of major military as well as societal change.[1] Indeed, like earlier revolutions in warfare, the RMA that began in the late twentieth century – also dubbed "transformation" and "network-centric warfare," among other descriptors – both incorporated and drove technological innovation that had an important role beyond the military sphere. Just as the railroad – the exemplar of the Industrial Age – had important civilian and strategic uses, so inventions that have marked the current Information Age – Global Positioning System, say – have had a dual role. Connections between the military and civilian spheres do not end with innovation, of course, as war is a human activity, which reflects, and is influenced by, society. Currently in the West, warfare is conducted by societies averse, if not to suffering casualties, then to participating in long, inconclusive conflicts. The chapters in this volume by Christopher Barron, Peter Tikuisis, and H. Christian Breede speak to this aversion. What the RMA offers to modern militaries, then, is the promise of short, sharp interventions making the resort to limited war tempting.[2]

By examining the changes in the way that war has been fought over the past four hundred years, my aim is to historicize the current RMA – synonymous with the United States and characterized as "the new American way of war" – and highlight the connections that have driven, and continue to drive, revolutions in warfare and intervention since the early modern period.[3] Throughout the history of warfare, humans have sought out advantages over enemy forces, in part by applying new advances in technology, generally with the aim of doing maximum damage to an enemy at minimal cost to one's own forces thereby mitigating the risk involved in going to war. Short wars are desirable not simply for the obvious reasons of minimizing the human and material costs, but because the longer the war the more time that chance can come into play. Present efforts, aimed largely at mitigating the uncertainty of warfare – Clausewitz's "fog of war" – with the technologies of the Information Age, have a lengthy pedigree in that militaries have long sought to make the resort to force quick, decisive, and even humane. But despite the innumerable changes to the ways in which war has been fought, its purpose remains immutable. War, as Clausewitz put it, is "an act of force to compel our enemy to do our will."[4]

In spite of the rhetoric about "war made new," proponents of the current revolution note that, like its historical antecedents, the RMA is a process of changing "how wars are fought and won" and not a paradigm shift in war itself.[5] These past revolutions have involved the harnessing of new technologies by armed forces and their incorporation into new military doctrines, causing the resulting obsolescence of old doctrinal and organizational concepts. Typical of revolutionaries of all stripes, those pushing military transformation have often been fervent in their belief that change is imperative if not inevitable. Certainly, history is replete with examples where those who failed to adapt to changes in warfare faced defeat, if not destruction. As one interwar military revolutionary warned, "victory smiles upon those who anticipate changes in the character of war, not upon those who wait to adapt themselves after the changes occur."[6] Sixty years later, a like-minded military historian affirmed that "for the United States and other countries that aspire to be first- or second-tier powers, there is no alternative but to stay abreast of the changes – tactical and technological, conventional and 'asymmetric' – transforming the modern battlefield."[7] In military affairs as in evolutionary biology, the maxim is "transform or perish."

But where trouble has arisen for the would-be military revolutionary has been in applying the technological and doctrinal changes to strategic thinking and planning and hence to the overall conduct of warfare.[8] To return to Clausewitz, the Prussian military theorist offered up another fundamental truth that is worth being mindful of two centuries later: war is driven by a "remarkable trinity" composed of violent emotion, the interplay of probability and chance, and rational calculations of policy.[9] The current RMA has placed a large emphasis on technology as a means of mitigating the influence of the first two factors, subordinating them and making warfare a predictable enterprise. As the West's experience in Afghanistan, Iraq, Libya, and now Syria has shown, technology is not a panacea and war remains nasty and difficult.

Now at least in the modern period, the first military revolution occurred as a result of gunpowder. This gunpowder revolution, from the 1500s to the mid-1800s, was centred in Europe, where it had its most profound impacts on society and government. Whereas prior to this revolution, warfare had involved commanders applying some mixture of light infantry, heavy infantry, light cavalry, heavy cavalry, and luck (preferably en masse), the introduction of gunpowder had a devastating effect on the battlefield. Massed mobs of soldiers fell by the wayside with the trend favouring professional armed forces, resulting in the need for troops to be drilled, for strict discipline, and for non-commissioned officers (NCOs) and a trained and relatively educated officer corps as opposed to feudal chains of command. These developments were all aimed at creating lines of fire or, in the case of artillery and naval cannons, at using mathematics with devastating effect. As this revolution took hold in Europe over three centuries, the size of armies grew, which in turn necessitated more officers, more arms, and longer logistical tails, while establishing and defending far-flung outposts of empire required more sailing ships and shipwrights. Paying for the revolution was expensive. So along came capital markets and the consolidation and centralization of the state, the only type of entity capable of raising the funds needed to train, arm, and deploy these forces.[10]

And deploy them European powers did. The early modern period saw almost continual warfare, with religion, dynastic succession, and the emerging concept of the "balance of power" proving to be major drivers of combat. The fighting took place not just across the continent but also in newly seized overseas territories, for sail proved to be as revolutionary as gunpowder. Slowly, European states expanded outwards into Asia, Africa, and the Americas, meeting with mixed success: guns, steel, but especially germs proved potent in the "New

World," far less so in the "Old World," where the Ottomans, Chinese, and Mughals proved adept at this new form of warfare, especially on land; "a military shift" in favour of the West occurred only in the period 1775–1815.[11] These forty years, the dawn of the modern era, were important, too, because they saw the rise of armies that far overshadowed the professional armies of the early modern period. With the upheaval wrought by the toppling of the *ancien régime*, these forces were deployed in almost continual warfare across much of the world.[12]

With the Great Powers (Austria, Prussia, Russia, France, and Britain) exhausted from twenty-five years of revolution and war, the Congress of Vienna brought nominal peace to Europe, where the balance of power held. Military innovation did not stop, however, and the next military revolution came about as the output of the Industrial Revolution intensified. Advances in naval warfare were plentiful: steam, shell guns, screw propellers, armour, and rifled ordnance. Of the lot, steam had perhaps the most important impact in that by allowing fleets to move quickly and purposefully across vast territory it altered time and space.[13] The importance of these technological advances led to a sense among elite opinion throughout Europe, the United States, and Japan that naval power was a reflection of national power, prompting the flowering of naval strategy.[14]

On land, meanwhile, rifling, breech-loading guns, and quick-firing artillery made armies capable of greater and more accurate rates of fire. Mass retained its importance, with conscript armies growing in size across Europe. The impact of these developments was plain to see in the casualty rates of the American Civil War, a conflict that also made evident the utility of railways.[15] From the 1850s onward, cheap steel had led to the spread of railroads across Europe as well as in North America. The advent of the telegraph and, later, the telephone shortened distances even further. Soon enough the state was capable of arming and mobilizing *national* armies, deploying them in short order, and ensuring that they could be quickly and easily supplied or moved as needed. The employment of many of these elements in the wars of German unification – and the failure of Prussia's opponents to adapt – proved the worth of industrialized warfare for the many Europeans who had ignored developments in the United States.[16]

Taking note of the changing way of warfare in a 1904 debate at the Royal Geographic Society, Leo Amery predicted that "the successful powers will be those who have the greatest industrial basis ... those people who have the industrial power and the power of invention and of science will be able to defeat all others."[17] Unsurprisingly, Amery, a young journalist who would soon rise to be First Lord of the Admiralty, was an ardent imperialist, for not only was industrial power an important driver of military power but so too was colonial power: the European Great Powers could pay for their expansive militaries by drawing upon the human, financial, and material resources of their massive empires. With relative peace in Europe after 1815 the power of European states had grown immense, as had the desire for overseas possessions. By the dawn of the twentieth century, the new imperialism had taken hold, and the West – and Japan, which had fully, eagerly, and shrewdly embraced industrialization – held suzerainty over most of the globe.[18]

The Industrial Revolution and the concentration of power among the handful of European imperial states meant that the wars of empire were decidedly asymmetric, making intervention and expansion easy options. In the "scramble for Africa" and in the consolidation of empires from the Caucuses to the American West, the new tools of industrial warfare proved their worth. Overall, and in contrast to the wars of European expansion in the early modern period, the colonial wars of the modern era were largely one-sided. As Hilaire Belloc put it in 1898, "Whatever happens, we have got / The Maxim gun, and they have not."[19] But Spain's frustrating experience against guerrillas in Cuba, Philippine resistance to the Americans, and British difficulties in suppressing the Boers showcased the problems that modern armies faced when confronted with determined, well-armed enemies who refused to fight in pitched battles. "Small wars" would prove particularly infuriating for the imperial powers, because while conquering foreign lands was relatively easy, controlling them required a sustained effort through "savage wars of peace."[20]

Belloc's maxim aside, the slaughter of the Great War was so immense because all of the warring parties were similarly armed. Despite gas and machine guns, it was quick-firing artillery and breach-loading, personal weapons that accounted for the vast majority of the killing.[21] The scale of the bloodshed necessitated calling up millions of soldiers so that the massive conscript armies of the war overshadowed the *levée en masse*. Mass itself did not prove enough, leading Basil Liddell Hart to lament that "the indigestible mass of infantry is the cause of our military nightmare."[22] Placing the state

under arms generated other nightmares, shown most spectacularly
in the collapse of the Romanov dynasty, though all the belligerents
experienced violent upheaval and political problems as a result of
mass conscription and wartime deprivation.[23] The casualties, the
stalemate, and the domestic pressures led the various belligerents
to seek out new ways of winning the war, putting faith in technology – tanks, airplanes, submarines – none of which proved decisive
in themselves. Indeed, the pre-war technological innovations, along
with the examples of the German wars of unification and the Russo-
Japanese War of 1904–05, created an expectation that war could
be short and sharp. But the Great War had not ended in Christmas 1914. The "progress of weapons," Liddell Hart contended in
1932, "has outstripped the progress of the mind – especially in the
class who wield weapons. Each successive war of modern times has
revealed the lag due to the slow pace of mental adaptation."[24]

In the wake of the "war to end all wars," strategists put their
minds toward preparing for the next conflict. For instance, the
wartime technological developments proved too little, too late for
J.F.C. Fuller, who complained that as the war progressed the armies
involved became "not more intelligent and scientific, but more brutal, ton upon ton of human flesh being added, until war strengths
are reckoned in millions in place of thousands of men."[25] Forecasting ahead, Fuller saw tanks as an answer to a future stalemate
by offering the promise of a strategic breakthrough and a speedy
advance that would avoid a lengthy war of attrition. Putting stock
in strategic bombing – a grandiose title indicating the high expectations placed upon it – other futurists contended that aircraft
laden with bombs could provide a quick, decisive victory. Foremost
here was Giulio Douhet, who emphasized the necessity of punish-
ing an opponent's populace as the means of achieving a speedy triumph. Whereas the collapse of the German war effort had been
partly achieved through a lengthy naval blockade, Douhet predicted
that, with bombers, the same results could be achieved in a matter of days. "A complete breakdown of the social structure cannot
but take place in a country subjected to this merciless pounding
from the air," he wrote, and the people, "would rise up and demand
an end to the war before the army and navy will be defeated."[26] In
the United States, Billy Mitchell saw a similar potential for airpower,
though his focus was on destroying an enemy's war industry.[27] In

both formulations, and in wider thinking about warfare during the interwar period, technology offered the promise of the quick victory that had eluded the warring powers in the Great War.

In many ways, the war of 1939–45 was a continuation of the 1914–18 conflict. Certainly, the Industrial RMA continued in force: mobility and communication intensified, while equipment developed using notions that sprang from the First World War – tanks, bombers, aircraft carriers – and the doctrines surrounding them, were put to the test. Further, since the early modern period, war and the expansion of the state had marched in lockstep, and with this type of war approaching Clausewitz's ideal type of "total war," the state reached the apogee of its power. The scale of the Second World War was unprecedented, thanks in part to strategic bombing, which nevertheless fell far short of expectations.[28] But the conflict's peculiar ending generated fears about a final war. "Thus far the chief purpose of our military establishment has been to win wars," observed Bernard Brodie, the father of nuclear strategy. "From now on its chief purpose must be to avert them."[29]

With the nuclear revolution making a conventional war in Europe unwinnable, postwar attention focused on "limited wars" and "low-intensity conflicts," terms that became intensely popular from the 1950s to the 1970s. These conflicts were fought not in Europe but in the decolonizing world. And what were limited wars for the Western powers were "wars of national liberation" for anti-colonial and Third World forces, an indication of the differing importance assigned to these struggles, though imperialism saw some last gasps of brutality in Kenya, Malaya, Algeria, and across the Portuguese empire. Against determined foes, Western powers proved largely impotent when it came to waging or at least winning these conflicts. Moreover, the devastation wrought by the Second World War left European states weak and increasingly hesitant about engaging in lengthy interventions. Europe's preference was for butter not guns – nor empire. The United States proved similarly inept at fighting a limited war in Vietnam – nor did its superiority win a victory in Korea – though it engaged in successful police actions throughout the Caribbean.[30] Failure in Southeast Asia, in spite of the preponderance of American power, led the United States to employ guerrilla warfare by funding and arming insurgents in Nicaragua, Afghanistan, and Southern Africa.

At this point, we reach the advent of the modern RMA, which began in the late 1970s. Washington, looking for a means of countering Moscow's overwhelming numerical advantage in conventional arms, harnessed the nascent power of Silicon Valley and the burgeoning American edge in satellite and communications technology. The result was a shift from "brute force to brain force."[31] Advances in precision-guided munitions (used in Vietnam) and what would come to known as C4ISR (command, control, communications, computer, intelligence, surveillance, and reconnaissance) led to the "AirLand Battle" doctrine that prescribed a "deep battle" aimed at destroying an enemy's command and control, transport, and logistics infrastructure, and force concentrations. Soviet strategists were aware that this "military-technical revolution" gave the United States distinct advantages over their own forces.[32] Thankfully, American power – and the balance of nuclear terror – proved decisive in deterring any Soviet advance into Western Europe, thus precluding a test of this new doctrine against its intended target.

That the new technologies of this revolution would serve as a force multiplier against the USSR was beneficial not simply because of the numerical superiority of the Communist Bloc's militaries but because of the "Vietnam syndrome" and the perceived reluctance of the American people to suffer casualties and to tolerate a long, vexing, and expensive war – precisely the same weariness Western Europeans had shown to the wars fought at the end of empire. Partly in response to public revulsion against the debacle in Vietnam, the US military became an all-volunteer force (AVF). This shift from a conscript to a professional force left the United States with fewer uniformed personnel. As the US military engaged in a post-Vietnam regenerative process, it seemed that the recourse to smaller armed forces – akin to the professional armies of the early modern period – signalled, like the nuclear revolution, the end of total warfare. The concluding chapter to this volume by Breede raises other interesting issues surrounding the implications of switching to an AVF.

Indeed, as the Cold War order collapsed and as the new millennium approached, some excited observers forecast an end to state-centric warfare. One hopeful commentator chalked this development up to the military revolution, which "may mark the closing of that era of warfare dominated by large military forces and equally large scopes of military operations. This RMA may usher in a new period of military contraction and a return to wars fought for limited objectives by valuable forces too precious to waste in mass attrition-style warfare."[33] If history had ended along with the East-West ideological struggle, then why not major warfare?

Of course, there had been a large conflict at the end of the Cold War era. But the ease with which the US military had deployed the AirLand Battle doctrine to defeat Saddam Hussein's forces and uphold collective security seemed to herald a "new world order" in many ways. "By God," President George H.W. Bush is supposed to have exclaimed, "we've kicked the Vietnam syndrome once and for all!"[34] Bush oversaw not just this quick victory but also the careful transition from the Cold War to the post–Cold War order, during which American preponderance turned into US primacy, both in geostrategic terms, as well as on the battlefield. The Gulf War had showcased what the melding of American technological and military prowess could accomplish, namely "a quantum leap in the quick flow of information" as well as "a quantum leap in bombing accuracy."[35] Some of the enthusiasm, especially about the utility of air power, was overblown – most of the munitions had, in fact, been "dumb" bombs – but the notion that technology could make wars quick and decisive was one with a long pedigree and its time seemed to have arrived.

As the Gulf War showed, this RMA (the term soon rose to widespread prominence), which multiplied the power of conventional forces, gave an undoubted edge to those who mastered it. And driven by a desire to maintain "full-spectrum dominance," the United States poured money into advancing this revolution.[36] Overall, the RMA focused on using C4ISR to reduce the fog of war and thereby limit the role that chance played in warfare. Satellites, unmanned aerial vehicles (UAVs), and airborne target acquisition and coordination platforms such as the Joint Surveillance Target Acquisition Radar System (JSTARS) and Airborne Warning and Control System (AWACS) planes, all brought air power "to a point where it has finally become truly strategic in its political effects."[37] Beyond precision, the RMA also emphasized "jointness" between air, land, and naval forces. In terms of the latter, there was an important shift in naval doctrine from open ocean warfare to littoral operations and the projection of naval power from sea onto land, not just through seaborne aircraft but also through cruise missiles, which would soon be emblematic of RMA warfare thanks to television coverage. And while there were gripes that the RMA was of greater benefit to the other armed services than to the army, on land the trend was toward smaller, more rapidly mobile, and flexible ground forces that could be highly dispersed but still controlled centrally. Moreover, individual ships and soldiers possessed the ability to "see" the entire battlefield and call in support as needed. Overall, the modern soldier was a "far more lethal creature" than his predecessors and no longer "a mass consumable of war."[38] Lastly, interoperability, not just between the armed services of a particular country but also between allied forces, became the *sine qua non* of RMA as it applied to NATO, though the withering away of conscript armies in Europe has provided added impetus for the embrace of new technologies. The search for interoperable forces meant that in the 1990s and 2000s, the NATO allies sought to keep pace with the United States, no mean feat given the costs of modern military equipment.[39]

Modern armies, principally those of the United States and its allies, now had a great capacity to conduct reconnaissance and to use this intelligence to acquire and then destroy targets, all with relatively little collateral damage, at least in comparison to the world wars, and with little risk to their own forces. In the Persian Gulf, belatedly in Bosnia, and then in Kosovo, Western governments used their dominance to pursue intervention in short wars. One critic would correctly characterize this as "risk-transfer war," and would proclaim it to be the "New Western Way of War."[40] But the idea that technology could transfer risk had motivated thinking on airpower since the advent of airplanes. And the RMA did indeed focus overwhelmingly on air power as the way to avoid long, grinding wars. Suddenly, mass was out of style:

> Today the traditional notion of massing a large ground force to confront an opponent, particularly on a "field of battle" is largely rendered archaic. The precision air attacker overcomes the battlefield by attacking at ranges far in excess of the most powerful artillery. What can be identified can be targeted so precisely that unnecessary casualties are not inflicted. Thus, increasingly, war is about destroying or incapacitating *things* as opposed to *people*. It is now about pursuing an *effects-based* strategy, rather than an *annihilation-based* one, a strategy that one can *control* an opponent without having to destroy him.[41]

The utility of the effects-based approach was put to the test in Kosovo. Precision munitions and C4ISR allowed NATO forces to dominate the battlespace, there were virtually no casualties on the coalition side, and relatively few Serbian civilians were killed. However, the use of precision airstrikes against the Serbians had not prevented the bombing of the Chinese embassy in Belgrade, a rather spectacular blunder. More importantly, a seventy-eight-day air campaign was needed to achieve the West's strategic aims, even though, when the war began on 24 March, there was the "almost universal assumption among NATO's leaders that the operation would last no more than two to four days."[42] Like construction projects, wars rarely seem to end on schedule or on budget – one thinks of the Europeans who set out in August 1914 under the assumption that the war would be over by Christmas.

Even so, the technological prowess on display in the Balkans, beamed live to a global audience, reinforced the notion that this period was the "Unipolar moment," with the United States alone maintaining full-spectrum dominance and the ability to project power in multiple theatres.[43] Unsurprisingly, many of the foremost revolutionaries were neo-conservatives, who saw the RMA not only as a means of ensuring US military primacy and, therefore, hegemony, but as a way of allowing the United States to intervene abroad, quickly, effectively, and, most importantly, bloodlessly. "America has long been more powerful than all but a handful of countries, so the cost of intervention in small states had always been low," noted one proponent of a more vigorous posture, and, "in the post–Cold War world, the price of exercising power appears low once again."[44] Liberal interventionists also embraced the ease with which US primacy and the RMA would allow the West to prevent gross violations of human rights. "Empire Lite" had wide appeal.[45]

And with the 9/11 Wars came opportunities to apply the awesome power of the Revolution in Military Affairs. In a piece recounting "the first US cavalry attack of the twenty-first century," Secretary of Defense Donald Rumsfeld wrote that "[w]hat won the battle for Mazar-i-Sharif – and set in motion the Taliban's fall from power – was a combination of the ingenuity of the US Special Forces; the most advanced, precision-guided munitions in the US arsenal, delivered by US Navy, Air Force, and Marine Corps crews; and the courage of valiant, one-legged Afghan fighters on horseback."[46] Mobility, precision force, joint operations – the Afghan War from 2001 to

2002 had all the hallmarks of "a new way of war."[47] Waging new wars with trim, networked forces appealed to Rumsfeld, who had entered the Pentagon devoted to the RMA; under his watch transformation (his preferred term) continued apace. Many shared his enthusiasm, particularly after the Iraq War in 2003, where "shock and awe" led quickly and decisively to "mission accomplished." The campaign had been "a walkover" as "[n]o army had ever travelled faster with fewer casualties."[48] Belying the reserved demeanour of the English, John Keegan exulted, "The Americans came, saw, conquered."[49] Even more so than the Gulf War, this lopsided victory proved what the sole superpower could accomplish with the fruits of the Information Age and a doctrine devised to win a conventional war against a first-rate military power but employed against a much weaker foe.

Technological wizardry had produced stunning results in the interventions in Afghanistan and Iraq but as was soon clear, it had done little to prepare the United States for the difficult task of counter-insurgency – to say nothing of nation building. More worrisome was that Pax Americana had its share of discontents and yet the advances wrought by the military revolution proved inadequate for waging and winning "war amongst the people."[50] The belief that the Iraq intervention would be a short war and that regime change would be a simple task had negated long-term planning. Furthermore, Rumsfeld's emphasis on his transformation agenda had "helped blind military and political leaders to a serious focus on the political objective of the war," which was viewed as little more than a "targeting drill."[51] The Americans, along with the British, found themselves in combat that was chaotic, close, and brutal. A heady tonic, the RMA had offered the tantalizing prospect of short, sharp, bloodless wars. As Western powers discovered in Afghanistan and Iraq, and later in Libya, intervening was easy; controlling outcomes was much more difficult and required "boots on the ground" and a sustained effort that increasingly weary publics grew unwilling to support.[52] Although transformation did much to lift the fog of war in these conflicts, it failed to neutralize emotion and the uncertainties and unintended consequences unleashed by warfare.

The difficulties that the United States and its allies faced in "learning to eat soup with a knife" were reminiscent of the small wars of empire, where the record of Western powers was decidedly mixed.[53] For transformation enthusiasts the problem was clear: "Our aging way of war had run head-on into a future organizational concept – the fighting network."[54] Offering hopeful tracts emphasizing the importance of the RMA for counter-insurgency warfare, they under-scored the need to push transformation farther and faster, thereby turning the army in particular into a lean, loose fight force akin, in many respects, to the insurgents themselves. For the United States to prosper in modern wars against unconventional foes, it was nec-essary for the Pentagon to cut "away the bureaucratic fat to turn bloated Industrial Age hierarchies into lean Information Age net-works capable of utilizing the full potential of high-tech weapons and highly trained soldiers."[55] As more recent operations in Afghan-istan, Iraq, and the Horn of Africa indicate, armed UAVs, Special Forces, and smaller units of conventional soldiers are effective instruments, while the use of the Stuxnet virus against Iran indicates the potency of cyberwarfare. As Christopher Barron demonstrates in his chapter, it took time to adapt.

The trend is toward further transformation of the American military, particularly through the use of robotics, has been stultified by inertia from elements within the Pentagon that remain uncon-vinced by the need to slim down. Severe defence budget cuts are also imposing constraints and a revision of the transformation agenda. To address this trade-off, Rumsfeld's successors have thus far taken up the challenge of maintaining the American qualitative advantage over the long term, but with a balanced approach that might best be seen as evolution, not revolution.[56]

Looking forward, problems are apparent with the transformation process. The sustainability of the transformation process is of cen-tral concern for one of the stated puzzles in the volume, namely that future military capabilities are made uncertain by budget cuts, with the potential to exacerbate technological gaps between allies. The high price of advanced equipment in an age of austerity in much of the West is a roadblock (see Breede's conclusion for a further discussion). Moreover, the technology behind transformation and the doctrines undergirding it are no longer the specific preserve of the United States and its allies. As states and non-state actors work to acquire, mitigate, or nullify the tools of network-centric warfare, the advantages that it provides to the West are temporary. Further-more, like Britain at the height of its power, the United States faces the challenge of maintaining forces needed to fight in multiple the-atres and the related conundrum of developing a military capable of balancing a rising China through the emerging doctrine of Air/Sea Battle, deterring medium powers such as Iran and North Korea, and engaging in limited interventions in the Near East and Africa (see the contributions by Bob Martyn, as well as those by Jan von der Felsen, and Ali Dizboni and Peter Gizewski). Force multiplication through the RMA gives the United States the ability to respond to these multiple threats, by letting the American military – and the militaries of its allies – do more with less. Yet as one supporter of transformation has noted, many of his compatriots have eschewed "the traditional threat- or problem-based approach to thinking about war," arguing "instead for the urgent necessity of exploiting certain technologies to transform war," with the result that the RMA has been designed to be defeat "relatively poorly equipped enemies in conventional combat" rather than defeating rivals and enemies who are designing their forces in ways that counter US military pre-eminence.[57] Transformation for the sake of transformation makes for poor strategy, just as technology alone will not win wars. Banquo's ghost haunted Macbeth, just as Clausewitz's spirit haunts the RMA enthusiast.

NOTES

1 The classic work is Michael Roberts, *The Military Revolution, 1560–1660* (Belfast: Boyd, 1956).

2 On aversion to defeat, see Adrian Lewis, *The American Culture of War: The History of U.S. Military Force from World War II to Operation Iraqi Freedom* (London: Routledge, 2007); Christopher Gelpi, Peter D. Feaver, and Jason Reifler, *Paying the Human Costs of War: American Public Opinion and Casualties in Military Conflicts* (Princeton, NJ: Princeton University Press, 2009); Dominic Tierney, *How We Fight: Crusades, Quagmires, and the American Way of War* (New York: Little, Brown and Company, 2010). On the temptations of war, see Christopher Coker, *Waging War without Warriors? The Changing Culture of Military Conflict* (Boulder, CO: Lynne Rienner, 2002); Robert Mandel, *Security, Strategy, and the Quest for Bloodless War* (Boulder, CO: Lynne Rienner, 2004); Andrew Bacevich, *The New American Militarism: How Americans Are Seduced by War* (Oxford: Oxford University Press, 2005); and Mikkel Vedby Rasmussen, *The Risk Society at War: Terror, Technology and Strategy in the Twenty-First Century* (Cambridge, UK: Cambridge University Press, 2007).

3 Antullo J. Echevarria II, *Reconsidering the American Way of War: US Military Practice from the Revolution to Afghanistan* (Washington, DC: Georgetown University Press, 2011), 27.

4 Carl von Clausewitz, *On War*, trans. Michael Howard and Peter Paret (Princeton, NJ: Princeton University Press, 1976), 75.

5 Max Boot, *War Made New: Technology, Warfare, and the Course of History, 1500 to Today* (New York: Gotham, 2006); Elinor Sloan, *The Revolution in Military Affairs* (Montreal: McGill-Queen's University Press, 2002), ix; Andrew N. Liaropoulos, "Revolutions in Warfare: Theoretical Paradigms and Historical Evidence – The Napoleonic and First World War Revolutions," *Journal of Military History* 70 (2006): 370; Clifford J. Rogers, "'Military Revolution' and 'Revolution in Military Affairs': A Historian's Perspective," in *Toward a Revolution in Military Affairs?*, eds. Thierry Gongora and Harald von Riekhoff (Westport, CT: Greenwood Press, 2000), 22; and Andrew F. Krepinevich, "Cavalry to Computer: The Pattern of Military Revolutions," *The National Interest* 37 (1994): 30.

6 Giulio Douhet, *The Command of the Air*, trans. Dino Ferrari (New York: Coward-McCann, 1942), 30.

7 Boot, *War Made New*, 409.

8 On the connection between technology, doctrine, and strategy over the past five hundred years, see the essays in Peter Paret, ed., *Makers of Modern Strategy: From Machiavelli to the Nuclear Age* (Princeton, NJ: Princeton University Press, 1986).

9 Clausewitz, *On War*, 89.

10 Michael Duffy, ed., *The Military Revolution and the State, 1500–1800* (Exeter, UK: University of Exeter Press, 1980); William H. McNeill, *The Pursuit of Power: Technology, Armed Force, and Society since A.D. 1000* (Chicago: University of Chicago, 1982); Brian M. Downing, *The Military Revolution and Political Change: The Origins of Democracy and Autocracy in Early Modern Europe* (Princeton, NJ: Princeton University Press, 1992); and Bruce D. Porter, *War and the Rise of the State: The Military Foundations of Modern Politics* (New York: Free Press, 1994).

11 Jared Diamond, *Guns, Germs, and Steel: The Fates of Human Societies* (New York: Norton, 1997); Jeremy Black, *War and the World: Military Power and the Fate of Continents, 1450–2000* (New Haven, CT: Yale University Press, 1998), 154; Geoffrey Parker, *The Military Revolution* (Cambridge: Cambridge University Press, 1988); and John Darwin, *After Tamerlane: The Global History of Empire* (London: Allen Lane, 2007), 47–156.

12 David A. Bell, *The First Total War: Napoleon's Europe and the Birth of Warfare as We Know It* (New York: Houghton Mifflin, 2007); and Paul W.

Schroeder, *The Transformation of European Politics, 1763–1848* (Oxford: Oxford University Press, 1994).

13 Benjamin Cooling, *Gray Steel and Blue Water Navy: The Formative Years of America's Military-Industrial Complex, 1881–1917* (Hamden, CT: Gazelle, 1979); Jon Sumida, *In Defence of Naval Supremacy: Finance, Technology, and British Naval Policy, 1889–1914* (Boston: Unwin Hyman, 1989); and Ray Walser, *France's Search for a Battle Fleet: Naval Policy and Naval Power, 1898–1914* (New York: Garland, 1992).

14 Alfred Thayer Mahan, *The Influence of Sea Power upon History, 1660–1783* (Boston: Little, Brown and Company, 1890); and Julian Corbett, *Some Principles of Maritime Strategy* (London: Longman, Green and Company, 1911).

15 Brian Holden Reid, *The American Civil War and the Wars of the Industrial Revolution* (London: Cassel Military, 1999).

16 Dennis Showalter, *The Wars of German Unification* (London: Bloomsbury, 2004); and Geoffrey Wawro, *Warfare and Society in Europe, 1792–1914* (London: Routledge, 2000).

17 Quoted in W.R. Louis, *In the Name of God, Go! Leo Amery and the British Empire in the Age of Churchill* (New York: Norton, 1992), 54–5.

18 On Japan's experience, see Meirion Harries and Susie Harries, *Soldiers of the Sun: The Rise and Fall of the Imperial Japanese Army* (New York: Random House, 1991).

19 Hilaire Belloc, *The Modern Traveller* (London: Edward Arnold, 1898); and Daniel R. Headrick, *The Tools of Empire: Technology and European Imperialism in the Nineteenth Century* (Oxford: Oxford University Press, 1981).

20 The classic contemporary study of small wars is C.E. Calwell, *Small Wars: Their Principle and Practice* (London: HM Stationary Office, 1906 [1896]); and see H.L. Wesseling, *The European Colonial Empires, 1815–1919* (London: Pearson, 2004); and V.G. Kiernan, *Colonial Empires and Armies, 1815–1960* (Montrea: McGill-Queen's University Press, 1998).

21 David Stevenson, *Armaments and the Coming of War: Europe 1904–1914* (Oxford: Oxford University Press, 1996); David Edgerton, *The Shock of the Old: Technology and Global History since 1900* (Oxford: Oxford University Press, 2007), 138–59.

22 B.H. Liddell Hart, *The Remaking of Modern Armies* (London: John Murray, 1927), 17.

23 See David Stevenson, *Cataclysm: the First World War as Political Tragedy* (New York: Basic Books, 2004), 161–78, 215–41, and 263–302.

24 B.H. Liddell Hart, "War and Peace," *English Review* 54 (1932), 408.

25 J.F.C. Fuller, *The Reformation of War* (London: Hutchinson, 1923), 103.

26 Douhet, *Command of the Air*, 52; and see Azar Gat, *Fascist and Liberal Visions of War: Fuller, Liddell Hart, Douhet, and Other Modernists* (Oxford: Oxford University Press, 1998); and Barry R. Posen, *The Sources of Military Doctrine: France, Britain, and Germany between the World Wars* (Ithaca, NY: Cornell University Press, 1984).

27 Tami Davis Biddle, *Rhetoric and Reality in Air Warfare: The Evolution of British and American Ideas about Strategic Bombing, 1914–1945* (Princeton, NJ: Princeton University Press, 2004); and Joe Maiolo, *Cry Havoc: How the Arms Race Drove the World to War, 1931–41* (New York: Basic Books, 2010).

28 Robert Pape, *Bombing to Win: Air Power and Coercion* (Ithaca, CT: Cornell University Press, 1996).

29 Bernard Brodie, "The Absolute Weapon," in Thomas G. Mahnken and Joseph Maiolo, eds., *Strategic Studies: A Reader* (London: Routledge, 2008), 213; and Robert Jervis, *The Meaning of the Nuclear Revolution* (Ithaca, CT: Cornell University Press, 1990).

30 James William Gibson, *The Perfect War: Technowar in Vietnam* (New York: Atlantic Monthly Press, 1986).

31 Alvin and Heidi Toffler, *War and Anti-war: Survival at the Dawn of the 21st Century* (New York: Warner, 1993), 8.

32 Keith L. Shimko, *The Iraq Wars and America's Military Revolution* (Cambridge: Cambridge University Press, 2010), 26–52; Williamson Murray and MacGregor Knox, "Thinking about Revolutions in Warfare," in *The Dynamics of Military Revolutions, 1300–2050*, eds. MacGregor Knox and Williamson Murray (Cambridge: Cambridge University Press, 2001), 2–4.

33 Jeffrey R. Cooper, "Another View of the Revolution in Military Affairs," in *In Athena's Camp: Preparing for Conflict in the Information Age*, eds. John Arquilla and David Ronfeldt (Santa Monica, CA: RAND, 1997), 112–13. See John Mueller, *Retreat from Doomsday: The Obsolescence of Major War* (New York: Basic Books, 1989); Martin van Creveld, *The Transformation of War* (New York: Free Press, 1991); John Keegan, *A History of Warfare* (New York, Random House, 1993); Mary Kaldor, *New and Old Wars* (Cambridge: Polity, 1998); and Michael Mandelbaum, "Is Major War Obsolete?," *Survival* 40 (1998), 20–38.

34 Quoted in George C. Herring, "America and Vietnam: The Unending War," *Foreign Affairs* (Winter 1991/1992): 104.

35 Robert Citino, *Blitzkrieg to Desert Storm: The Evolution of Operational Warfare* (Lawrence, KS: University Press of Kansas, 2004), 290; and Boot, *War Made New*, 321. A cautious assessment is Thomas A. Keaney and Eliot A. Cohen, eds., *Revolution in Warfare? Air Power in the Persian Gulf* (Annapolis, MD: Naval Institute Press, 1995).

36 William Owens, *Lifting the Fog of War* (New York: FSG, 2000), 12.

37 Benjamin Lambeth, *The Transformation of American Airpower* (Ithaca, NY: Cornell University Press, 2000), 297.

38 Eliot A. Cohen, "Change and Transformation in Military Affairs," *Journal of Strategic Studies* 27 (2004), 403–4.

39 Michael O'Hanlon, *Technological Change and the Future of Warfare* (Washington, DC: Brookings, 2000).

40 Martin Shaw, *The New Western Way of War* (Cambridge: Polity, 2005).

41 Richard Hallion, *Storm over Iraq: Air Power and the Gulf War* (Washington, DC: Smithsonian Institution Press, 1997), x.

42 Benjamin Lambeth, *NATO's Air War for Kosovo: A Strategic and Operational Assessment* (Santa Monica, CA: RAND, 2001), 232; and see Andrew Bacevich and Eliot Cohen, eds., *War over Kosovo: Politics and Strategy in a Global Age* (New York: Columbia University Press, 2001).

43 Charles Krauthammer, "The Unipolar Moment," *Foreign Affairs* (1990): 23–33.

44 Max Boot, *The Savage Wars of Peace: Small Wars and the Rise of American Power* (New York: Basic Books, 2002), xx; Donald Kagan and Frederick Kagan, *While America Sleeps: Self-Delusion, Military Weakness, and the Threat to Peace Today* (New York: St. Martin's, 2000); and William Kristol and Robert Kagan, "Toward a Neo-Reaganite Foreign Policy," *Foreign Affairs* (July/August 1996): 18–32.

45 Michael Ignatieff, *Empire Lite: Nation-Building in Bosnia, Kosovo and Afghanistan* (Toronto: Penguin, 2003); and Samantha Power, *A Problem from Hell: America and the Age of Genocide* (New York: Basic Books, 2002).

46 Donald Rumsfeld, "Transforming the Military," *Foreign Affairs* 81 (May/June 2002): 20–32.

47 Richard B. Andres, Craig Wills, and Thomas G. Griffith, "Winning with Allies: The Strategic Value of the Afghan Model," *International Security* 30 (2005/2006), 127.

48 Van Creveld, *Changing Face of War*, 248; Boot, *War Made New*, 400.

49 John Keegan, *The Iraq War* (New York: Knopf, 2004), 1.

50 Sir Rupert Smith, *The Utility of Force: The Art of War in the Modern World* (New York: Knopf, 2005).

51 Frederick Kagan, *Finding the Target: The Transformation of American Military Policy* (New York: Encounter Books, 2006), 359; Francis Fukuyama, *America at the Crossroads: Democracy, Power, and the Neoconservative Legacy* (New Haven, CT: Yale University Press, 2006).

52 Alan J. Kuperman, "A Model Humanitarian Intervention? Reassessing NATO's Libya Campaign," *International Security* 38 (2013), 105–36.

53 John Nagl, *Learning to Eat Soup with a Knife: Counterinsurgency Lessons from Malaya and Vietnam* (Chicago: University of Chicago Press, 2002); and Chad C. Serena, *A Revolution in Military Adaptation: The US Army in the Iraq War* (Washington, DC: Georgetown University Press, 2011).

54 John Arquilla, *Worst Enemy: The Reluctant Transformation of the American Military* (Chicago: Ivan Dee, 2008), 7; John Arquilla, *Networks and Netwars: The Future of Terror, Crime, and Militancy* (Santa Monica, CA: RAND, 2001); and Thomas G. Mahnken, *Technology and the American Way of War since 1945* (New York: Columbia University Press, 2008).

55 Boot, *War Made New*, 473.

56 Robert Gates, "A Balanced Strategy: Reprogramming the Pentagon for a New Age," *Foreign Affairs* (January/February 2009): 29–40; and Ashton B. Carter, "Running the Pentagon Right: How to Get the Troops What They Need," *Foreign Affairs* (January/February 2014): 101–12.

57 Kagan, *Finding the Target*, 362–3.

2

Disasters as Security Threats: Mapping Humanitarian Assistance Needs and Priorities for the Canadian Armed Forces

RACHEL LEA HEIDE

Since 2005, the Canadian Armed Forces (CAF) has been involved in six humanitarian assistance operations around the world.[1] It is likely that countries in distress will continue to call upon the government of Canada (GOC) to send the CAF to help provide humanitarian assistance,[2] especially in light of the increasing likelihood of disasters in the developing world, as indicated by current security environment trends. Furthermore, based upon past practices, it is likely that the GOC and the CAF will continue to address as many disasters as force posture and readiness will allow. In fact, one of the six missions in the 2008 Canada First Defence Strategy (CFDS) stipulates that the CAF must be able to "deploy forces in response to crises elsewhere in the world for shorter periods."[3]

In order to help the CAF better anticipate where humanitarian disasters might occur and what type of tasks a relief mission might entail, this chapter will analyze strategic trends[4] around the globe that may affect the frequency, and indicate the potential locations, of future humanitarian assistance missions outside of Canada. This chapter will discuss the indicators for natural and man-made disasters, where these events could potentially occur, and what kind of operations the CAF might be called upon to carry out. Potential causes of natural disasters requiring intervention include climate change (extreme weather, drought), resource scarcity (food and water shortages), and unstable geography (volcanoes, earthquakes, coastal flooding). Foreseeable causes of man-made disasters include state, ethnic, or religious clashes; overpopulation pressures; and failure of large urbanized areas. Based on the projection of strategic trends, humanitarian assistance operations in the near future are most likely to occur in sub-Saharan Africa, Asia, and the Middle East.

NATURAL DISASTERS

Natural disasters can generally be grouped into climatic or geological catastrophes, such as resource scarcity and unstable geography. Since water and food shortages can be caused by climatic phenomena (such as floods or droughts), analysis of the resource scarcity is included. Regardless of the type of disaster, at the point of disaster itself, it is likely that external humanitarian assistance is required to provide food, water, shelter, and medical aid. These disasters might also lead to mass migration, where people flee the devastated area in search of improved and safer circumstances. This often means that displaced persons end up in refugee camps. If the host nation does not have adequate food and water resources for the displaced people, the human suffering will persist in the refugee camps until outside humanitarian assistance comes. This next section examines the three forms of natural disasters: climate change, resource scarcity, and unstable geography.

Climate Change

Environment Canada defines *climate change* as "changes in long-term weather patterns caused by natural phenomena and human activities that alter the chemical composition of the atmosphere through the build-up of greenhouse gases which help trap heat and reflect it back to the earth's surface."[5] Climate change can lead to natural disasters requiring humanitarian assistance in one of two ways: through extreme weather or by affecting rainfall and agricultural patterns. Climate change will continue to increase the frequency and intensity of severe weather, including violent storms and their consequent damage, flooding of populated and urban areas, coastal erosion and rising sea levels' threatening those living in littoral areas, as well as drought and heat waves. Extreme weather events that result in a natural disaster could lead to extreme damage to city infrastructure, the mass destruction of housing, the inability of people to access food and water, and large numbers of deaths. Affected people in paralyzed urban centres or remote and isolated rural areas could require humanitarian assistance and shelter. If people had enough advance notice, or if there was too much devastation to survive in the affected area, people would likely flee, thus resulting in mass migration and refugee camps that burden the economic sustainability of neighbouring regions and countries that became reluctant host nations. These displaced people would also require humanitarian assistance for basic needs.[6]

Climate change has also been linked to changes in weather, rainfall distributions, and agricultural patterns. Trends analysis indicates that wet regions will likely see an increase in rainfall and that arid regions will become drier. Although too much rain can negatively impact crop production by preventing proper growing conditions in time for harvest, the more frequent consequence will be droughts that directly affect crops already in production. Droughts also prevent the growth of future crops. Degradation of agricultural lands and food and water shortages are not the only consequences of droughts. Lack of precipitation also leads to desertification, where areas become deserts.[7] Desertification affects approximately two-thirds of the world's countries, which happen to cover one-third of the earth's surface and where 1 billion people (20 per cent of the global population) live.[8] Sub-Saharan Africa is at the greatest risk of suffering from decreases in rainfall, drought, and desertification. Darfur and South Sudan are currently suffering from drought, and the countries susceptible to desertification are Chad, Darfur, Eritrea, Mali, Niger, and the Saharan margins. Lack of rainfall, prolonged drought, and desertification can lead to the same natural disaster consequences as extreme weather. People without food or water require humanitarian assistance. If mass migration occurs, the resulting refugee camps will require humanitarian assistance to meet basic needs and address the continuing suffering.[9]

Resource Scarcity

In general, resource scarcity could be a catalyst for conflict, which in turn could threaten individuals' security or lead to a mass exodus of a war zone. National resentments and frustrations arise when there is uneven distribution of, or access to, resources. This leads to competition for the resources (such as energy, minerals, food, and water), and some groups will try to gain access and control through aggression and war. If conflict did lead to a humanitarian disaster where large groups of people were displaced and lacked shelter and sustenance, food and water shortages are likely to lead to mass starvation, mass migration, and the consequences of refugee camps needing humanitarian assistance.[10]

There are currently insufficient supplies of potable water and food in the developing world. Twelve of the world's fifteen water-scarce countries are located in the Middle East and North Africa (MENA) region, which is the most water-scarce region of the world. Water stress is also felt in sub-Saharan Africa, South and Central Asia, and China where less precipitation and increasing evaporation are leading to decreased water availability. The melting of the Himalayan glaciers also contributes to the region's decrease in water supplies. Scientists predict that the Himalayan glaciers will have disappeared by 2023; this will result in the loss of a major water supply for 750 million people in the Himalaya-Hindu-Kush region, as well as China, Bangladesh, India, and Pakistan. This will lead to mass suffering and mass migration as people move to find new sources of sustenance. Humanitarian assistance will be required in refugee camps and in regions where people remained behind despite the lack of water.[11]

Food shortages will lead to the same consequence: people starving in devastated regions and in refugee camps. In both instances, humanitarian assistance will be needed. Food shortages result from a variety of causes: population growth, lack of arable land, desertification, and inadequate rainfall. Internal or inter-regional disputes over food supplies could result. Protests and riots could erupt among those who cannot access or afford food, thus destabilizing a region and leading to a potential eruption of violence that the local government might not be able to stop without external intervention of stabilizing forces. If large enough masses of people lack basic needs, such as food, then humanitarian assistance will be required. Six million people in the Mali area are at risk for food insecurity. Africa's crop yields are predicted to decrease by 50 per cent before 2030. It is expected that populations from sub-Saharan Africa will migrate to the Middle East, Mediterranean area, and Europe to flee food and water scarcities. Humanitarian assistance will be required in the regions of Africa that are experiencing food shortages to the point of disaster and hosting refugee camps.[12]

Unstable Geography

Natural disasters are increasingly likely due to unstable geography. Habitation has increased in volcanic and seismic areas. Settlements, especially large urban areas, in low-lying coastal and littoral regions, are vulnerable to extreme weather that could involve intensified seasonal rains, tropical cyclones, storm surges, and tsunamis. Almost all of these weather events will likely result in destructive coastal flooding, forcing people to flee. Coastal inundation of highly populated areas is a threat to Southern Asia, China, Bangladesh, Maldives, the Indian East Coast, and the East Asian Archipelagoes. Humanitarian assistance will be required for those trapped in the devastated area and for people who fled and ended up in refugee camps where host nations cannot accommodate the needs of the displaced people.[13]

These three forms of natural disasters breed similar results: an acute need for food, water, and shelter. Militaries are well equipped to respond to such crises, as they can quickly provide large-scale assistance within an established organizational framework.

DISASTERS OF HUMAN ORIGIN

Disasters of human origin requiring humanitarian assistance is generally some form of conflict; humanitarian assistance would be needed to alleviate the suffering of a particular group of people targeted by the conflict or to help reduce the suffering of people in refugee camps who fled the conflict. Stabilization operations might also be necessary to end the fighting and restore peace to an area. The following is a discussion of factors that can cause instability, which in turn could result in conflict and a man-made disaster requiring external assistance. These factors include geopolitics, inequality, demographics, urbanization, and conflict.

Geopolitics

Conflict – whether diplomatic or violent – is generated when divisions, competition, and rivalries arise between groups of people. States can be rivals of other states, thus dividing a region. A state can be fragmented along ethnic, cultural, or religious lines. Religions and ideologies can have extremists pitted against moderate and mainstream believers. Further group divisions include identity, race, nationality, class, caste, clan, tribe, and area of origin.[14]

Fragile and failed states are another cause of instability that could lead to conflict. A weak or fragile state that may fail is generally characterized by poor governance; lack of human security; lack of economic and social development; poverty; and corruption. The majority of these are located in Africa and Asia; the top seven states most likely to fail include Somalia, the Democratic Republic of Congo, Sudan, South Sudan, Chad, Afghanistan, and Haiti. Other areas of instability exist in the Middle East, Central and South Asia, and Latin America. Specific states in danger of failing are Yemen, Central African Republic, Côte d'Ivoire, Nigeria, Guinea, Guinea-Bissau, Iraq, North Korea, and Pakistan. In fragile and failed states, the extreme poverty, chaos, and armed clashes could push people to flee as refugees in order to escape injustice, starvation, and conflict. Neighbouring nations can be destabilized by the domestic unrest and the refugee flows. Intervention – humanitarian assistance or stabilization forces – becomes necessary as civilian casualties and suffering mounts with no sign that the conflict can be solved and stopped internally.[15]

Inequality

A variety of social stresses can lead to discontent, which in turn could be the eventual root of tensions and conflict. Global inequalities are brought to light through mass communications, especially the Internet. Once the magnitude of the disparities between the West and the developing world become known in real-time detail, this knowledge fuels grievances and anger among politically charged individuals and groups in the developing world. Another social stress is poverty and the inability to better one's existence and escape the suffering and limitations that comes from having very little financial means. Poverty is rampant in Africa (sub-Saharan Africa especially) and Asia. Poverty rates are increasing for already struggling regions: South America and the Caribbean are not able to meet their projected poverty reduction rates. No progress has been made in reducing poverty in many sub-Saharan African countries. Sub-Saharan Africa and Latin America have the highest levels of income inequality, and Europe and Central Asia have seen their poverty rates increase.[16]

Demographics

Demographic trends in population increases and youth bulges can lead to tensions, unrest, and potentially conflict. The world's population is expected to reach 8.8 billion by 2040. Much of this growth is going to take place in developing countries, such as Sudan, Somalia, Darfur, and Rwanda. Rapid growth is expected in sub-Saharan Africa, Afghanistan, and the Palestinian territories. Large and rapid population growth will be detrimental if the state is unable to expand its economy, infrastructure, services, and social safety net fast enough to provide education and employment opportunities and if it lacks the resources to have adequate food, water, and shelter for everyone. If a state cannot accommodate the needs of its entire people, then those who are suffering will become discontent, perhaps to the point of violent protest or aggression against those who are not lacking to the same degree.[17]

Many developing countries also face the challenge of youth bulges, where people between the ages of twelve and twenty-four account for over 50 per cent of the population. This demographic trend is occurring in regions that already lack proper education, social services, housing, and employment opportunities. With such a large proportion of the population entering the phase of life where one would typically pursue an education and then move into a life-sustaining career and start a family, the competition will be heightened for the scarce positions and opportunities. Consequently, these regions will likely experience much unrest as this large proportion of the population will become dissatisfied because they cannot attend high school or university, find gainful employment after graduation, or afford housing or marriage. Mass protests that may destabilize a government or lead to violence are not inconceivable. Impoverished youth lacking hope for economic improvement could turn to terrorist organizations as a means of gaining social legitimacy or income. Countries with youth bulges are three times more likely to experience armed insurrections, *coups d'état*, or civil wars. The top ten states that have youth bulges are located in sub-Saharan Africa; the next five are in the Middle East. Central Asia is another region challenged by this potentially destabilizing demographic trend.[18]

Urbanization

A variety of destabilizing trends converge with the occurrence of urbanization. The increase in the size of urban centres is taking

Table 2.1
Megacity population projected to 2025

Urban Agglomeration	Population (millions)
Tokyo, Japan	36.4
Bombay, India	26.4
Delhi, India	22.5
São Paulo, Brazil	21.4
Mexico City, Mexico	21.0
New York–Newark, US	20.6
Calcutta, India	20.6
Shanghai, China	19.4
Karachi, Pakistan	19.1
Kinshasa, Dem. Republic of Congo	16.8
Lagos, Nigeria	15.8
Cairo, Egypt	15.6
Manila, Philippines	14.8
Beijing, China	14.5
Buenos Aires, Argentina	13.8
Los Angeles–Long Beach–Santa Ana, US	13.7
Rio de Janeiro, Brazil	13.4
Jakarta, Indonesia	12.4
Istanbul, Turkey	12.1
Guangzhou, Guangdong, China	11.8
Osaka–Kobe, Japan	11.4
Moscow, Russian Federation	10.5
Lahore, Pakistan	10.5
Shenzhen, China	10.2
Madras, India	10.1
Paris, France	10.0

Source: United Nations, *World Urbanization Prospects: The 2007 Revision*, 10.

place mainly in the developing world. Consequently, population growth will be concentrated in the urban centres of less developed countries. While the developing world is already feeling pressures from resource shortages and inadequate infrastructure, rapid urbanization will only increase these stresses. City failure (the collapse of governance and control) or food and water shortages could lead to chaos, violence, or mass migration.[19]

Megacities are urban agglomerations of more than 10 million inhabitants. According to a United Nations urbanization report, 80 per cent of the increase in megacities will take place in the developing world. In 2007, there were nineteen megacities; by 2025, this number will increase to twenty-seven. Ten per cent of the world's population will be living in megacities. Large cities are urban centres with 5 to 10 million inhabitants. It is predicted that 7 per cent of the world's population will be living in large cities by 2025. In 2007, there were thirty large cities in the world; by 2025, this number will increase to forty-eight. By the same year, 75 per cent of large cities will be located in the developing world.[20]

The regional and geographical location of megacities and large cities makes them susceptible to destabilizing factors. Because of their size and their location in developing countries that are struggling to provide stable governance and modern amenities, it is likely that these cities will be impoverished shanty towns that are congested, polluted, and lacking running water and sewers. Discontented residents could turn to violent protest, attempts to overthrow the government, or terrorist or extremist organizations to change their situation. Civil unrest would only be accelerated if the urban centre was located in a failed or fragile state. Failure of a megacity could occur if the government was unable to provide essential services or if a governance vacuum occurred in part, or all, of the city. Large numbers of people would be subjected to chaos, disease, food and water shortages, disrupted employment and economies, and potentially a humanitarian crisis as living in the failed city devolved into fighting for one's survival.[21] In short, large urban centres magnify the risks of collapse.

Megacities and large cities face an additional threat, due to their geographical location. The expansion of these cities is occurring in the littoral (coastal areas that are within 100 kilometres of a shoreline). Currently, 60 per cent of the world's population lives within 100 kilometres of the sea while 70 per cent live within 300 kilometres of a seacoast. Littoral areas are vulnerable to environmental risks such as extreme weather and flooding. If an environmental disaster occurred in a megacity located in the littoral, large numbers of people would become casualties; many would flee in search of safety, and the resulting humanitarian crisis might be beyond the capability of external aid organizations and defence forces. Whether it be dissatisfaction that requires stabilization operations or a humanitarian crisis that requires assistance and relief, crises in a large urban area would affect unprecedented numbers of people.[22]

Conflict

A conflict, in large enough proportions, could necessitate intervention with humanitarian assistance or stabilization operations. Many of the previously mentioned trends could either directly or indirectly result in conflict. Although conflict is typically thought of as man-made, the clash could have originated over food or water sources or competition for natural resources. Specific groups of people can be targeted for annihilation through ethnic cleansing or genocide, resulting in death and displacement of people. In Sudan, ethnic cleansing produced 2 million refugees. Genocide has been committed in a number of African states by sub-state tribal groups. With regards to ethnic strife, a line of instability has been noted from Morocco to Pakistan, where Shias, Sunnis, Kurds, Arabs, Persians, Jews, Pashtuns, and Baluch feel religiously and physically threatened by the existence of other groups.[23]

Conflict can also have geopolitical roots. During the Arab Spring, citizens of Syria, Tunisia, Yemen, Mali, Mauritania, and Burkina Faso tried to change the government regimes with which they were dissatisfied. Conflict also occurs when one state decides to assert power over another sovereign nation or when governance in a failed or fragile state collapses or is challenged by other internal competing sources of power. Regional economic disparity is another potential driver for conflict, as recently prosperous states channel their new wealth into aggression to attain goals previously out of reach, or as impoverished nations attack those who have a coveted source of wealth. In states that were once stable or that are now fragile, the pressures from mass migration and refugee flows can result in ethnic, religious, or territorial tensions that might eventually escalate into conflict.[24] No matter what the cause of conflict, large groups of people could suffer from lack of resources, could be displaced and forced to seek refuge elsewhere, or could be physically in danger. In any case, humanitarian assistance intervention may be required and decided upon by the international community.

CONVERGENCE AND CONSEQUENCES

Whether natural or man-made, disasters will have similar consequences. Most notable are the consequences of migration in particular and destabilization in general for the country in question.

Consequences of Migration

For all the potential causes of disasters discussed, humanitarian assistance will likely be needed – either in the place where the disaster occurred or at a refugee camp in a neighbouring region or country. People cannot always flee for safety because of injury, illness, poverty, employment obligations, small children, or family ties. Hence, there will always be people needing medical shelter, food, and water assistance in the disaster area. Nevertheless, there will also always be people who flee en masse an area devastated by storms, floods, droughts, earthquakes, or conflict in search of safety or food and water supplies. When mass migration occurs, it is unlikely that everyone will be successful in finding adequate food and water, as well as permanent shelter and employment to sustain a reasonable existence. Consequently, people who have nowhere else to go will probably resort to refugee camps, dependent upon the host nation for food, water, and make-shift shelter.

Disaster areas and refugee camps could potentially need humanitarian assistance. Some neighbouring regions might have the space, money, food, and water resources to maintain large refugee camps without detrimental hardship to the host nation. Nonetheless, this is not always the case; refugees living in dense and unsanitary conditions are prone to infectious disease, and they might have stopped in a region that does not have the capacity or resources to cope with such a large influx of people. The establishment of refugee camps will likely disrupt the economic and social balances of the host nation causing resentments between native citizens and displaced persons, potentially leading to conflict. Ethnic, religious, or economic differences can arise, causing the people in the refugee camps to suffer just as much as they did before they migrated.

If tensions rise between the displaced people and the host nation's citizens, or among ethnic groups making up the refugees, conflict might arise, and intervention by stabilization operations may be needed. The devastated areas could also require reconstruction aid, and if local governments are overwhelmed, stabilization operations might also be warranted. The developing world will be especially vulnerable due to widespread existing poverty and city governance that does not have adequate emergency management. Thus, whether at the site of the disaster, conflict, or place of refuge, humanitarian assistance operations will likely be required. Whether or not foreign military assistance is requested depends upon the severity of the disaster and the capacity of the host nation and non-governmental organizations (NGOs) to respond adequately to the human suffering.[25]

Consequences of Destabilization

Destabilizing factors that could lead to conflict can be both natural and man-made. Lack of food creates instability as people suffer from malnutrition and hunger and consider moving elsewhere. Climate change will exacerbate existing food and water shortages and could potentially be the tipping point for a humanitarian disaster. Economic disparity and poverty are destabilizing as people grow increasingly dissatisfied with their state of want, perhaps to the point of pushing for political change or aggression against neighbouring states. Demographic trends in the developing world, such as youth bulges and urbanization, can be destabilizing, seeing as poor living conditions, unemployment, and dissatisfaction with lack of government programs could lead to violent protests.[26]

The existence of fragile and failed states is also destabilizing; if a state fails, whatever governance did exist likely would be replaced by chaos. Eventually, other forms of informal organization will move in to fill the vacuum, some of which might be linked to terrorists, international crime, or ethnic persecution. Mass movements of people trying to escape and alleviate their suffering are destabilizing, putting unexpected resource and financial demands on the host nation, and causing civil unrest among those who resent the pressure being placed on their home economy and resource base or who dislike the particular ethnic or religious group that has arrived. If these factors were destabilizing enough and lead to conflict, the international community might be required to undertake stabilization operations to restore the peace in addition to humanitarian operations to address the shelter, water, and medical needs of the mass groups of people suffering because of the conflict.[27]

PREPARING A CANADIAN RESPONSE

It must be acknowledged that disaster will not strike in every location where it has been identified as possible, nor will external assistance necessarily be required for every humanitarian emergency that occurs. Furthermore, the GOC cannot send aid and assistance to every disaster that occurs around the world; it simply does not have the resources to do so. When the GOC does choose to provide assistance for a disaster, civilian government departments (CGDs) will be tasked first. The CAF will be called upon only as a last resort when it has suitable capabilities for the situation that all other CGDs and NGOs lack. Although the CAF will not be sent on every humanitarian mission operated by the GOC, and although not every disaster will require CAF capabilities, it is prudent for the CAF to be aware of what disasters could occur, where they might happen, and what the surrounding circumstances could entail. From this awareness, the CAF could ensure that it had the adequate training, capabilities, force posture, and readiness in order to respond as quickly and efficiently as possible.

After conducting an anticipatory analysis of strategic trends, a scenario set could be created based on the results to further analyze readiness levels and capability gaps for these possible situations and missions. This would be done by populating the scenarios to determine the amounts of supplies, equipment, and personnel that are required and to quantify any deficiencies or gaps in capabilities for each scenario, mission, and location. Once readiness levels have been determined, call-up for any of these scenarios (or similar missions) should be faster since thought and preparation have already gone into these specific humanitarian assistance deliberations. These scenarios could also be used for joint CAF training purposes or for training with CGD partners to increase co-operation and integration levels. Nine scenarios that follow from this anticipatory analysis include five natural disaster scenarios and six man-made disaster scenarios: Severe Weather Damage, Extreme Heat and Drought, Food Shortage, Water Shortage, Geological Event, Fragile and Failed States, Civil War, Ethnic or Religious Clashes, Poverty Pressures, Overpopulation Pressures, and Failed Urban Area.

The CAF's past experiences in both combat and humanitarian assistance missions provide lessons on capabilities that are imperative for effective humanitarian assistance operations in the future. The CAF must continue to conduct civil-military co-operation with ease. The CAF is sent to disaster areas to help support host nation governments, NGOs, and CGDs from Canada by providing emergency assistance until these civilian entities are able to take over the provision of these services. Close co-operation throughout the entire operation and transition period to redeployment improves efficiency and provides more comprehensive aid to victims. Part of the coordination process is devising the CAF's exit strategy and the appropriate metrics for determining when the host nation and NGOs are capable of taking over the assistance mission, thus allowing the CAF to end its presence and return to Canada.[28]

The acquisition of intelligence is another important capability. Intelligence is needed as soon as a disaster strikes so that the GOC can determine if CAF presence is required and so that the CAF can ascertain what capabilities it will need to prepare to deploy. Intelligence is required throughout the operation, to discern the location and needs of victims, to identify any security risks, and to monitor the progress that is being made toward turning over responsibilities to civilian organizations. Having native-language speakers is an important human intelligence asset (for example, the CAF sent French-speakers to Haiti in 2010 and Tagalog-speakers to the Philippines in 2013). This enables the CAF to communicate directly with local citizens, find out their needs, and inform them of the aid and services being provided, without anything being lost in translation. To ensure and enhance communications between the CAF and Canadian CGDs, interoperability of communications and information systems should be a priority. The greater the ease of communication, and the more universal the coordination of civilian and military assets, the more effective the humanitarian assistance mission will be. This provides a more effective aid experience for the victims.[29]

CONCLUSION AND WAY AHEAD

The anticipatory trends analysis determined that there are two types of disasters. Natural disasters include geological disasters (earthquakes, tsunamis, volcanoes, and landslides) and climatic disasters (tornadoes, floods, blizzards, heavy storms). Disasters of human origin could be unintentional (such as an accidental chemical spill) or intentional (conflict over a variety of potential disagreements). In either case, the disaster brings about suffering to significant segments of the population, and given the magnitude of the emergency, neither the people nor their state government have the capacity to alleviate and mitigate the suffering on their own. People have lost their homes, lack food and water, and are probably suffering injuries and medical emergencies.

Current trends indicate that disasters requiring humanitarian assistance operations are most likely to occur in sub-Saharan Africa, Asia, and the Middle East. More specifically for natural disasters, drought, and desertification will likely affect sub-Saharan Africa (Chad, Darfur, Eritrea, Mali, Niger, South Sudan, and the Saharan margins). Sub-Saharan Africa will also suffer food and water shortages; additional water shortages are expected to occur in the Middle East, North Africa, South and Central Asia, China, and the Himalaya-Hindu-Kush region. Unstable geography disasters are likely in Southern Asia, China, Bangladesh, Maldives, East India, and the East Asian Archipelagoes. Regarding man-made disasters, the top seven states likely to fail include Somalia, the Democratic Republic of Congo, Sudan, South Sudan, Chad, Afghanistan, and Haiti. Other states that are in danger of failing are Yemen, Central African Republic, Côte d'Ivoire, Nigeria, Guinea, Guinea-Bissau, Iraq, North Korea, and Pakistan. Rapid population growth is expected to occur in sub-Saharan Africa, Afghanistan, and the Palestinian territories, and the top fifteen states with youth bulges are located in sub-Saharan Africa and the Middle East.

Based on security environment analysis, it appears likely that expeditionary humanitarian assistance missions will continue as a trend in future military operations. Security environment trends indicate that disasters (both natural and of human origin) are likely to increase in frequency, and Canada has willingly responded each time countries have requested help to recover from overwhelming disasters.

To demonstrate how the government of Canada and the Canadian Armed Forces can further increase Canada's preparation for potential humanitarian assistance missions, this chapter demonstrates the value of conducting a periodic anticipatory analysis of security environment trends. Identifying what will likely cause natural and man-made disasters in the future, as well as suggesting where these are most likely to occur, enables the CAF to prepare for specific types of humanitarian assistance operations as well as the conditions of specific locations. When the security environment changes, the trends analysis should be updated on a regular cycle to ensure no new circumstances are missed. From this awareness, the CAF could ensure that it had the adequate training, capabilities, force posture, and readiness to respond as quickly and efficiently as possible when the GOC decides to deploy the CAF in response to humanitarian crises around the world.

NOTES

1 Operation Structure (response to 24 December 2004 tsunami in South-
  east Asia, December 2004–March 2005); Operation Plateau (response to
  8 October 2005 earthquake South Asia, 14 October–4 December 2005);
  Operation Unison (support to the Hurricane Katrina Relief Efforts in the
  United States, 2005); Operation Horatio (response to August 2008 hurri-
  canes in Haiti, 10–27 September 2008); Operation Hestia (response to 12
  January 2010 earthquake in Haiti, 13 January–1 April 2010); Operation
  Renaissance (response to 7–8 November 2013 Typhoon Haiyan in Philippines, 13 November–16 December 2013).
2 A humanitarian operation "is an international military operation conducted where the primary task is purely to assist agencies of the humanitarian enterprise in the delivery of humanitarian assistance. It does not
  include a security function for the relief effort. Requests for military assets
  normally only occur when civil agencies cannot respond in a timely manner, or when they lack the requisite capacity." Canada's Department of
  National Defence, *Humanitarian Operations and Disaster Relief Operations
  BGJ-005-307 FP-040* (Ottawa: J7 Doctrine 2, 2005), 1–4.
3 The CFDS outlines a total of six missions which the CAF must maintain the
  capability to conduct. They are as follows: (1) Conduct daily domestic and
  continental operations, including in the Arctic and through NORAD; (2)
  Support a major international event in Canada, such as the 2010 Olym-
  pics; (3) Respond to a major terrorist attack; (4) Support civilian authorities during a crisis in Canada such as a natural disaster; (5) Lead and/
  or conduct a major international operation for an extended period; and
  (6) Deploy forces in response to crises elsewhere in the world for shorter
  periods. Government of Canada, Canada First Defence Strategy (Ottawa:
  Department of National Defence, 2008) accessed 1 August 2014, http://
  www.forces.gc.ca/en/about/canada-first-defence-strategy.page.
4 The research methodology for this study consisted of looking at future
  trends analyses that were prepared by the defence departments of Canada
  and its two closest allies. These documents include the following: United
  Kingdom's Ministry of Defence, *Strategic Trends Programme: Global Strategic
  Trends – Out to 2040* (London: Development, Concepts, and Doctrine
  Centre: January 2010) accessed 4 April 2014, https://www.gov.uk/gov-
  ernment/uploads/system/uploads/attachment_data/file/33717/GST4_
  v9_Feb10.pdf; United States' Department of Defense, *The Joint Operating
  Environment 2010* (Suffolk, VA: United States Joint Forces Command,
  2010) accessed 4 April 2014, http://www.peakoil.net/files/JOE2010.pdf;
  Canada's Department of National Defence, *The Future Security Environment*

2008–2030: Current and Emerging Trends (Ottawa: Chief of Force Development, 2010); and Canada's Department of National Defence, *The Future Security Environment 2013–2040* (Ottawa: Chief of Force Development, 2013). From these studies, the author looked for events and outcomes that could lead to a disaster situation where Western military assistance might be requested. This collection of trends was then sorted into two categories: potential causes of natural disasters and potential causes of man-made disasters.

5   Government of Canada, "Climate Change Definition," accessed 22 August 2013, Environment Canada's Definitions and Glossary website, online at http://www.ec.gc.ca/ges-ghg/default. asp?lang=En&n=B710AE51-1#section3.

6   DCDC, *Global Strategic Trends*, 11, 16, 21, 26, 54, 105; JFCOM, *Joint Operating Environment*, 32; CFD, *FSE 2013–2040*, 24, 39; CFD, *FSE 2008–2030*, 40, 41; J.J. Messner and Kendall Lawrence, "Failed State Index 2013: The Troubled Ten," The Fund for Peace, 24 June 2013, accessed 27 June 2013, http://library.fundforpeace.org/fsi13-troubled10.

7   Desertification "is the degradation of the land in arid, semi-arid, and sub-humid dry areas caused by climatic changes and human activities. It is accompanied by a reduction in the natural potential of the land and a depletion in surface and ground-water resources. But above all, it has negative repercussions on the living conditions and the economic development of the people affected by it." A.P. Koohafkan, "Desertification, Drought, and Their Consequences," Food and Agriculture Organization of the United Nations, accessed 10 September 2013, http://www.fao. org/sd/epdirect/epan0005.htm.

8   Koohafkan, "Desertification, Drought, and Their Consequences."

9   DCDC, *Global Strategic Trends*, 11, 21, 26, 106; CFD, *FSE 2008–2030*, 32, 40; Messner and Lawrence, "Failed State Index 2013: The Troubled Ten."

10 DCDC, *Global Strategic Trends*, 10, 11, 15, 16, 24, 26, 114; CFD, *FSE 2013–2040*, iii, 24; Emily Meierding, "Climate Change and Conflict: Avoiding Small Talk about the Weather," *International Studies Review* 15, no. 2 (June 2013): 200.

11 DCDC, *Global Strategic Trends*, 11, 112, 114; CFD, *FSE 2008–2030*, 40, 43, 71; CFD, *FSE 2013–2040*, 17, 34, 35.

12 DCDC, *Global Strategic Trends*, 11, 24, 114; JFCOM, *Joint Operating Environment*, 29, 30; CFD, *FSE 2008–2030*, 1, 2, 39, 40; CFD, *FSE 2013–2040*, 24; Messner and Lawrence, "Failed State Index 2013: The Troubled Ten."

13 DCDC, *Global Strategic Trends*, 114–15; JFCOM, *Joint Operating Environment*, 33, 57; CFD, *FSE 2008–2030*, 24, 40; CFD, *FSE 2013–2040*, 3–4.

14 DCDC, *Global Strategic Trends*, 10, 15, 61; JFCOM, *Joint Operating Environment*, 45; CFD, *FSE 2013–2040*, 24; Fund for Peace, "Failed State Index" 2013, accessed 26 Jun 2013, http://ffp.statesindex.org/.

15 DCDC, *Global Strategic Trends*, 10, 58, 61, 62, 73, 115; JFCOM, *Joint Operating Environment*, 50; CFD, *FSE 2008–2030*, 3, 73; CFD, *FSE 2013–2040*, iii, 23–4; David Carment, Simon Langlois-Bertrand, Yiagadeesen Samy, "Assessing State Fragility, with a Focus on the Middle East and North Africa Region: A 2014 Country Indicators Report for Foreign Policy Report" (Ottawa, Norman Paterson School of International Affairs, Carleton University, 30 December 2014), 2, 4, 5.

16 DCDC, *Global Strategic Trends*, 11, 12, 15, 16, 24; CFD, *FSE 2008–2030*, 26, 27, 28; CFD, *FSE 2013–2040*, 24, 42.

17 DCDC, *Global Strategic Trends*, 10, 15, 24, 55, 61; JFCOM, *Joint Operating Environment*, 12.

18 CFD, *FSE 2008–2030*, 30–1.

19 DCDC, *Global Strategic Trends*, 2; JFCOM, *Joint Operating Environment*, 57, 58; CFD, *FSE 2008–2030*, 22; CFD, *FSE 2013–2040*, iii.

20 CFD, *FSE 2008–2030*, 22–3; United Nations, *World Urbanization Prospect: The 2007 Revision*, (New York: United Nations, 2008), 9–10.

21 Ibid., 22–4.

22 Ibid., 23–4.

23 DCDC, *Global Strategic Trends*, 16, 73, 106; JFCOM, *Joint Operating Environment*, 6, 41, 48–9.

24 CFD, *FSE 2008–2030*, 2, 4, 12, 27, 31, 41, 75; CFD, Fund for Peace, "Failed State Index."

25 DCDC, *Global Strategic Trends*, 97; JFCOM, *Joint Operating Environment*, 15, 33; CFD, *FSE 2008-2030*, 22, 28, 41; CFD, *FSE 2013–2040*, iii; Fund for Peace, "Failed State Index."

26 CFD, *FSE 2008–2030*, 1, 2, 17, 31, 33, 39, 43, 103.

27 Ibid., 1, 3, 18, 22, 67, 73, 74.

28 David Carment, *Effective Defence Policy for Responding to Failed and Failing States* (Calgary, AB: Canadian Defence and Foreign Affairs Institute, 2005), 12, 17, accessed 29 October 2015, http://www4.carleton.ca/cifp/docs/archive/EffectiveDefencePolicyFailedStates.pdf.

29 Ibid., 14, 29, 31; US Department of Defense, *Lessons from Civil-Military Disaster Management and Humanitarian Response to Typhoon Haiyan* (Yolanda) (Pearl Harbor-Hickam, HI: Center for Excellence in Disaster Management and Humanitarian Assistance, 2014), 33–4, 38.

3

The Strategic Impact of Improvised Explosive Devices in the US Military

CHRISTOPHER BARRON

Since 2002, close to 3,700 Americans have been killed by improvised explosive devices (IEDs) during operations in Iraq and Afghanistan. Tens of thousands more were maimed. The signature wounds of the twenty-first-century soldier – traumatic brain injuries and multiple limb amputations – stem directly from IEDs.[1] On the battlefield, uncertainty in placing the next footstep or driving outside existing tire tracks created a braking effect on small-unit movement and manoeuvre, and slowed the pace of missions. This gelatinous state trickled upward to the operational level; pace and tempo slowed everywhere, not just where an IED was found or struck. The constant spectre of IEDs and suspicion of local civilian complicity stymied campaign plans reliant upon close interactions with civilian populations. But for all the destruction and frustration created within the tactical and operational realms, the real damage from IEDs occurred at the strategic level. The steady stream of casualties and destroyed vehicles – courtesy of the IED – presented via television, print, and Internet, was a key contributor to the decline in domestic support for the wars.[2]

The employment of IEDs had a game-changing effect on the way the United States conducted military operations in the 9/11 Wars, and the response it elicited in terms of money, time, and energy was massive. Little more than a year into the US-led occupation of Iraq, the commander of US Central Command acknowledged the long-term challenges posed by the IED by explicitly calling for a "Manhattan-like project" to solve the problem.[3] Yet despite the subsequent efforts to combat these relatively simple weapons, the IED routinely maintained its position as the leading cause of casualties to US forces in both Iraq and Afghanistan. This chapter will offer three propositions: one, that the IED should not have surprised the United States as there was ample evidence of the threat throughout the twentieth century; two, that the US response to the IED did not solve the problem; and three, that the IED has a bright future in both tactical, asymmetric warfare and long-term, strategic deterrence against Western combat forces.

NOTHING NEW

The IED's ability to project an influence far beyond Ramadi's streets and Helmand's orchards is remarkable considering that most of the devices are little more than crudely assembled landmines, reliant upon technologies and tactics predating the twenty-first century. Yet its appearance and effectiveness in the last decade and a half still surprised the United States, although it should have been simple to forecast. The names occasionally changed – homemade landmine, booby trap, IED, roadside bomb, explosive hazard, et cetera – but the practice of detonating high explosives underneath or near unsuspecting targets on the battlefield was neither new nor uncommon prior to the West's focus on South and Central Asia. The landmine has long been a proven weapon and an asymmetrically perfect fit for war against the United States and its allies, and the evidence was there for those willing to look.

For the United States, there was never a shortage of opportunities to learn about the dangers from hidden explosives on the battlefield. Painful lessons could be learned from its own experiences and the missteps of others. The historical precedents for the landmine go back at least as far as the early Ming dynasty, when warring Chinese factions used gunpowder-filled buried shells as mines. Four hundred years later, during the American Civil War, both Union and Confederate forces used rudimentary mines on the battlefield.[4] These early applications of mine warfare are important, but it was not until the twentieth century that the concept of the portable landmine really blossomed.

The First World War is typically remembered for trench warfare, chemical weapons, and the advent of armoured vehicles. It was this latter event – the rise of the tank – that spawned the development of modern landmines. In response to the successes of British and French tanks during 1917, Germany developed anti-tank mines and placed them in patterns designed to maximize the impact on large formations.[5] At the same time, German soldiers established the habit of laying smaller anti-personnel mines and booby traps at road intersections, or when they withdrew from occupied areas. These nuisance mines did little to affect overall strategies, but they were more than enough to cause fear among allied soldiers and foreshadowed future tactics.

The Second World War saw a massive expansion in the role played by landmines, largely from technical and design innovations. The Germans developed the feared "S-mine," which could be triggered in multiple ways, and launched its main charge into the air before detonating and spraying shrapnel.[6] Finnish troops pioneered the use of tripwire-initiated fragmentation mines mounted on wooden stakes – a design that lasted for over fifty years.[7] Rommel's minefield at El Alamein (the infamous Devil's Garden) required attacking British forces to breach for nearly five miles, and Soviet minefields at Kursk helped the Red Army destroy 1,500 German tanks.[8] Nuisance mining of abandoned areas by departing forces continued as during the First World War. For better or worse, mines became an acknowledged and accepted figure on the modern battlefield. Just twenty years later in South Vietnam, their use would become a dominant form of warfare.

During the Vietnam War, mines and explosive booby traps had a devastating effect on US forces far beyond anything the Americans had experienced in either of the world wars. The statistics are grim. A Defense Intelligence Agency report revealed that landmines caused roughly 65 per cent of Marine Corps casualties in 1965.[9] From 1967 to 1968, nearly 10,100 US casualties in Vietnam came from mines and other explosive booby traps; in some American units, they accounted for nearly half of the total casualties.[10] By late 1970, more than 10,700 US Marines had been killed in Vietnam; 2,600 – nearly one in four – had been killed by mines, booby traps or other (non-indirect fire) explosions.[11] Other estimates put mine and mine-type casualties at nearly 33 per cent of the total number of American casualties for the war.[12]

These unprecedented casualty rates were the result of several factors, including advantageous terrain, the fluid nature of counter-insurgency combat and the remarkable skill of the Viet Cong (VC) and North Vietnamese Army (NVA) in manufacturing their own mines and IEDs from dud bombs and stolen US munitions.[13] But most important was the shift from using mines primarily as defensive tools to slow down attackers, to utilizing them as full-fledged offensive weapons. Mines were still used to protect positions and facilities, but the VC and NVA took the First and Second World Wars' concepts of nuisance mining to an entirely new level. US troops encountered mines and booby traps as part of complex enemy ambushes on patrols and convoys, as well as individual nuisances designed to maim and terrorize.[14] They found their own mines had been lifted at night and moved to commonly used paths and routes; fear of stepping in the wrong place became palpable. As one soldier put it, "We'd rather take on a thousand [enemy] in a firefight than have to walk through a known minefield."[15] The sentiment is meaningful, and one wonders: how much worse is the unknown minefield?

The use of mines continued long after the United States left Vietnam; Cambodia, Angola, and Mozambique all saw extensive mine warfare in the following years. The Rhodesian and South African armies – modern, well-equipped Western forces – dealt with mine strikes so often that they developed sophisticated vehicles designed to help defeat buried mines and IEDs.[16] For years, the Irish Republican Army utilized IEDs, often achieving spectacular results. In 1979, they attacked British Army elements near Warrenpoint with two well-placed IEDs, resulting in the death of eighteen British soldiers.[17] Other than date and location, the attack is nearly indistinguishable from the type that would plague US forces in Iraq. Throughout the 1980s, the US-backed forces fighting communism around the world faced similar threats. The Contras used mines against the Sandinistas in Nicaragua, frequently to devastating effect.[18] In Afghanistan, the US-supported Mujahedeen gained hard-earned experience with mines and IEDs as both victims and perpetrators. More recently, Hezbollah routinely used IEDs to attack Israeli Defense Forces in southern Lebanon and eventually succeeded in killing a senior general officer. Russian forces in Chechnya – in armoured vehicles comparable to US models – repeatedly absorbed lethal IED attacks; during the Second Chechen War, graphic videos of attacks were available to anyone with Internet access. Replace the green Russian equipment with American tan vehicles and the videos are indistinguishable with those eventually produced in Iraq.

STILL SURPRISING

None of this is intended to argue that landmines, booby traps, or IEDs are always critical to military success. What it did do, however, is demonstrate that these weapons have been an increasingly common battlefield threat for nearly a hundred years, and while they may not have singlehandedly won wars, they have extracted a terrible toll on the battlefield. This makes the American lack of preparation in dealing with this threat troublesome.

Despite the price paid, the lessons of Vietnam simply did not sink in. Some in the United States believed that the style of fighting there was an aberration, and that if the United States fought the Vietnam War again, it would somehow avoid the operational and strategic mistakes, and win the war; indeed, conventional wisdom still holds (wrongly, some would argue) that the United States never lost on the battlefield.[19] And there was solace found in focusing on the threat of open warfare in Europe against the Soviet Union. Much of the AirLand Battle doctrine of open warfare, deep strikes, and fast-paced tempo had little in common with the slow and messy nature of light infantry fighting a counter-insurgency.[20] But why were the later experiences of our allies and rivals seemingly ignored? Perhaps that came from the post–Cold War fascination many within the defence community had regarding the much-discussed Revolution in Military Affairs (RMA). Conceptually, the RMA allowed the United States to achieve swift, decisive victories through expanded intelligence, surveillance, and reconnaissance (ISR), increased situational awareness and command and control, and the use of precision munitions.[21] Rapid victories had the added benefit of eliminating the need for costly ground campaigns. Operation Desert Storm and the subsequent air campaigns over Bosnia and Kosovo were embraced as supporting evidence, minus the inconvenient reality of the NATO peacekeepers' struggles with Balkan minefields. The allure of the RMA was immensely appealing to acolytes of air power as well as some within the ground services, despite the Army and Marine Corps's natural affinity for believing that true victory required putting boots on the ground, or committing what T.R. Fehrenbach called "proud legions."[22]

As Asa McKercher points out in the first chapter of this book, these revolutions in military affairs are not the "specific preserve of the United States."[23] Rather, the science and technology works for both sides in a conflict equally – it cuts both ways. What advantage one side gains the other can just as easily realize. An advantage gained can quickly become a costly loss. Regardless of whether the cause was wishful thinking about Vietnam, fascination with bloodless victories or even a hubristic belief that what happened to the Russians or Israelis simply couldn't happen to the best-trained, best-equipped, and best-led military in the modern era, little was done to effectively address the threat of mines and IEDs. Ironically, from a countermine or counter-IED readiness standpoint, the never-ending debate on preparing for high- or low-intensity conflicts seems to have been irrelevant: US equipping and training decisions resulted in capabilities suited for neither. Over the years, soft-skin Jeeps were replaced by equally vulnerable high-mobility multi-purpose wheeled vehicles (HMMWVs). Bulky and hard to use metal detectors were replaced by slightly less bulky, yet still difficult to use detectors. Explosive-sniffing canines, one of Vietnam's few success stories, were allowed to nearly disappear from the inventory and took years still to re-introduce as part of the 9/11 Wars decades later. Even the equipment issued to armoured units that were expected to breach massive minefields in a high-intensity war was inadequate. Derided as "farm implements," it consisted chiefly of notoriously unreliable rocket-launched demolitions mounted on outdated platforms or towed behind under-armoured vehicles.[24]

Training was equally neglected. Despite a great renewed interest throughout the US military on realistic training during the 1980s and 1990s, the training renaissance stopped short of truly addressing the mine and IED threat.[25] Combat training centres focused heavily on direct-fire engagement between armoured forces, the use of indirect fires and air-ground integration. Breaching large minefields or clearing a few buried mines at road intersections relied on outdated and unreliable equipment, and routinely resulted in significant casualties.[26] Because of this, countermine training was often viewed as a distraction and as something that prevented units from focusing on their "actions on the objective." The idea that getting to the objective was itself a serious problem was not internalized by the military, and this combination of subpar *matériel* and incomplete training did little to prepare the US military for the IED, which

appeared almost immediately after the initial successes in March
and April of 2003.

Fully examining what helped feed and accelerate the IED's role
as the weapon of choice – the overestimation of Iraqi "good will"
toward the United States, a gross misjudgment on the condition of
Iraqi essential services, the disbanding of the Iraqi Army and the
failure to secure Iraqi munitions storage facilities – will continue for
years and is far beyond this chapter's scope. What matters is that
the United States was unprepared when the first reports of roadside
explosions coalesced into a disturbing trend. Admirably, commanders at all levels quickly recognized that their equipment, organizational structures and tactics were inadequate in addressing the IED
threat. Unfortunately, they simply lacked the capability to keep the
roads open and protect their troops, and the leaders knew it.

THE (EXPENSIVE) RESPONSE

The American response to the IED eventually snowballed into a
nearly all-consuming effort at individual, unit, theatre and service
levels. The threat was severe enough to force the United States back
to the drawing board on equipment, tactics, organizational structures, training, policy, and doctrine. To improve survivability, units
modified vehicles by lining floorboards and cargo beds with Kevlar
blankets and sandbags. Welders and mechanics applied heavy steel
sheets to undercarriages and doors. Official safety processes struggled to keep up with ad hoc modifications; in one case, a transporta-
tion unit permanently mounted the hull of an armoured personnel
carrier – a light tank of sorts – onto the back of a five-ton truck, creating a survivable and transportable weapons platform.[27] Some units
taped remote controllers for toy cars onto their vehicles in an attempt
to pre-detonate remotely controlled IEDs, and diesel engine glow
plugs were suspended in front of engines to spoof infrared sensors.[28]

Eventually, more sophisticated *matériel* made its way into Iraq
and Afghanistan. Robots equipped with cameras and manipulating
arms were used to create safer stand-off distances between troops
and suspected IEDs. HMMWV variants with armour plating, heavy
ballistic windows, internal air conditioning, and stronger suspen-
sions arrived in-theatre. Armour kits became available for previously
unprotected support and logistics vehicles while personal protective
equipment to include flame-retardant clothing and shatter-proof

glasses was fielded. Electronic warfare equipment (such as the counter radio-controlled IED electronic warfare, or CREW system) was developed to jam signals from the cellphones and garage-door openers used to remotely trigger IEDs.[29] Over $100 million was spent on state-of-the-art handheld sensors that used ground-penetrating radars and improved algorithms to detect buried IED components. And a staggering $45 billion was spent to produce the more than 27,000 mine-resistant, ambush-protected (MRAP) vehicles, massive armoured trucks with V-shaped hulls based on earlier South African and Rhodesian designs.[30]

Tactics and procedures were constantly revised, often after painful trial and error or in response to the enemy's exploitation of weaknesses and established patterns. Leaders stressed personal discipline and every movement became a combat patrol, regardless of whether the troops were infantry or quartermasters. An emphasis on small-unit tactics and patrolling fundamentals returned as units learned that sloppiness was quickly punished by an enemy with superb reconnaissance skills. Counter-IED working groups were created to help commanders synchronize efforts and better measure effectiveness. Units devised methods to attack networks and go after the critical links – financiers, bomb-makers and leaders – and not just expendable IED "emplacers" (the people who actually buried the bombs). This was combined with the concept of treating IED events as crime scenes, and using a forensics approach to help convert information into evidence and intelligence.[31]

Previously unimaginable changes to organizational structures were made. Troops school-trained in intelligence analysis were assigned to infantry and armour companies, Navy officers were assigned directly to Army units to coordinate electronic warfare operations and engineer formations solely dedicated to counter-IED were created on a large scale.[32] At the theatre level, new organizations were created to track and study IEDs. These units brought together intelligence, explosive ordnance disposal (EOD), law enforcement, and engineer functions to coordinate critical resources and help convert overwhelming amounts of data and information into usable intelligence. And the importance of ISR blossomed at every level, facilitated by the use of unmanned aircraft systems (UAS) and persistent surveillance platforms. From the small and hand-launched to the large and plane-sized, UAS offered a variety of sensors that troops could use to help detect insurgents and IEDs.[33]

Along with these changes in structure, equipment, and thinking, the US military put an increasingly heavy focus on training, both pre-deployment and in-theatre. The training typically fit into two categories. The first was primarily concerned with how to physically operate and maintain the seemingly endless stream of new and updated equipment. The second – and arguably far more important – dealt with learning to fight, individually and collectively, in an environment where the IED was the main threat. More than two hundred distinct training courses and programs were developed and delivered by contractors and military personnel at home stations, training centres and mobilization stations.[34] To manage these processes, numerous new organizations were created to fund and synchronize counter-IED initiatives, and chief among them was the Joint IED Defeat Organization (JIEDDO), the Department of Defense–level office with the overarching responsibility for counter-IED within the United State.[35]

Just as the earlier review of IED and landmine history was not intended to be all-inclusive, neither was this summary of US efforts to improve counter-IED capabilities. Organizational responsibilities, the MRAP program, the rise of the UAS and the shift to attacking networks deserve their own lengthy studies. But the summary does show the breadth and scale of the US response to the IED. The effort cost billions of dollars and touched nearly every element of the Army and Marine Corps as well as select functions in their sister services. For example, JIEDDO spent approximately $24 billion through 2012.[36] Much of the funding was allocated to an enormously diverse profile, including experimental technologies, ISR platforms, commercial off-the-shelf equipment, realistic training facilities, and the establishment of intelligence-training programs.[37] Some JIEDDO funds were parcelled out to other organizations working counter-IED directly for the services or personnel in-theatre. An additional $45 billion – by far the largest counter-IED expenditure – went to the MRAP program, which did not deliver in strength until 2007.[38] The $69 billion spent between these two efforts does not count the Overseas Contingency Operations (OCO) funding that the services also received, some of which went to other organizations working counter-IED, so the real sum committed to counter-IED is likely several billion more.

The wars in Iraq and Afghanistan cost an estimated $1.38 trillion through 2012, according to a Congressional Research Service report examining the cost of military operations since 9/11.[39] The $69 billion spent on counter-IED equates to 5 per cent of the total cost of the wars, meaning that at least one in every twenty dollars was spent on the IED threat. Whether this massive effort and expenditure was successful is debatable. Despite a few dead-end initiatives and the friction caused by the constant influx of new equipment, many counter-IED initiatives yielded positive results. Troops in up-armoured trucks and MRAPs survived blasts that would have killed them in other vehicles.[40] Insurgents virtually abandoned remotely triggered IEDs as sophisticated CREW systems created protective electro-magnetic bubbles around patrols while airborne sensors facilitated intelligence-driven operations. Integrating EOD with manoeuvre, intelligence, and engineer units served as the cornerstone for the collection of forensics and attacking enemy networks.[41] And the counter-IED training funded by JIEDDO and other key entities helped better prepare many of the 2.5 million American service members who have served in Iraq and Afghanistan.[42]

These were all undeniable successes, but it is important to note that these did not occur in a vacuum. While the United States and its closest allies enhanced their ability to fight in an IED environment, the insurgents also improved their skills. The strength and sophistication of IEDs changed to meet increases in armour and detection. Individual artillery shells were replaced by clusters of five or six, all simultaneously detonated. Homemade bulk explosive charges grew into the hundreds of pounds. Ingenious hiding places were used: under road surfaces and in potholes; cars, carts and bicycles; overpasses and guard rails; trash and dead dogs; trees and canals. Sunni suicide bombers wearing explosive vests or driving explosive-filled cars wreaked havoc.[43] Explosively formed penetrators emerged in Shia-dominated regions and proved easy to conceal and disturbingly effective.[44] US electronic warfare successes pushed insurgents to use newer technologies that were more difficult to defeat. Bomb-makers developed infrared detectors, hair-thin command wires and pressure switches, often crudely assembled from plastic bowls, springs, or hacksaw blades. Threat evolution was constant and the thousands of monthly attacks gave superb feedback to insurgents looking for US vulnerabilities. To truly gauge the level of success the United States had with its counter-IED efforts, we need to look at three key metrics: the number of IED attacks, the number of casualties, and the ratio of detection to detonation.

During the war in Iraq, US troops were targeted with more than 120,000 IEDs, with August 2006 to July 2007 as the most active twelve-month period when 30,822 IEDs were found or detonated.[45] IED attacks on US troops in Afghanistan began in 2002, and by early 2013 the total exceeded 75,000. The sheer number of IEDs encountered is enough to cast some doubt on the success of a $69-billion solution, as every detonation chipped away at American credibility. When it finally came, the reduction in IEDs in Iraq tracked closely with the reduction in violence in general. Counter-IED efforts deserve some credit, as improved equipment and better targeting practices allowed US troops to survive blasts and degrade IED networks. However, a case can be made that the decrease in violence was much more dependent on the effects created by improved counter-insurgency (COIN) strategies, the Sunni Awakening, and aggressive tactics employed against Sunni and Shia extremists during the troop surge.[46]

While every IED detonation damaged the American image, effective blasts were the worst, and it is this metric that reveals sharper evidence on the shortfalls of the counter-IED effort. In total, 3,517 service members were killed in action or died of wounds received in Iraq.[47] Of those, 2,207, or nearly 63 per cent of the total combat deaths, were killed by IEDs.[48] The deadliest was 2007, when IEDs accounted for almost 70 per cent of US combat deaths during the troop surge.[49] Of the 32,245 wounded in Iraq, 21,743 – over 67 per cent – were the result of IEDs.[50] Data from Afghanistan is similarly painful. As of early February 2014, IEDs caused 963 of the total 1,849 US combat deaths, or just over 52 per cent.[51] As in Iraq, the percentage of wounded is higher than killed; 19,443 were wounded in combat with 12,034, or roughly 62 per cent from IEDs.[52] Discounting years with low enemy activity, the rates are consistently high. These are sobering but not surprising statistics. The wide-scale use of IEDs and high casualty rates are what the United States should have expected, based on Vietnam, Chechnya, Lebanon, and other conflicts in and among a civilian population. That these numbers were so high, despite the time, money, and energy dedicated to the problem, should be troubling to Western nations.

The ability to detect an emplaced IED prior to its detonation ("find and clear") was obviously a critical factor in preventing casualties, as even the hardest armour had its limits nor could every IED cell be eliminated. The costs of vehicle-mounted ground-penetrating radars, handheld detectors, aerial-detection platforms, and the training to teach personnel how to identify IED indicators ran into the billions of dollars. Yet IED find-and-clear rates remained stubbornly constant despite the money spent and the nearly myopic focus on counter-IED missions by intelligence, manoeuvre, EOD and engineer units. In 2009, 55 per cent of the IEDs in Afghanistan were found prior to detonation. Four years later in 2013, that rate had increased slightly, but plateaued at 65 per cent.[53] In Iraq, early find-and-clear rates were erratic, but settled to roughly 40 per cent by early 2005, and slowly increased to their peak at just over 70 per cent for a brief period in late 2008.[54] After 2008, rates gradually decreased to 50 per cent by mid-2010.[55] Despite the enormous sums of money spent on training and equipment for counter-IED, the inescapable conclusion is that on average, the best the United States could expect to find would be only two of every three IEDs prior to detonation. This is hardly a solved problem.

Clearly, the key indicators show that the IED was not defeated and in fact had a stubbornly constant impact. Adding to the frustration are several unintended consequences that the US military will struggle with for years to come. The partial success achieved in two limited ground campaigns required the constant, repeated deployment of nearly every explosive ordnance disposal detachment unit in the military, to include the Air Force and Navy.[56] The $45-billion MRAP program produced thousands of vehicles that offer increased survivability, but have limited mobility and utility in areas outside the Middle East and Central Asia; they remain modes of transportation, rather than true combat vehicles from which teams, squads, and platoons can fight.[57] Many of the more successful individual counter-IED systems, such as handheld detectors, are still not captured as enduring *matériel* requirements, and several of the more promising ISR sensors rely far too heavily on "soda straw," narrow apertures to effectively support counter-IED missions at lower levels.[58] These are all serious issues that the US military must address as it prepares for life after Iraq and Afghanistan.

FUTURE TRENDS AND IEDS

The history of the IED and the US attempts to defeat it beg several remaining questions. Can the IED be taken off the battlefield, or at least made negligible? What will the future hold for the IED, and what should the United States do about it in the coming years of reduced defense budgets? Experience gained from the last one hundred years – the First and Second World Wars, Vietnam, North Ireland, Lebanon, Chechnya, Iraq, and Afghanistan – seems to suggest that the IED isn't going anywhere. Whether they're called booby traps, roadside bombs, or landmines, IEDs are a permanent facet of the modern battlefield. Despite the West's best efforts, the science and technology never came through, likely coming as no surprise to US Marine Corps Lieutenant General James Mattis who said in 2005 that "for … a country that can put a man on the moon in ten years or build a nuke in two and a half years of wartime effort, I don't think we're getting what we need from technology."[59] The threat from IEDs is not a static, predictable problem to solve, like splitting atoms for the Manhattan Project or calculating lunar orbits for the Apollo program. The unpleasant truth may be that despite a US cultural preference for finding technological solutions to complex problems, IEDs are now a permanent condition of the modern battlefield. Future enemies will not be blind to the success that IEDs had against the world's best-trained and best-equipped military; they are too cheap, easy and effective to forsake as weapons. They serve as extensions of the imagination: flexible and adaptable to changing environments. This adaptability makes it difficult to divine exactly how it will be used or evolve in the future. Based on its past employment, however, we can predict four broad ways in which the weapon will likely be used against Western forces:

Anti-Access / Area Denial

IEDs will be employed in large numbers at airfields, ports, and other key locations that offer potential for use as entry points into a theatre or intermediate staging bases. If used in sufficient quantity, IEDs will prevent Western forces from quickly massing on their initial objectives and prevent them from establishing lodgments – actions critical to force projection. Initial casualties could be extremely high, and attempts to conduct deliberate area clearance could easily overwhelm the limited capabilities available to initial entry forces, particularly as the United States and several of its allies continue with deeper cuts to their armies. The potential of this scenario will contribute to Western reluctance to commit ground forces.

Disruption of Lines of Communication

This approach would basically recreate many of the attack patterns seen in Iraq and Afghanistan, where frequently used routes were continuously seeded with large, anti-vehicle IEDs, often in conjunction with direct-fire ambushes. The initial intent would be to severely restrict US operational mobility, while the long-term intent would be to affect Western public opinion through a steady flow of casualties, destroyed vehicles, and increased costs. The very reason why the IED is so attractive as a weapon is that it is cheap, homemade and can have a sustained impact beyond the confines of the battlefield in which it is employed. The IED – used in this way – would shift the focus of the mission to one of simply surviving on the roads rather than engaging with and destroying the will of the enemy to fight.

Traditional Obstacles

Altering the geography to impede the movement of soldiers has been a constant feature of battlefields. Such obstacles range from destroying bridges to prevent units from crossing rivers, to knocking down trees across roads to slow the advance of armies. IEDs are no different. These obstacles are not only used to impede movement or channel it in a specific direction but also to provide a measure of protection against incursion. A booby-trapped door to an insurgent safe house, or a network of buried homemade explosives along a road are examples of ways in which IEDs can be used as an obstacle to be cleared, rendered safe, and removed, all at the expense of time, exposure, and risk to those who come across them. IEDs are often detonated at the beginning of a more complex attack involving small arms and hand-launched explosives (the ubiquitous rocket-propelled grenade, or RPG) and are designed to demoralize dismounted combat soldiers, and create a "thickening" of the battlefield. Moreover, because the detonation of an IED is arbitrary in many cases (a pressure-plate cannot discern between an armoured vehicle and a family car), they develop mistrust within host-nation populations. Success with this method will have a strategic effect on Western countries similar to the previous method coupled with greater insecurity as perceived by the local population.

Precision Munitions

IEDs will be used as an improvised precision munition, terminally guided, or placed and triggered near specific high-value targets by an individual willing to give up their lives for the sake of the single act of detonating a bomb on a specific target. Suicide-bombing attacks against key persons or interests will be used to publicly demonstrate Western weakness, provoke tension between Western and host-nation security forces, and gain support from sympathizers across the globe.

As varied as these employment techniques are, they all share the fact that they use the lethality of the IED to exploit weaknesses in the high value that Western nations place on the lives of their military members. Couple that lethality with a widespread proliferation of bomb-making knowledge and skills, and the IED means that relatively weak opponents can quickly turn an already challenging security environment into something virtually unmanageable by Western forces.

CONCLUSION

The IED directly challenges the idea of quick and bloodless military operations, and by promising that any gains will come only at a terrible price, it deters the United States and its allies from committing ground forces to a long-term effort. To echo one of the research questions listed in Stéfanie von Hlatky's introduction, the IED challenge has contributed to the war-weary political climate and has arguably changed the threshold for military intervention involving boots on the ground. This is seen clearly in the American public's aversion to ground combat in Libya and Syria, a feeling associated with "war fatigue" after over a decade of fighting in the 9/11 Wars. That weariness is a direct result to the thousands of young men and women killed and maimed by IEDs.

What this means is that the United States and its traditional warfighting partners, like the UK and Australia, have some soul searching to do. If they still want the ability to project a sustained and persistent force that is capable of intervening and effecting true change in some troubled corner of the globe, they need to recognize that air, sea, and cyber platforms alone will not end ethnic cleansing, terrorism or civil war. The move toward the AirSea Doctrine within the United States is a siren's song, and will likely end the same as the previous fascination with the RMA. To do the truly hard tasks requires committing Fehrenbach's proud legions and putting boots on the ground. The problem is that the IED is going to guarantee that tomorrow's soldier is going to be just as vulnerable as his predecessors. Vietnam, Chechnya, Iraq, and Afghanistan are proof of that. And if a nation, its leaders, and its public do not have the stomach for the price IEDs will extract, then the thirty-pound jug of homemade explosives can be just as effective of a strategic deterrent as a nuclear weapon.

NOTES

1 Christiaan N. Mamczak and Eric A. Elster, "Complex Dismounted IED Blast Injuries: The Initial Management of Bilateral Lower Extremity Amputations with and without Pelvic and Perineal Involvement," *Journal of Surgical Orthopaedic Advances* 21 (2012). See also US Government Accountability Office, *Mild Traumatic Brain Injury Screening and Evaluation Implemented for OEF/OIF Veterans, but Challenges Remain* (Washington, DC: US Government Accountability Office, 2008).

2 Numerous polls show a steady decline of public support for the wars in Iraq and Afghanistan, coinciding with rising casualties in each theatre. See John Mueller, "The Iraq Syndrome," *Foreign Affairs,* November/December 2005, http://www.foreignaffairs.com/articles/61196/john-mueller/the-iraq-syndrome. Also see Gallup polling from a random sample of 1,022 people, collected 7–10 March 2013, http://www.gallup.com/poll/161399/10th-anniversary-iraq-war-mistake.aspx. The supporting data includes Iraq, Afghanistan, and Vietnam for comparison.

3 Rick Atkinson, "The Single Most Effective Weapon against Our Deployed Forces," *Washington Post,* 30 September–3 October 2007, http://www.washingtonpost.com/wp-dyn/content/article/2007/10/02/AR2007100202366.html. General Abizaid used the analogy in an unpublished memorandum to the undersecretary of defense. Atkinson wrote that the originator of the idea was Abizaid's deputy, Air Force Lieutenant General Lance Smith. The initial intent was "stopping the bleeding" from an "IED problem (that was) out of control," as Lieutenant General Richard Cody told one of his staffers. By 2008, it had evolved to "defeat(ing) the systemic use of IEDs to strategically influence our citizens and leaders," as per Lieutenant General Thomas Metz's testimony

to Congress. See US Congress, House of Representatives, Committee on Armed Services, Oversight and Investigations Subcommittee, *Defeating the Improvised Explosive Device (IED) and Other Asymmetric Threats: Today's Efforts and Tomorrow's Requirements,* 110th Cong., 2nd sess., 16 September 2008. For additional views, see Andrew Smith, *Improvised Explosive Devices in Iraq, 2003–2009: A Case of Operational Surprise and Institutional Response,* Letort Papers (Carlisle, PA: Strategic Studies Institute, 2011), 13. Smith's timing of Abizaid's "Manhattan" request is earlier than Atkinson's and others.

4   Lydia Monin and Andrew Gallimore, *The Devil's Gardens* (London: Pimlico, 2002), 42, 45–6.

5   Ibid., 43–5.

6   Ibid., 49.

7   Ibid.

8   Ibid., 53–5.

9   US Defense Intelligence Agency and US Army Foreign Science and Technology Center, *Landmine Warfare – Trends and Projections,* DST-1160S-019-92 (Washington, DC, December, 1992), section 2-1. This declassified study has been used as reference material for several books written about landmines as well as some of the documents supporting the International Convention to Ban Landmines.

10 Herbert L. Smith, *Vietnam, 1964–69 (Landmine and Countermine Warfare)* (Washington, DC: US Department of Defense, 1972), 1.

11 Associated Press, "Booby Traps a Major Killer in Vietnam War," 9 September 1970, accessed 18 February 2014, http://news.google.com/new spapers?nid=950&dat=19700909&id=Dd4LAAAAIBAJ&sjid=hFcDAAA AIBAJ&pg=3855,1850946. The AP article refers to unnamed Pentagon sources who say that "as many as half the [at that time] 43,000 Americans who have died in the Vietnam War may have been killed by booby trap devices." Interestingly, the article also refers to the use of dogs to detect explosives and training on enemy techniques, two ideas that would be resurrected for use in Iraq and Afghanistan.

12 Smith, *Vietnam, 1964–69,* 28

13 "Vietnam Era IED Production," YouTube video, from the Canadian documentary *Vietnam: The 10,000 Day War* produced in 1980, posted by "pissedonpolitics.com," 5 January 2007, http://www.youtube.com/ watch?v=HFjvkJ_NkQk. The clip shows Vietnamese soldiers and guerrillas harvesting components from dud US munitions and converting them to IEDs.

14 Monin and Galimore, *The Devil's Gardens,* 72–3.

15 Smith, *Vietnam, 1964–69,* 22.

16 J.R.T. Wood, "The Pookie: A History of the World's First Successful Landmine Detector Carrier," 2005, accessed 21 January 2014, www.jrt-wood.com/article_pookie.asp. The Pookie was developed by the Rhodesian Army after losing numerous personnel to African nationalist guerrilla attacks involving Soviet-made landmines. The steep V-hull concept eventually migrated to the South African Defence Force, which was also losing significant numbers of soldiers to landmines. The design proved extremely effective against underbelly attacks from conventional landmines.

17 General Sir Mike Jackson, "Gen Sir Mike Jackson Relives IRA Paras Bombs," *Telegraph*, 5 September 2007, http://www.telegraph.co.uk/news/worldnews/1562283/Gen-Sir-Mike-Jackson-relives-IRA-Paras-bombs.html.

18 Monin and Galimore, *The Devil's Gardens*, 95–7.

19 Barack Obama, "Remarks by the President at 93rd Annual Conference of the American Legion," public speech, Minneapolis Convention Center, Minneapolis, MN, 30 August 2011.

20 Douglas W. Skinner, *AirLand Battle Doctrine* (Alexandria, VA: Center for Naval Analyses, September 1988), 3–5, 11.

21 Stephen Metz and James Kievet, *Strategy and the Revolution in Military Affairs: From Theory to Policy* (Carlisle, PA: Strategic Studies Institute, 1995), v, 1–2. Metz and Kievet also describe one of the risks involved with pursuing the RMA, namely that it would struggle against threats that "operate in widely dispersed fashion and emit a limited electronic signature … [have] cellular organizations… [are] insurgents [that] intermingle with the population … [and] need only succeed in a limited number of military missions to attain desired psychological objectives." This describes the nature of the threat in Iraq and Afghanistan nearly perfectly.

22 T.R. Fehrenbach, *This Kind of War: A Study in Unpreparedness* (New York: MacMillan, 1963). Fehrenbach's seminal work on combat during the Korean War is revered by many in the US, UK, and Australian militaries' ground components. His quote, "[Y]ou may fly over a land forever; you may bomb it, atomize it, pulverize it and wipe it clean of life – but if you desire to defend it, protect it, and keep it for civilization, you must do this on the ground, the way the Roman legions did, by putting your young men into the mud," is viewed as a prescient rebuttal to airpower proponents.

23 See Asa McKercher's chapter in this volume.

24 Major Harry Greene, "The Grizzly and the Wolverine: Alternatives to an Orchestrated Ballet of Farm Implements," *Engineer Bulletin Online* (August 1996), http://www.fas.org/man/dod-101/sys/land/

docs/960800-greene2.htm, accessed 13 February 2014. As of the mid-2000s, standard mechanized engineer minefield- and obstacle-breaching operations were conducted from platforms that the Infantry and Armor branches had abandoned twenty to thirty years prior. *Farm implements* was – and still is – a term of extreme derision.

25 Author's personal experience while serving as a combat engineer officer from 1992 to 2014 to include training rotations at the Combined Maneuver Training Center in Germany, the National Training Center at Fort Irwin, California, and the Joint Readiness Training Center at Fort Polk, Louisiana, as well as an assignment as an observer/controller at the National Training Center at Fort Irwin, California, from 2000 to 2002.

26 Author's personal experience. Casualty rates for simulated minefield-breaching operations at the Combat Training Centers typically exceeded 30 per cent of the attacking force. Frequently, this resulted in the temporary suspension of the training event, to allow the unit to reconstitute itself and move on to other training objectives, without ever actually successfully breaching or bypassing the minefield.

27 This Frankenstein's monster is parked, without any explanatory museum plaque, near the main parade field at Fort Leonard Wood, Missouri. Its display seems equal parts homage to American ingenuity and precautionary tale.

28 Adam Higginbotham, "U.S. Military Learns to Fight Deadliest Weapons," 28 July 2010, http://www.wired.com/magazine/2010/07/ff_roadside_bombs/.

29 Ibid.

30 Yasmin Tadjdeh, "The MRAP: Was It Worth the Price?," *Foreign Affairs*, October 2012.

31 Gerald M. Muhl, *Defeating Improvised Explosive Devices (IED): Asymmetric Threat and Capability Gaps*, Strategy Research Project (Carlisle Barracks, PA: US Army War College, 23 March 2011), 4–5, 13.

32 Atkinson, "The Single Most Effective Weapon against Our Deployed Forces."

33 Joint Improvised Explosive Device Defeat Organization, *2010 Annual Report* (Crystal City, VA: JIEDDO, 2010), 13–19. The 2010 annual report is a good example of what JIEDDO focused on as the war in Iraq was drawing down and the war in Afghanistan was at its most violent point to date. Pages 13–14 give a good summary of where the money went for that particular fiscal year and the wide range of programs. Subsequent pages show the variety of systems developed, including UAS for counter-IED; this does not include classified programs.

34 Brad Martin, Thomas Manacapalli, James C. Crowley, Joseph Adams, Michael G. Shanley, Paul Steinberg, and Dave Stebbins, *Assessment*

of Joint Improvised Explosive Device Defeat Organization (JIEDDO) Training Activity (Washington, DC: RAND, 2013), 11–13. RAND identified 252 training programs and courses that received JIEDDO funding or support.

35 Atkinson, "The Single Most Effective Weapon against Our Deployed Forces." Atkinson gives a good history of the thought processes and events that went into the development of JIEDDO. JIEDDO's unclassified website also provides some background on their creation, https://www.jieddo. mil/index.aspx.

36 Peter Cary and Nancy Youssef, "JIEDDO: The Manhattan Project That Bombed," *Center for Public Integritiy*, 10 August 2011, http://www.publicintegrity.org/2011/03/27/3799/jieddo-manhattan-project-bombed; and Amber Corrin, "Wars Wind down, but Counter-IED Agency Sees More Bombings," *Defense Systems*, 12 February 2012, http://defensesystems. com/articles/2012/02/16/jieddo-strategic-plan.aspx. JIEDDO expenditures are calculated by combining the $1.4 billion for JIEDDO's predecessor (the transitional joint team between the original twelve-man army task force and JIEDDO) in 2005, the $17 billion spent by JIEDDO through 2010, the $3.4 billion allocated for 2011, and the $2.4 billion allocated for 2012.

37 JIEDDO, *2010 Annual Report*, 13–15.

38 Andrew Feickert, *Mine-Resistant, Ambush-Protected (MRAP) Vehicles: Background and Issues for Congress* (Washington, DC: US Library of Congress, Congressional Research Service, 2010), 1, and Tadjdeh, "The MRAP: Was It Worth the Price?" The CRS report notes that as of 2010, IED attacks against MRAPs had a casualty rate of 6 per cent compared to 22 per cent for up-armoured HMMWVs.

39 Amy Belasco, *The Cost of Iraq, Afghanistan and Other Global War on Terror Operations Since 9/11* (Washington, DC: US Library of Congress, Congressional Research Service, 2011), table I. The CRS report uses enacted funds for 2001–11, and requested funds for 2012. It does not include funds not directly war-related, to include funds for hospitals, medical facilities, and barracks, although an argument can be made that the stress of continuous war operations drew attention – and money – toward previously neglected areas. The overall numbers from CRS are substantially lower than the $4 to $6 trillion proposed in a recent study (Linda J. Blimes, *The Financial Legacy of Iraq and Afghanistan* [Harvard, MA: Harvard Kennedy School, 2013]) that includes long-term medical care and benefits. The reports referenced in this paper use only operational costs for the Second World War, Iraq, and Afghanistan.

40 Details on MRAP resistance to IED effects is classified, but the open-source, first-hand experience of personnel with time in both MRAPs and up-armoured HMMWVs is overwhelmingly consistent in noting that MRAPs

routinely maintained hull integrity against IED-charge sizes that shattered up-armoured HMMWVs.

41 Colonel Patrick Kelly, "TF Troy Counter-IED Update," briefing slides to the NDIA Global EOD Conference, Emerald Coast Convention Center, Fort Walton Beach, Florida, 30 April 2010; see also Commander, Joint Task Force Paladin, "Overview and Lessons Learned," briefing slides, Bagram, Afghanistan, June 2012. Both briefs show the nature and success of the integration of EOD units with other types of formations, and the importance of a forensics-based approach to attacking IED networks.

42 Blimes, *The Financial Legacy of Iraq and Afghanistan*. Blimes states that as of May 2013, roughly 2.5 million have served in Iraq and Afghanistan. She relies on Defense Department data, and does not double count personnel for multiple deployments.

43 Jessica Bernstein-Wax, "Studies: Suicide Bombers in Iraq Are Mostly Foreigners," *McClatchy DC*, 8 August 2007, http://www.mcclatchydc. com/2007/08/08/18791/studies-suicide-bombers-in-iraq.html. Berstein-Wax's source material includes data and commentary from Robert Pape of the University of Chicago. Pape runs the university-affiliated Chicago Project on Suicide Terrorism, which has collected significant data on suicide bombers in Iraq; more than 75 per cent were foreign born, with Saudi Arabia providing the most.

44 Bill Roggio, "Iraqi Troops Find EFP Factory in Sadr City," *Long War Journal*, 30 October 2008, http://www.longwarjournal.org/archives/2008/10/ iraqi_troops_find_ef.php. The article highlights an Iraqi Army raid on a Shia militia cache point that resulted in the actual capture of the presses and milling equipment required to make high-quality explosively formed penetrators (EFPs).

45 Data from JIEDDO J-9, derived from Combined Information Data Network Exchange (CIDNE) and US Forces – Iraq historical records, email message to the author, 14 February 2014. Data shows monthly totals of IED events. May 2007 was the most active month in Iraq, with 3,613 IEDs. June 2012 was the most active for Afghanistan (to date) with 2,052.

46 Tom Bowman, "As the Iraq War Ends, Reassessing the U.S. Surge," NPR, 16 December 2011, http://www.npr.org/2011/12/16/143832121/as-the-iraq-war-ends-reassessing-the-u-s-surge. The NPR story gives a good initial starting point for discussions about what really was responsible for the success in Iraq. Some argue that it was mostly due to a Shia-Sunni reconciliation, while others argue that would have never occurred were it not for the 30,000 extra troops that allowed the United States to put massive pressure on extremists and insurgents. The debate on the surge will

probably generate as many books as did the debate on the merits of the
Tet Offensive in Vietnam.

47 US Military Casualties – Operation Iraqi Freedom (OIF) and US Mil-
    itary Casualties – Operation New Dawn (OND) Defense Casualty Analysis
    System.

48 JIEDDO, "Human Cost."

49 Ibid.

50 Ibid. and US Military Casualties – Operation Iraqi Freedom (OIF) and US
    Military Casualties – Operation New Dawn (OND) Defense Casualty Analy-
    sis System.

51 JIEDDO, "Human Cost."

52 Ibid.

53 Data from Combined Joint Task Force Paladin Operations Research and
    Systems Analysis, derived from the Combined Information Data Network
    Exchange (CIDNE), email message to the author, 3 March 2014.

54 Anthony H. Cordesman, Charles Loi, and Vivek Kocharlakota, *IED Metrics
    for Iraq: June 2003 – September 2010* (Washington, DC: Center for Strategic
    and International Studies, 2010). Cordesman et al. use data from JIEDDO.
    Interestingly, there is an initial spike in find-and-clear rates for Iraq in late
    2003, but it bottoms out in 2004 when only roughly one-third of all IEDs
    were found prior to detonation. The informal idea that equipment and
    training limitations combined with threat evolution and competency will
    prevent the United States from ever getting much above the two-thirds
    find rate has gained traction over the last several years.

55 Ibid.

56 Michelle Tan, "Dwell Time Increases to 2 Years Next Month," *Army Times*,
    4 September 2011, http://www.armytimes.com/article/20110904/
    NEWS/109040311/Dwell-time-increases-2-years-nextmonth. See also
    Oriana Pawlik and Stephen Losey, "Leaders Seek Relief for the Busi-
    est, Most-Stressed Airmen," *Air Force Times*, 2 December 2013, accessed
    3 March 2014, http://www.airforcetimes.com/article/20131202/
    CAREERS/311180002/Leaders-seek-relief-busiest-most-stressed-airmen.
    Engineer Route Clearance, Military Working Dog and Military Intelli-
    gence units also suffered from reduced dwell time when compared to
    other types of units.

57 Defense Industry Daily, "High Afghan Exit Costs Force US Military
    to Contemplate End of Era," 16 December 2013, http://www.defen-
    seindustrydaily.com/mraps-shipping-post-coin-needs-019723/. The
    heavy weight and high centre of gravity of most MRAPs makes them dif-
    ficult to employ off-roads in many areas. US forces in Korea rejected

the MRAP after a lengthy test for suitability of use on the Korean peninsula. See also Jon Rabiroff, "MRAP No Good for Korea, 2ID Decides," *Stars and Stripes*, 16 August 2013, http://www.stripes.com/news/pacific/mrap-no-good-for-korea-2id-decides-1.235725.

58 Interview with several project directors at the Cold Regions Research and Engineering Lab (CRREL), Hanover, NH, 16 January 2014. CRREL has been an integral part of several UAS technologies provided to deployed US forces.

59 Atkinson, "The Single Most Effective Weapon against Our Deployed Forces." Lieutenant General Mattis commanded the Marine Corp Combat Development Command at the time, and made the statement shortly after fourteen Marines were killed by a single IED in Iraq.

PART TWO

Trends

4

The Decline of Combat Casualties: Trends and Implications

PETER TIKUISIS

War is the ultimatum confronting adversaries from a failure to resolve a political dispute peacefully with the tragic consequent loss of human life. While warfare has occupied most of civilized human history,[1] war's character has and continues to evolve. In the last hundred years, for example, as a somewhat simplistic but illustrative generalization, the First World War could be considered a chemist's war, the Second World War a physicist's war, and the Cold War an intelligence war.[2] A significant portion of post–Cold War and future warfare might be aptly described as a "grey war,"[3] characterized by complexity, confusion, and above all, uncertainty as to the identity of the adversary. In a grey war, the adversary uses conventional weapons, asymmetrical threats, and irregular tactics to challenge the operational effectiveness, ethics, and legality of countermeasures. Cyberattacks and "disruptive social behaviour"[4] add to the complexity of adversarial options. In large part, these challenges have spawned the recognition of the "human domain" as the essential foundation for future joint force development.[5] Yet, despite these variations in the transformation of warfare, the loss of life remains a persistent feature of war. Put simply, technology has and continues to change the *character* of war, but the *nature* of war remains unchanged; it is about killing.[6]

Casualties, however, are on the decline. Indeed, the number of deaths (civilian and military) in major conflicts has declined markedly over time[7] and has continued to do so even recently[8] with a

further projected decline.[9] Although weapon lethality has steadily
increased,[10] so have improvements in troop protection[11] and combat casualty care[12] that collectively have contributed to a marked
decrease in troop casualties. Other more phenomenological factors, such as the increasing reliance on technology for fighting at
a distance, societal pressure for less bloodshed, and the evolutionary shift from kinetic to non-kinetic warfare, are also contributing
to fewer casualties. This chapter focuses on this trend by examining the chronological decline of combat troop casualties.[13] It investigates whether current trends, primarily focused on US combat
casualties, point to a future time when casualty numbers might no
longer be a significant determinate of conflict termination, especially with unpopular interventions.[14] The implicit assumption is
that wars paid only in treasure, rather than blood, should be more
politically acceptable and sustainable. Are recent changes in the
character of war brought about by rapid advances in technology and
shifting societal norms starting to change the nature of war as well?

METHODOLOGY

The appropriate unit of measure of combat casualties is not trivial. Casualty rates are sometimes simply reported as the percentage
of the troops that served[15] and are occasionally reported as a percentage of the home-nation population. However, neither of these
metrics is sufficiently informative since the number of casualties per
conflict can vary widely depending on the size of the force, and on
the duration and intensity of the conflict. Indeed, George Kuhn has
suggested that force size, which has generally declined since the
Second World War,[16] conflict duration, and operational scenarios
should all be factored into any meaningful expression describing
casualty rates.

One approach is to express the number of casualties per total
number of troops served over the duration of the conflict, yet this
metric is also potentially ambiguous. For example, suppose that 100
casualties occurred in the first year of a conflict involving 10,000
troops for a casualty rate of 10 per 1,000 troops per year (1 per
cent). If the conflict extended for another year with an additional
150 casualties among 15,000 replacement troops, then the casualty rate suggested above would be 250/25,000 troops/2 years =
5 per 1,000 troops per year (0.5 per cent), or half the single year
rate even though the ratio of casualties to number of troops per

year is unchanged. This ambiguity is due to the division of the total number of troops irrespective of how long they served.

A better ratio would be the total number of casualties divided by the total number of troop-years. To borrow from the above example, the sum of troop-years equals 25,000 (i.e., 10,000 + 15,000) for a resultant casualty rate of 1 per cent per troop-year.[17] Unfortunately, however, reliable historical data on troop-years are scarce.

An alternative approach adopted herein is to normalize the average number of casualties per year by the peak number of troops served, which is more readily available and invariant to how long all troops served in the conflict. Using the above example once again, this metric would yield a casualty rate of 250/15,000 peak number of troops/2 years = 8.3 per 1,000 peak number of troops per year (0.83 per cent) with the understanding that this value is generally lower than that obtained by normalizing the total number of casualties by the sum of troop-years, if known.[18] We use the metric involving peak troop number to define the casualty to troop ratio (CT ratio). It is also understood that the number of troops involved in actual combat is usually a small fraction of the total number deployed, which will add variability to the analysis. However, to minimize this variability, we limit our analysis to military interventions since the Second World War conducted by a single nation (the United States, in this case) involving combat troops.

Using the above metric, the chronological trend of combat casualties suggests a reduction over time that, if reliable, points to a future convergence of the CT ratio to unity.[19] Consequent policy implications, not of the convergence itself but of its underlying causes, are considerable, potentially reflecting a greater reliance on technology to replace human combatants with alternative means of conducting "hard" warfare concomitant with changes in operational doctrine. The purpose of this study is to present an analysis of this decreasing casualty trend with a specific focus on US combat casualties in major military interventions since the Second World War.

DATA

US combat casualty data were obtained from the Military Intervention by Powerful States (MIPS) database.[20] The selection of cases was based solely on whether ground combat was the primary type of force used (i.e., where "the intervening state deployed more than 2,000 combat-ready troops and conducted ground combat operations").

Fourteen interventions between the Second World War and 2003 qualified,[21] however, three interventions were excluded and one was updated for this study. Two of the three interventions (Operation Blue Bat 1958 Lebanon and Operation Uphold Democracy 1994–95 Haiti) were excluded since no combat actually took place. The third case (Lebanon, 1982–84) was excluded from the analysis since the vast majority of casualties were the result of a suicide bombing (Beirut, 23 October 1983). Operation Enduring Freedom (OEF, 2001 Afghanistan) was updated to include recent data. Finally, Operations Iraqi Freedom (OIF) and New Dawn (OND) in Iraq were combined and added to the analysis as a single case. Table 4.1 provides descriptions of the final twelve selected US interventions including the peak number of troops deployed, the duration of the intervention, and the total number of troop casualties.

ANALYSIS

Table 4.1 also provides the casualty to troop ratio obtained by dividing the total number of casualties by the product of the peak number of troops served (in thousands) and the duration of the conflict (converted into years). Statistics of the campaign in Afghanistan were truncated to the end of 2012 for this analysis. Casualty statistics for Afghanistan and Iraq were obtained from *Military Times*.[22]

The logarithm of the CT ratio (see table 4.1) was regressed against the start year of the intervention. The resultant exponential fit ensured that any projection beyond the study period would remain above zero (i.e., it could only approach zero asymptotically). The 1962 intervention in Thailand (case 4) with an exceptionally high CT ratio of 260.9, which is at least two orders of magnitude higher than the four lowest ratios, is considered an outlier and was excluded from the regression, although it is reconsidered later on. The best fit with the remaining eleven cases is given by CT ratio = $e^{(83.46 - 0.0412 \cdot \text{start year})}$; $r = 0.632$; $p = 0.037$, which extrapolates to a convergence of unity (i.e., CT ratio = 1) in 2025. This is shown in figure 4.1 where the CT ratio is plotted against the start year of the intervention (see table 4.1 for the closed-circle data points; not shown is the data point for the 1962 intervention in Thailand). The half-period of the CT ratio is 16.9 years[23] meaning that the ratio is reduced by half approximately every 17 years.

Table 4.1
Peak number of troops, conflict duration, casualties, and CT ratio

Case	Year(s)	Location	Troops (peak)	Duration (days)	Total casualties	CT ratio	ln CT ratio
1	1950	South Korea	340,833	96	5,145	57.4	4.05
2	1950–53	North Korea	440,000	1,030	32,000	25.8	3.25
3	1962–73	Vietnam	543,482	4,013	58,209	9.7	2.28
4	1962	Thailand	5,000	68	243	260.9	5.56
5	1965–66	Dominican Republic	20,463	510	47	1.6	0.50
6	1983	Grenada	7,355	48	19	19.6	2.98
7	1989–90	Panama	27,500	42	26	8.2	2.11
8	1991	Kuwait	541,425	43	269	4.2	1.44
9	1992–93	Somalia	30,000	152	14	1.1	0.11
10	1993	Somalia	4,000	241	29	11.0	2.40
11	2001–12	Afghanistan	109,200	4,103	2,160	1.8	0.57
12	2003–11	Iraq	218,500	3,208	4,400	2.3	0.83

Notes: Interventions were (1) Korean War: defence of South, (2) Korean War: unification, (3) Second Indochina War, (4) Cease-fire collapse: Nam Tha, Laos, (5) Op Power Pack, (6) Op Urgent Fury, (7) Op Just Cause, (8) Op Desert Storm, (9) Op Restore Hope–UNITAF, (10) Op Continue Hope–UNOSOM, (11) Op Enduring Freedom (although OEF continued beyond 2012, it was truncated for this analysis), and (12) Ops Iraqi Freedom and New Dawn.

Source: Patricia L. Sullivan, "War Aims and War Outcomes: Why Powerful States Lose Limited Wars," *Journal of Conflict Resolution* 51, no. 3 (June 2007): 496–524, http://thedata.harvard.edu/dvn/dv/tsulli/faces/study/StudyPage.xhtml?globalId= hdl:1902.1/15519; httfp://projects.militarytimes.com/valor.

For comparative purposes, the number of casualties per year per home population (taken at the start of the intervention) was similarly regressed with the significant result (and caveats) that 1 combat death per year per 100,000 capita is projected in 2016 with a half-period of 8.2 years. This accelerated rate compared to the reduction in above CT rate is attributed to population growth.[24]

The open squares in figure 4.1 show the CT ratios for two Canadian combat operations, Korea (February 1951–July 1953) and Afghanistan (December 2001–July 2011) to demonstrate similarity to the US casualty trend. These CT ratios are approximately 25.4 (516 casualties[25]/8,123 peak troops[26]/2.5 years[27]) for the Korean campaign and 5.6 (158 casualties/2,922 peak troops/9.7 years) for the Afghanistan campaign.[28] Both ratios fall within the 95 per cent confidence interval of the US values.

Figure 4.1
CT ratio over time

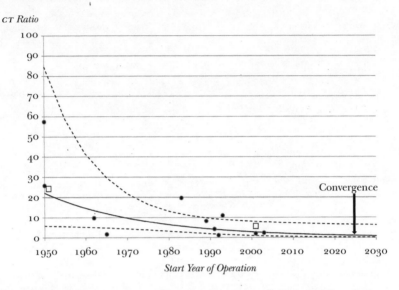

Notes: The solid line is the regressed/projected CT ratio and the dashed lines depict the 95 per cent confidence interval. "Convergence" indicates the year (2025) when the CT ratio is projected to reach unity. Canadian CT ratios for the Korean (1951) and Afghanistan (2001) campaigns are indicated by the open squares.

Sources: Obtained by the ratio of $ln2/0.0412$; Canadians in Korea, http://www.korean-war.com/canada.html; Herbert F. Wood, "Strange Battleground: The Operations in Korea and Their Effects on the Defence Policy of Canada" (Ottawa: National Defence, Queen's Printer and Controller of Stationary, 1966), 70, 276, and 286; based on first contact in February 1951 until armistice in July 1953 (Wood 1966); CBC, http://www.cbc.ca/news2/interactives/canada-afghanistan-casualties/.

DISCUSSION

Notwithstanding the small sample size of data used in this study and the rather large confidence interval of the data fit, the implication of this finding is profound, as it suggests that US casualties involving major combat operations is trending to a reduction of less than one per thousand peak number of troops per year of conflict after 2025. Additional data or different data selection criteria would undoubtedly alter the quantitative findings,[29] but not likely the qualitative conclusion of a progressive geometric reduction in casualties. Even a crude metric, such as the number of combat casualties per year per home population, indicates a significant geometric reduction.

Although this study has focused on US combat interventions, the above conclusion of combat troop casualty reduction pertains to all modern forces of advanced nations, noting in particular that the Canadian CT ratios for the Korean and Afghanistan campaigns both fall within the confidence interval of the US CT ratio (see figure 4.1). That is, combat casualties of future interventions similar in scale to those analyzed herein should also trend downwards to a convergence of a unit CT ratio, albeit at different rates and endpoints. In other words, while operational intensity in certain cases might skew or dislocate the downward trend, it is unlikely to reverse it.

A viable exception is the possibility of war between peer powers, which falls outside the parameters of this analysis. However, it is plausible that the CT ratio might still be low even if large troop numbers are involved. That is, while total casualties between major peer adversaries could be high, their numbers compared to peak troop numbers might be relatively low due to continued advancements in force preparation, protection, and casualty care.

Experience in past wars, with the corresponding trend of declining casualties, leads to two general comments that relate to how allies are likely to conduct military interventions in the future, a question posed in the introduction. The first is that this trend has an impact on public expectations related to the loss of life in times of war. Domestic publics in Canada, the United States, and other allied nations have come to expect low casualties and this impacts decisions leading to the use of force and certainly the type of military contribution deemed politically acceptable by the government.

The second comment is about force protection as an essential priority in the development of emerging military technologies, as also discussed in chapters 2 and 3 in this volume. Indeed, emerging technologies can further improve combatant performance, both physical and mental, and survivability, contributing to low combat casualties. Examples include counteracting fatigue and stress through advancements in biochronicity, pharmaceuticals, and genomics, and through human-machine interfacing and physical/physiological enhancements;[30] more effective training through virtual and immersive technologies;[31] modelling and training of critical and adaptive thinking in complex situations;[32] and improving battlefield survivability, such as tissue engineering to speed the healing process.[33]

Such advancements will continue to contribute to the reduction of combat casualties in parallel to a continued decline in troop

deployment. US overseas troop deployments[34] normalized by the
nation's population have decreased by approximately 70 per cent
since 1955. Coincident with this marked reduction is an increased
public awareness of conflict casualties, especially in an era of immediate global media coverage of violent conflicts and their dissemination
via social networks. High casualty levels are increasingly intolerable
in protracted and unpopular conflicts.[35] Indeed, as put forward by
RAND, "it is not so much the passage of time as the prevalence of a
particular class of operation that explains the apparent recent low
tolerance for casualties in U.S. military interventions."[36] Not surprisingly, the 2006 US counter-insurgency field manual stated that,
"at the strategic level, gaining and maintaining US public support
for a protracted deployment is critical."[37] The current field manual
states, "Where the U.S. is supporting a host nation, long-term success requires supporting viable host-nation leaders and institutions
that are legitimate and capable. The longer that process takes, the
more U.S. public support will wane and the more the local population will question the legitimacy of their own forces and government."[38] As Christopher Barron argues in chapter 3 of this volume,
weapons such as improvised explosive devices are employed not just
to target US soldiers deployed to Iraq but also to foment American
public opinion to question the mission as casualties mount and are
brought home. This connection between the soldier and the society they are charged to protect constitutes a major preoccupation
for political leaders and is connected to a broader theme in this volume, namely the conditions that will impact the conduct of military
interventions in the near future (next five to ten years).

Moreover, an analysis of a much larger dataset from which the
present study relied upon revealed no relationship between intervention outcomes and military capability,[39] indicating that "might"
is no guarantee of success,[40] as recently echoed by Karl Eikenberry.[41]
Consequently, future interventions might be executed more judi-
ciously with greater emphasis on brain versus brawn, resulting in
fewer casualties.

An important implication of these findings is that technological
solutions will be increasingly relied upon to replace human combatants in harm's way. In fact, US Army Training and Doctrine Command predicted that, "future battles will have unmanned systems
as forward sensors/observers detecting and identifying high-value
targets and calling for fires."[42] The precedent for remote weapon

deployment has already been established by US drone attacks of al Qaeda leadership since 2002.[43] Mechanical surrogates, such as (semi-) autonomous combat-capable robots, are also being developed to replace human combatants.[44] This operational advantage will also offer the additional benefit of alleviating public tension arising from operations in theatres of potentially lethal consequences, albeit with the associated legal and ethical dilemma of "fighting at a distance."[45] For example, compliance with just-war precepts of discrimination (between combatants and non-combatants) and proportionality (military gain relative to civilian harm) with the use of technological combatants is and will continue to be controversial and challenging to justify.[46]

The conduct of future warfare by other means (such as space- and cyberwarfare) might also supplant the requirement for large numbers of human combatants. Indeed, cyberwarfare is considered a very high-level threat that can potentially incapacitate national security, and without bloodshed.[47] Interestingly, Russia's "new generation warfare" guidelines for developing military capabilities by 2020 include a shift "from war in the physical environment to a war in the human consciousness and in cyberspace."[48] In other words, the human mind is the main battlespace to be dominated by influence,[49] a key guiding principle of information operations.[50]

What then are the implications for future force planning? It is not the convergence of combat casualties to a unit CT ratio, per se, but the reasons underlying this convergence that will ultimately impact force planning. Such planning will be increasingly reliant on technology to further protect and replace human combatants in kinetic operations with a concomitant transformation in operational doctrine to ensure an ever-decreasing CT ratio. This challenge cannot be taken lightly since, as noted earlier, casualty minimization is an essential condition for sustaining public support, especially for protracted expeditionary military interventions.

The challenge is further exacerbated by the trend of decreasing troop numbers. It is noteworthy that modular, multi-purpose, and rapidly responding smaller units will be preferentially deployed.[51] These smaller units include doctrines such as Canada's Directorate of Land Strategic Concepts' research into "tactical self-sufficient units" and American deployment of special operations forces.[52] With the use of these small, multi-purpose units, a single casualty can elevate the CT ratio appreciably, although this falls outside the present context of major military interventions (i.e., beyond single-purpose "surgical" strikes).

If "war is not a mere act of policy but a true political instrument, a continuation of political activity by other means,"[53] then any morally and legally defensible means are worthy of consideration with particular emphasis on non-lethal methods.[54] Indeed, the logical extrapolation from ongoing developments in influence science and cyber technologies points to a future of far fewer human combatants with even fewer combat casualties. In the interim, kinetic warfare will continue to exact a significant toll in human casualties, but the continued pace of developments in technology, social pressures, and operational doctrine will ultimately reduce combat casualties to the convergence of a unit CT ratio, presently projected in 2025 for the United States, and similarly anticipated for other advanced nations.

ACKNOWLEDGEMENTS

The author gratefully acknowledges the constructive advice of Anton Minkov and Aaron P. Tikuisis during the preparation of this chapter.

NOTES

1 John Keegan, *History of Warfare* (New York: First Vintage Press, 1993), 123–5.

2 Sara B. King, "Military Social Influence in the Global Information Environment: A Civilian Primer," *Analyses of Social Issues and Public Policy* 18, no. 1 (December 2011), 1–26.

3 Peter Tikuisis, Fred Buick, Andrea Hawton et al., "Futuristic Outlook on Human-Centric S&T," DRDC Toronto TM 2013-060 (Toronto Research Centre, ON, Defence R&D Canada, 2013), 7, http://cradpdf.drdc-rddc.gc.ca/PDFS/unc137/p538431_A1b.pdf.

4 Frank G. Hoffman, "Hybrid vs. Compound War. The Janus Choice: Defining Today's Multifaceted Conflict," *Armed Forces Journal* (October 2009), http://www.armedforcesjournal.com/hybrid-vs-compound-war/.

5 Essentially encompassing the full spectrum of cultural, institutional, technological, and physical dimensions of the human in-theatre;

see Frank G. Hoffman and Michael C. Davies, "Joint Force 2020 and the Human Domain: Time for a New Conceptual Framework?," *Small Wars Journal* (June 2013), http://smallwarsjournal.com/print/14125.

6 Carl von Clausewitz, *On War*, ed. Michael Howard, trans. Peter Paret (Princeton, NJ: Princeton University Press, 1984), 89.

7 Steven Pinker, *The Better Angels of Our Nature: Why Violence Has Declined* (New York: Viking, 2011), 297–305.

8 Peter Tikuisis and David R. Mandel, "Is the World Deteriorating?," *Global Governance* 21 (February 2014): 9–14; Bethany Lacina, "Explaining the Severity of Civil Wars," *Journal of Conflict Resolution* 50, no. 2 (April 2006): 276–89.

9 Håvard Hegre, Joakim Karlsen, Håvard Mokleiv Nygård, Håvard Strand, and Henrik Urdal, "Predicting Armed Conflict, 2011–2050," *International Studies Quarterly* 57, no. 2 (2013): 250–70.

10 Richard A. Gabriel and Karen S. Metz, "Lethality and Casualties," in *A Short History of War: The Evolution of Warfare and Weapons* (Carlisle, PA: Strategic Studies Institute US Army War College, 1992), 105–10, http://www.au.af.mil/au/awc/awcgate/gabrmetz/gabr0022.htm.

11 See for example Bob Reinert, "Bringing Immediate Protection to Soldiers," US Army, 17 February 2012, http://www.army.mil/article/73818/Bringing_immediate_protection_to_Soldiers/.

12 John B. Holcomb, Lynn G. Stansbury, Howard R. Champion et al., "Understanding Combat Casualty Care Statistics," *Journal of Trauma – Injury, Infection, and Critical Care* 60, no. 2 (February 2006): 397–401.

13 Herein casualties refer to military deaths.

14 Christopher Gelpi, Peter D. Feaver, and Jason Reifler, "Success Matters: Casualty Sensitivity and the War in Iraq," *International Security* 30, no. 3 (Winter 2006): 7–46.

15 Marcus Baram, "Overall, Afghanistan More Lethal for U.S. Soldiers than Iraq," *The World Post*, last modified 25 May 2011, http://www.huffingtonpost.com/2009/10/15/overall-afghanistan-more_n_319194.html.

16 George W.S. Kuhn, 1992. Total US troops per population have declined steadily by approximately 70 per cent since 1955, http://www.vetfriends.com/US-deployments-overseas/historical-military-troop-data.cfm.

17 More complicated mixtures of troop numbers, duration, and casualties than used in the text example would demonstrate that the troop-year normalization generally yields a different casualty rate than simply dividing the total number of casualties by the total number of troops. Specifically,

the former yields a higher rate than the latter if troops served less than one year and a lower rate if otherwise.

18 For example, suppose in a two-year conflict that five rotations of 1,500 troops each served eight months in overlapping periods such that 1,500 served in the first eight months, the second deployment of 1,500 troops began serving four months later, etc. until the final deployment of 1,500 troops began after sixteen months. The total number of troops served would be 7,500, the peak number of troops would be 3,000, and the sum of troop-years would be 5,000. Suppose further that each rotation suffered one casualty per month during their eight-month deployment for an over-all total of forty casualties. The net casualty rates would then be 0.53 per cent per 1,000 troops served, 0.67 per cent per 1,000 peak troops per year, and 0.80 per cent per troop-year.

19 Convergence can be gauged in numerous ways; herein we refer to one casualty per thousand peak number of troops per year of conflict. Projection to zero casualties is not considered a realistic option.

20 Patricia L. Sullivan, "War Aims and War Outcomes: Why Powerful States Lose Limited Wars," *Journal of Conflict Resolution* 51, no. 3 (June 2007): 496–524, http://thedata.harvard.edu/dvn/dv/tsulli/faces/study/StudyPage.xhtml?globalId=hdl:1902.1/15519.

21 Database is limited to the period 1946–2003.

22 "Honor the Fallen," *Military Times,* http://projects.militarytimes.com/valor.

23 Obtained by the ratio of *ln*2/0.0412.

24 United States Census Bureau, "International Programs," http://www.census.gov/ipc.

25 Canadians in Korea: "About the War," http://www.korean-war.com/canada.html.

26 Herbert F. Wood, "Strange Battleground: The Operations in Korea and Their Effects on the Defence Policy of Canada" (Ottawa: Queen's Printer and Controller of Stationary, 1966), 70, 276, 286.

27 Ibid. Based on first contact in February 1951 until armistice in July 1953.

28 CBC News, "Canada's Casualties in Afghanistan," CBC, last modified May 2014, http://www.cbc.ca/news2/interactives/canada-afghanistan-casualties/.

29 For example, inclusion of the 1962 intervention in Thailand would result in a projected CT ratio of less than one after 2019.

30 Academy of Medical Sciences, *Human Enhancement and the Future of Work* (London, UK, 2012), http://royalsociety.org/uploadedFiles/

Royal_Society_Content/policy/projects/humanenhancement/2012-11-06-Human-enhancement.pdf; Committee on Assessing Foreign Technology Development in Human Performance Modification, *Human Performance Modification: Review of Worldwide Research with a View to the Future* (Washington, DC: The National Academies Press, 2012), http://www.nap.edu/download.php?record_id=13480; Kenneth Ford and Clark Glymour, "The Enhanced Warfighter," *Bulletin of the Atomic Scientists* 70, no. 1 (2014), 43–53.

31 Kresimir Cosic, Sinisa Popovic, Marko Horvat et al., "Virtual Reality Adaptive Stimulation in Stress Resistance Training," in *NATO Science and Technology Organization* RTO-MP-HFM-205 (Brussels, BE, 2011): 4-1–4-18.

32 Anne-Marie Grisogono and Vanja Radenovic, "The Adaptive Stance – Steps towards Teaching More Effective Complex Decision-Making," in *Unifying Themes in Complex Systems, Vol VIII: Proceedings of the Eighth International Conference on Complex Systems.* New England Complex Systems Institute Series on Complexity, eds. H. Sayama, A. Minai, D. Braha, and Y. Bar-Yam (Cambridge, MA: NECSI Knowledge Press, 2011), 714–28, http://necsi.edu/events/iccs2011/papers/177.pdf.

33 Anthony D. Metcalfe and Mark W.J. Ferguson, "Tissue Engineering of Replacement Skin: The Crossroads of Biomaterials, Wound Healing, Embryonic Development, Stem Cells and Regeneration," *Journal of the Royal Society Interface* 4, no. 14 (June 2007): 413–37.

34 See Stat Planet: http://www.vetfriends.com/US-deployments-overseas/historical-military-troop-data.cfm.

35 Christopher Gelpi, Peter D. Feaver, and Jason Reifler, "Success Matters: Casualty Sensitivity and the War in Iraq," *International Security* 30, no. 3 (Winter 2006): 7–46; Bob Martyn's chapter in this volume.

36 RAND, "Public Support for U.S. Military Operations: The Relationship between Casualties and Public Support," RAND, http://www.rand.org/pubs/research_briefs/RB2502/index1.html.

37 US Army, *FM 3-24/MCWP 3-33.5: Counterinsurgency* (Washington, DC: Department of the Army, 2006), 1–24, http://www.militaryfieldmanuals.net/mwginternal/de5fs23hu73ds/progress?id=sDaSRZkBxi.

38 US Army, *FM 3-24/MCWP 3-33.5: Insurgencies and Countering Insurgencies* (Washington, DC: Department of the Army, 2014), 7–2, http://armypubs.army.mil/doctrine/DR_pubs/DR_a/pdf/fm3_24.pdf

39 Patricia L. Sullivan, "War Aims and War Outcomes: Why Powerful States Lose Limited Wars," *Journal of Conflict Resolution* 51, no. 3 (June 2007): 496–524.

40 For example, see Thomas L. Friedman, "It's Not Just about Obama," *New York Times,* 3 May 2014, http://www.nytimes.com/2014/05/04/opinion/sunday/friedman-its-not-just-about-obama.html?_r=1.

41 Karl Eikenberry, "The American Calculus of Military Intervention," *Survival* 56, no. 3 (2014): 264–71.

42 Thomas K. Adams, "Future Warfare and the Decline of Human Decision-Making," *Parameters* 31, no. 4 (2001): 57–71.

43 First publicly known targeted killing (Qaed Salim on 3 November 2002 in Yemen). Gary Solis, "Viewpoint: Drones, Modern War, and the US," *BBC,* 19 July 2012, http://www.bbc.co.uk/news/world-us-canada-18896236.

44 Chris Caroll, "Intelligent, Autonomous Robots Set to Change Combat Landscape," *Stars and Stripes,* 9 August 2012, http://www.stripes.com/intelligent-autonomous-robots-set-to-change-combat-landscape-1.185261; Robert O. Work and Shawn Brimley, *20YY: Preparing for War in the Robotic Age* (Washington, DC: Center for a New American Security, 2014), http://www.cnas.org/sites/default/files/publications-pdf/CNAS_20YY_Work-Brimley.pdf ; Aaron Ettinger's chapter in this volume.

45 "Morals and the Machine," *The Economist,* 2 June 2012, http://www.economist.com/node/21556234.

46 Kenneth Anderson and Matthew C. Waxman, "Law and Ethics for Robot Soldiers," *Policy Review* 176 (2012): 35–49.

47 Richard A. Clarke and Robert Knake, *Cyber War: The Next Threat to National Security and What to Do about It* (New York: Ecco, 2010), 67–8, 104–6, 226–8.

48 Janis Berzins, "Russia's New Generation Warfare in Ukraine: Implications for Latvian Defense Policy," National Defence Academy of Latvia, Center for Security and Strategic Research Policy Paper No. 2 (2014), 5, http://www.naa.mil.lv/~/media/NAA/AZPC/Publikacijas/PP%2002-2014.ashx.

49 Consider, for example, "I say to you that we are in a battle, and that more than half of this battle is taking place in the battlefield of the media," by Ayman al-Zawahiri in a translated version of letter to Abu Musab al-Zarqawi of al Qaeda, July 2005, as published by Global Security, http://www.globalsecurity.org/security/library/report/2005/zawahiri-zarqawi-letter_9jul2005.htm.

50 US Joint Chiefs of Staff, *JP 3-13: Information Operations* (Washington, DC, November 2014), I-2, http://www.dtic.mil/doctrine/new_pubs/jp3_13.pdf.

51 Karl Eikenberry, "The American Calculus of Military Intervention," *Survival* 56, no. 3 (2014): 264–71.

52 Jim Thomas and Chris Dougherty, "Beyond the Ramparts: The Future of U.S. Special Operations Forces" (Washington, DC: Center for Strategic and Budgetary Assessments, 2013), 1–5, http://www.csbaonline.org/publications/2013/05/beyond-the-ramparts-the-future-of-u-s-special-operations-forces/

53 Clausewitz, *On War*, 87.

54 Tracy J. Tafolla, David J. Trachtenberg, and John A. Aho, "From Niche to Necessity: Integrating Nonlethal Weapons into Essential Enabling Capabilities," *Joint Forces Quarterly* 66, no. 3 (2012): 71–9.

5

War-Weariness and Canadian Debates on the Use of Force: Back to Peacekeeping?

BOB MARTYN

Hans Morgenthau once observed that we appeared to be echoing 1793 France, where its new constitution declared that its people "do not interfere in the domestic affairs of others," which ushered in a "period of interventions by all concerned on the largest possible scale."[1] Where Morgenthau saw decolonization as a major intervention stimulus, we now cite ethnically splintered countries and jihadist movements. This chapter investigates whether or not peacekeeping operations, particularly within a Canadian context, are poised to make a comeback. Against background constraints of war-weariness, a tumultuous security environment, and budgetary limitations, this chapter will show that peace support operations (PSO) may appeal to government decision makers as a possible way ahead for the Canadian Armed Forces (CAF). This discussion includes the caveat that we should not mistake earlier blue-beret missions, and Canada's mythologized memory of such events, for what likely waits ahead.

The Berlin Wall's collapse signalled a busy time for Canada's military. Afghanistan was preceded by diverse operations that included Somalia, Haiti, three separate missions in the Balkans, and Rwanda. These all shared a lack of any threat to vital national interests, motivated predominantly by spreading a liberal world order. Following these missions with a more than decade-long engagement in Afghanistan, it is warranted to ask whether Canadians are war-weary. While it is intuitive that war-weariness attends *every* conflict – in reaction to deaths, prolonged absences from family and friends, massive economic outlays, and anxiety regarding war – has Afghanistan taken a greater toll than previous military interventions in the post–Cold War era? Could Afghanistan become Canada's "never-again" war, similar to Australia's view of the First World War with that country's troops seen as cannon fodder for causes of dubious national value? I argue that the threshold for embarking on similar interventions has likely increased, even if one merely extrapolates from decreasing approval trends as the war wound down; 74 per cent of Canadians overwhelmingly supporting the mission in 2002 plummeted to 58 per cent opposing by 2008.[2] The conflation of war-weariness with an entitled "peace dividend" can be compelling in national debates about Canada's role abroad. The core issue, then, is to engage in a rational assessment of when it is in a nation's best interest to intervene militarily. Public thinking on Afghanistan and current conflict is still evolving, influenced strongly by two ongoing factors: coverage of veterans' postwar medical issues, plus ongoing debates on the war's actual utility.

WAR-WEARINESS

There has been no shortage of negative attention drawn to veterans' health problems, suicides, and other support issues, such as the closure of Veterans' Affairs offices. By their very nature, these are emotionally charged issues and some players have shown no hesitancy in exploiting such sentiments; one need look no further than veterans clamouring for the immediate resignation of the former Veterans' Affairs Minister, claiming that they were "disrespected" by his tardiness to a meeting, notwithstanding his being delayed in Cabinet arguing on their behalf.[3] Although all suicides are tragic, suicide within Canada is the second-leading cause of male death in the age group generally employed by the military in combat. Those informed solely by Canadian media are unlikely to know that the CAF suicide rate has been consistent over the past decade, remains lower than the civilian average, is less than half that of the US Army, and actually decreased during recent media turmoil.[4]

Beyond medical issues, additional reticence to deploy combat troops is fuelled by increasing questions on the conflict's utility: whether we won or lost, at what cost in blood and treasure, and whether our efforts have provided the Afghans any lasting benefits. Although research questions the reality of a "CNN effect," there can be no doubt that political staffers closely monitor what information the electorate receives. Unfortunately, news stories seldom delved deeper than repeating the refrain "158 soldiers killed," focusing almost exclusively on ramp ceremonies in lieu of any reasoned assessment. In a potentially relevant twist to evaluating Afghanistan, only twenty-two of those killed were in direct combat. Most fatalities and the many horrific injuries resulted from crude homemade bombs, or improvised explosive devices (IEDs).[5] Such warfare largely denigrates the celebrated "honour" of the warrior fighting nobly against evil, which has inspired legend and literature throughout history. Discussants now, however, are almost exclusively academics and professional military as Canadian society has moved on, leaving only faded Support the Troops bumper stickers.

Those pondering the conflict face difficult questions, given that existing interpretations of how Canada behaves, or *should* behave, do not adequately explain our presence; debating points are nested within the reality that a majority of Canadians never truly understood the war. Notwithstanding the important governance precedent of two parliamentary votes taken to extend military involvement, at no time was the mission adequately justified to the public. Five years into the conflict, until 2006 when casualties started to increase, 70 per cent of Canadians believed that Afghanistan was a peacekeeping operation. This watershed year saw a clear division in the war's toll, with combat deaths and wounds jumping from 7 and 16 respectively to 115 and 514 by 2009, when the troop drawdown commenced in earnest.[6] The source of Canada's ignorance – be it taciturn government, sensationalist media, or disinterested population – is moot. People will be more skeptical of military interventions not tied to obvious, clear and present security threats, with goals and success criteria made clear.

Such reticence is not exclusively Canadian. A 2013 American survey concluded that 52 per cent want the United States to "mind its own business internationally," the highest figure in five decades of polling. Afghanistan reconstruction appropriations now exceed the Marshall Plan, which rebuilt sixteen nations, yet the outlook for success is increasingly bleak.[7] The British have expressed an equivalent desire to abandon a global policing role, although this is further tainted with blaming America for dragging them in against their better judgment.[8] Today's weariness is clearly analogous to the 1920s, after the "war to end all wars."

SECURITY CHALLENGES

Debating future interventions requires one to consider the prospective security circumstances into which we may deploy Canadian troops. While laying out specific forecasts may be akin to carnival fortune-telling, some readily identifiable trends can inform our thinking. Signs of global order breaking down proliferate. According to the 2013 Global Peace Index, 70 per cent of countries surveyed became less peaceful between 2008 and 2013. Of their twenty-two "peacefulness" indicators, seventeen worsened when averaged across all countries.[9] Russia's seizure of Crimea was the first time since 1945 that Europe witnessed such barefaced territorial conquest. Concurrently, a proxy war in Syria has left 250,000 dead and millions displaced at the time of writing, further destabilizing a region renowned for turmoil. Both Syria and Ukraine garnered tepid responses. Our revulsion for war reminiscent of the 1920s is thus poised for a transition into chaos reminiscent of the 1930s.

The obvious underlying premise is that absent superpower blocs bringing a semblance of order to international politics, we have a variety of powers, including nations, ideological movements, multinational corporations, and criminal terror groups, playing off among each other to further their ambitions. International politics is evolving from a system that was comparatively orderly in hindsight, into one that is far more disconcerting, with fewer behavioural regularities.[10] Russia's machinations seem almost a Machiavellian relief for its ruthlessly realist underpinnings. Such great power flashpoints will remain, with adjacent countries continuing to lack "the influence to play a decisive role in the very issues redefining their neighbourhoods."[11] However, such crises will not likely provide the demands for military interventions; that dubious honour lies with the growing number of smaller regional conflicts.

Many such localities are reappraising their previously dictated boundaries through the lens of ethnic, religious, and tribal dispersions. The majority of our future conflicts will not be between Huntington's "civilizations," but neighbours divided by history, with tensions often exacerbated by access to resources, be it food, water, or marketable reserves. For military thinking built upon conventional tank battles, this likely form of warfare seems new but is rather very old: low-level, endless warfare, often inextricable from political unrest. They will be fuelled by economic inequality, corruption, kleptocracy, and class injustices. As Thomas Friedman notes, "most of what threatens global stability today are crumbling states. Exactly how many can we rescue at one time?"[12]

A new feature of this older warfare that intervening forces will confront is the growth of social media. The aforementioned Global Peace Index showed an especially large increase in violent demonstrations, facilitated by texting and video services.[13] This empowerment provides everyone from average citizens to terrorists and religious zealots with the ability to gather an audience and disrupt; there is little requirement to show that their group actually *creates* positive change, rather merely promoting the message that getting rid of "what is" will magically spawn something outstanding in its place.[14] Nowhere is this more glaringly obvious than with Islamic State's (IS) horrific but also professionally produced online videos and publications – all of which demonstrate graphic design and public relations know-how. Grainy and low-budget has been replaced with high definition and high production value. Essentially, states are threatened with losing legitimacy as the costs of destabilizing decline relative to the costs of maintaining or restoring order.

FISCAL REALITIES

Largely for budgetary reasons, it has been stated that foreign policy and military decline resulted in Canada sleepwalking "its way to global irrelevance, squandering a proud tradition."[15] While many Canadians may agree, one must ask the follow-up question of whether they care. Money spent on defence must come from other portfolios, whether agriculture subsidies, provincial transfers, or debt repayment. This inward focus away from international politics is further exacerbated by weak economic recovery since 2008. Yet three factors continue driving annual spending increases: population growth; inflation, which is higher in defence procurement than in the general economy; and regulation creep, wherein governments add cost-accruing legislation but rarely remove any. With this in mind, Canada's spending on defence went from $12.3 billion to $18.9 billion during Afghanistan. It is now time to pay the piper.

To set the tone, last year commenced with the government clawing back $3.1 billion in military spending; currently at 1.1 per cent of its gross domestic product (GDP), Canada's defence-spending peers are Greece, Slovakia, and Ethiopia.[16] A briefing note prepared for the deputy minister of defence projected an additional cut of \$2.7 billion, which would put Canada behind Spain, Hungary, Luxembourg, and Lithuania as well. While NATO has established a guideline of 2 per cent of GDP, a position reinforced at the 2014 NATO Wales Summit, Canada calls this merely an "aspirational target," which it has no intention of meeting. The Parliamentary Budget Office has confirmed that, with the price of maintaining Canada's defence force structure increasing at 1.5 per cent per year, forecast spending will inexorably create an affordability gap mirroring the 1990s "decade of darkness"; capabilities must inevitably be lost.[17]

In directing budget cuts, the government specified there be no reduction in personnel numbers. Because wages account for more than half of the defence budget, this leaves operating expenses and acquisitions as targets for cuts.[18] The Canada First Defence Strategy (CFDS) anticipated that by 2014 military spending would have grown steadily due to six years of assured investment to refurnish the military with state-of-the-art equipment. Instead, the budget is now roughly equivalent to what it was before CFDS, providing significantly less money available to keep existing fleets operating. The curtailed budget of 2014 forced the army to park some 6,800 trucks with many of these vehicles being cannibalized for parts. The Navy has tied up half of its patrol vessels, and the Air Force cut back on CF-188 maintenance sparking pilot safety concerns.[19] The CFDS, beyond being criticized as a mere shopping list rather than any sort of strategy, was quietly shelved as being simply unaffordable.

Once again, the Canadian military faces a recurring problem of competing among itself for resources rather than forming any strategically guided consensus on objectives. This is particularly significant with major equipment purchases. The near-future's army will likely come out worst of the three services simply because navies and air forces are defined by their equipment, with their strategic effect being achieved through their weapons and the platforms on which they are mounted. The Royal Canadian Navy (RCN) and Royal Canadian Air Force (RCAF) combat infrastructure (made up of surface combatants and fighter aircraft respectively) is aging significantly, and they cannot perform their core duties in the absence of this equipment; it must be replaced soon.

For the RCN, between 2006 and 2012 the government announced replacement programs for the forty-four-year-old destroyers and the forty-five-year-old replenishment ships, as well as new Arctic/

Offshore Patrol ships; to date, not a single contract has been signed. Delivery dates are currently forecast for somewhere around 2020, with steel only just now (as of 2015) being cut in Canadian shipyard meeting even this date is highly improbable. The RCAF is in similar straits. Scant attention is paid to the success stories of the CC-117 Globemaster III and the CH-147 Chinook acquisitions, to focus on the negative publicity surrounding the on-again, off-again F-35 program. The Sea King helicopter has passed fifty years of service, with the SAR fixed-wing replacement aircraft right behind – the timeline equivalent of fighting the Korean War with the Wright Brothers' Flyer. These aircraft programs remain stalled with no firm delivery dates on the horizon. Unequivocally, the RCN and the RCAF are in dire need of revitalization or their capabilities will inexorably grind to a halt. What then, does this leave for the Canadian Army?

Because Afghanistan was almost exclusively an army fight, with Canadian troops dependent upon the US Air Force (USAF) and Royal Air Force (RAF) for requisite close air support, most recent acquisitions favoured the army. Nevertheless, strain of combat sees much of that equipment already well-worn and in need of refurbishment or replacement. As well, other capability gaps such as credible air defence or a readily deployable anti-tank system are not being rectified, with additional gaps projected as weapons and support systems age-out without replacement.

These trends will necessitate a greater embracing of "light infantry" as a default model – a view reinforced by the 2013 cancellation of the heavily armoured close combat vehicle program. This is not to say that mechanized infantry will wither away, but simply reaffirm that a major reason for having light infantry battalions is that we simply cannot afford to equip them with light-armoured vehicles (LAV). When deploying to Afghanistan, these light units would simply go through LAV III qualification training. This reality is not a mechanized versus a light infantry divide, but simply "the LAVs and the LAV-nots." While budget cuts are likely to hit the army hardest, Canada will not be bereft of land forces. In the concluding chapter to this volume, Breede makes a similar point, but here we see the details of fiscal realities that will shape future engagements abroad.

Pre-emptive deployment of special operations forces (SOF) demonstrates a cost-effective and politically acceptable approach to contemporary conflicts. From a Western perspective, avoiding negative headlines is a high priority, and SOF personnel address problems while the target country is "still on page eleven in the news, before it moves up to page two in the headlines."[20] They provide tactical guidance and training to indigenous forces, allowing those nations to solve their own security issues rather than requiring greater military intervention. These efforts also aid in professionalizing their militaries, which is essential to a fledgling democracy's stability. When the conflict does move to the front pages, as with the IS, the SOF training mission and provision of terminal guidance to CF-188 munitions is more acceptable to the electorate than deploying a mechanized brigade group; once again, it is a more sanitary option.

THE END OF GRAND STRATEGY

In addition to war-weariness, a complex security environment, and budgetary contraction, collective experiences in Iraq and Afghanistan have drawn attention to an associated issue, which is a dearth of strategic thinking. Long interventions certainly played a part in undermining support for such wars, but also for the wisdom that led into them. As Christian Leuprecht and Joel J. Sokolsky's chapter in this volume demonstrates, Canada has not defined a clear grand strategy, nor is it the only country that has stopped short of so doing. This realization is not limited only to the 9/11 Wars. The absence of a grand strategy continues with the leadership deficiencies in supporting post–Arab Spring transitions and in addressing Syria's ongoing crises by drawing repeated "red lines" that when crossed, simply mean the drawing of a new one. This leaves a cumulative message of weakness. Retired Canadian Army General Lewis MacKenzie is rightfully dismissive, stating that NATO's "rhetoric about Ukraine is meaningless, because Russia knows NATO is incapable of taking on any high-risk intervention – anywhere."[21]

With the US government pondering "four defeats in Fourth Generation War – Lebanon, Somalia, Iraq, and Afghanistan," one notes silence from the military in contrast with the post-Vietnam generation of military reformers: "[T]oday the landscape is barren. Not a military voice is heard calling for substantive change. Just more money, please."[22] A senior Canadian officer recently serving with US-Africa Command expressed similar concerns, noting that, "strategy died in our [W]estern world over a decade ago. Now hash-tag activism drives 'operational art.'"[23] It is within this vacuum that the Department of National Defence must create strategically coherent plans, based upon clear policy goals. It appears doubtful that any such overarching plan existed after the 1950s, as subsequent policy statements (1964, 1971, 1987, 1994, and 2009) all read merely as justification for a priori government decisions.[24] History adds a further suggestion that intervention triggers may come as a surprise since planners have a tendency to merge the unfamiliar with the improbable, assuming the latter to be less worthy of in-depth consideration. Prior to the 9/11 attacks, for example, government strategists had not considered unconventional strategic shocks as highlighted by the 9/11 Commission, "imagination is not a gift usually associated with bureaucracies."[25]

In crafting our strategic plans, several things suggest that the aforementioned global instability is more than a blip. Details of each crisis differ, yet common features abound. Early crisis participants were relatively young, urban, wealthy, and somewhat educated. They were angry about economic stagnation, official corruption, governments' arbitrary use of power, and their lack of representation in decision making.[26] Many uprisings featured demands for liberal democracy and the rule of law, which encouraged our support, while in several others a return to brutal authority has been championed as an answer to chaos or Western intervention. These varied realities should inform policy-makers' thinking about Canadian grand strategy.

FOREIGN AND DEFENCE POLICY DECISION MAKING

Foreign policy, our ability and willingness to act in the world, is simplistically about three things: interests, values, and leverage. While political interest and Canadian values are readily understood, leverage is a function of the economic and military resources we can bring to bear, coupled with our coalition partners' unity of purpose.[27] Essentially, do we have the leverage to sustainably shift things our way at a price we can afford? Given the number of potential flashpoints, there is no shortage of opportunities for Canadian military intervention. Trigger points beyond clear humanitarian efforts are always an interesting topic: why bomb Libya but not Syria? Even humanitarian intervention decision making is puzzling. Despite international law's norm of non-intervention, such actions are not uncommon; motivation is the major variable. Comparing 2003 Iraq and Darfur for example, one sees a military intervention to install a more preferred regime in Iraq despite being decried as illegitimate. Concurrently, willingness to end Darfur's genocide was largely apathetic, despite being considered legitimate under international law and having the potential to save countless lives.[28] Such examples highlight that intervention triggers, rather than being based largely upon legal or altruistic principles, remain very much discretionary and self-interest based.

Theoretically, intervention decisions should come down to what is best for Canadian security, trade influences, and being seen as a team player by allies. There are minimal military threats to our national security, being in a "fireproof home, far from flammable materials," as we are. Failed states were portrayed as key Canadian security concerns in both the Liberals' 2005 *International Policy Statement* and the Conservatives' aforementioned 2008 CFDS. While both documents quickly passed their "best-before" date, they still provide insight into both governments' thinking. They asserted that such states potentially warrant intervention, being sources of international instability as terrorist sanctuaries and contributors to social and economic instability spilling across neighbouring borders and indeed back to Canada.[29] Nonetheless, given our positioning within the global economy and the wakeup call of the 2008 financial crisis, I suspect that we will see international priorities increasingly linked to trade and economic stability. Government thinking may therefore emphasize opportunity costs of ameliorating risks to trading routes or supplies, intervening to gain favour of trading partners, and effects of a "go/no-go" decision on various domestic constituents – immigrant and Canadian-born.

One notable change to intervention judgment occurred within Canada's domestic polity. The 1970s Pavlovian anti-militarism has recently matured into a more nuanced view in which the dedicated Left now provides the most persistent calls for military intervention, focusing upon the downtrodden and oppressed.[30] Perhaps this is the fallout of a generation that does not remember the Cold War, but knows only Rwanda, Iraq, and Afghanistan. While they are strident in their calls to "do something" to promote the liberal world order, their level of personal sacrifice is very circumscribed: low-risk, low-cost peace support operations may seem to be the perfect prescription. In the end though, intervention triggers will remain

the unforecasted occurrences in the realm attributed to Harold
Macmillan of "events, dear boy, events." As noted, with hashtag
activism driving strategic thinking, domestic politics make coherent
long-term programs difficult, with policies increasingly appearing
to be developed by advertising agencies in response to election-
cycle imperatives. Many of these imperatives are, of course, driven
by finances.

LOOKING AHEAD

What does all this portend for future military intervention? The
twenty-first century has already seen no shortage of violence, but
notwithstanding Russia's renewed assertiveness, major conventional
war seems unlikely at the moment. Our political leaders should nevertheless remember that "the military provides the glint of steel that
ultimately makes diplomacy work."[31] A credible military capability
that gives pause to those whose interests run afoul of ours is still
vitally necessary if we do not wish to confirm that we have indeed
sleepwalked our way into global irrelevance. With an accountant's
mindset curtailing our strategic thinking though, Canada's ability
to field and sustain a significant, balanced combat force is looking
dismal. While our military is renowned for having risen to similar
challenges in the past, they may simply be unable to pull that rabbit
out of the hat one more time. Our options may be limited to deployments such as providing airlift into Mali supporting France's Operation Serval, or the RCN's Operation Artemis Arabian Sea patrols.
More recently, deploying RCAF fighter-bombers and support aircraft against the Islamic State through Operation Impact can be
seen as a logical outcome of reluctance to see more negative publicity of soldiers' bodies returning home; such a campaign is perceived as "clean" and garners widespread public support. Regardless
of the efficacy of such airpower operations, they also meet the government's need to be seen by our allies as being a dependable
team player.[32]

The army's emasculated combat capabilities, coupled with war-
weariness and risk-aversion, however, may see a renewed interest in
PSO as a way ahead for military interventions. While the Conference
on Defence Associations Institute claims that the "days of humanitarian military interventions are over," I would argue the opposite,

if only because that will be one of the few options remaining.[33] One increasingly hears terms such as *peacemaking* and *humanitarian intervention* underlying calls for deployments, often from middle-class liberals traditionally accustomed to peace. In other words, perhaps foreign involvement under the rubric of helping others is growing in popularity.

Timely and effective military intervention providing stability for follow-on economic and political assistance has proven to be a cost-effective way of mitigating post-conflict violence.[34] Canada certainly has the command, planning, and logistic wherewithal to benefit UN-type operations. Choosing to provide troops to lower-risk missions has the added benefit of appealing to those voters, and hence politicians, steadfastly adhering to the myth of Canada as a premier peacekeeping nation. Put bluntly, however, Canada's peacekeeping self-image of unarmed, blue-hatted troops embraced by two sides of former-combatants is too historically scarce an occurrence to ponder. Those who cling to such myths would equally cross the city of New York's Central Park and noting how much safer it had become, believe that humanity is inherently more peaceful while dismissing any NYPD role.[35] The reality is that while Chapter VI peacekeeping missions previously produced mixed results, they are virtually non-existent now, having been supplanted by Chapter VII peacemaking. Of the seventeen current PSO, only five are mandated under Chapter VI and these were all established between 1948 and 1978; missions over the past four decades have been of the more robust, but more hazardous, peacemaking variety.[36]

If we are to go down the PSO path, therefore, we must do so with eyes wide open. A policy to which our government clings is liberalizing economies, introducing democracy and improve governance overall to discourage rampant corruption, patronage and nepotism. Regrettably the mantra of "stabilize, privatize, democratize" has not proven particularly successful. The complex processes of stopping warfighting and changing economic and political systems have either reinforced pathologies or introduced new ones. Humanitarian intervention has been labelled as "synonymous with Western interference and cultural imperialism."[37] Groups have been prone to exploit elections to enflame harmful competition along ethnic lines or through angry religious rhetoric, as well as to misappropriate foreign aid for political purposes. Canadian troops experienced this first-hand during the early Balkans involvement, where nationalist overtones and fear-mongering marshalled the electorate and voting effectively crushed the fledgling democracies.[38] Those missions were compelled to convert from blue-beret UN peacekeeping into multiple NATO-led peacemaking missions.

Growing evidence now strongly suggests that liberalizing economics and politics may actually be a harmful remedy for recently warring societies, particularly those with a history of colonial or strongly directed political-economic systems. In short, active competition underpins both capitalism and democratic elections and these societies may not be in the mood for our imposing further antagonism.[39] Perhaps this should not be surprising. Widespread democracy in Europe is barely over a century old and that was an uphill struggle. We may be accused justifiably of repeatedly trying to plant democracy in infertile soil. Michael Ignatieff once observed that "liberal civilization ... runs deeply against the human grain and is achieved and sustained only by the most unremitting struggle against human nature."[40] Economically, even advanced societies feature groups claiming they did not receive their entitlement or fair share; it is too easy to blame other factions, fomenting renewed hatred.

There are numerous factors making these operations a more multi-faceted endeavour than war's comparatively straightforward gunfight; such deployments are increasingly complex and we are only beginning to understand nuances that eluded us previously. For example, problems occur if intervention forces are seen as actively supporting one faction to the detriment of the other, removing incentives to compromise. Other complications arise if the mission priority is to get in and out as rapidly as possible, encouraging local warlords to feign compliance and allow intervention forces to disarm much of their opposition prior to recommencing violence. These missions routinely see that the people most capable of organizing a local polity are often the least desirable – the warlords and criminals who prefer to selectively cripple the state, creating areas for their own rule of law.[41] Our history of stabilizing conflicts under the banner of "Responsibility to Protect" is altruistically to prevent genocide and ethnic cleansing. However, there is evidence that this perversely *increases* such violence by encouraging disgruntled substate groups to rebel, expecting intervention to protect them from inevitable state retaliation.[42] Actual intervention, however, is often too late or feeble to prevent reprisals.

CONCLUSION

As Basil Liddell Hart noted over a half-century ago, limiting war is wise because the avoidance of extremes in warfare tends to facilitate a more lasting peace.[43] Many current global crises are textbook examples of intense societal clashes, particularly those drawn along ethnic lines or featuring no culture of conflict resolution, exacerbated by ineffective political institutions. Nonetheless, nation-building costs are comparatively modest. For example, at the height of its military operations in Iraq, the United States was spending almost $4.5 billion per month; this is more than the UN spends to run all seventeen of its current missions for a year.[44] Yes, this is somewhat of an apples-oranges comparison, but I submit that such missions may pre-empt more costly full-scale interventions.

In the current context, defence budget cuts have unmistakable implications for future capabilities and the allocation of resources. Fiscal realities have set the conditions wherein the RCN and RCAF must receive the lion's share of funding. Deploying these elements has the additional political benefit of being seen as "clean," when contrasted with soldiers fighting and dying on the nightly newscast. For the army, there may be few options beyond peace operations. Complex, often vicious, PSO are not for the faint-hearted. Canada will be doing its soldiers no favours with such missions. Given current war-weariness, risk-aversion, and budgetary restraint, the government may see great international utility and domestic favour in expanded involvement in peacemaking operations. One can only hope that they are not marketed domestically as a return to a golden era of peacekeeping.

NOTES

1 Hans Morgenthau, "To Intervene or Not to Intervene," *Foreign Affairs* 45 (April 1967): 425–36.
2 "In Depth: Canada's Military Mission in Afghanistan," CBC *News*, last updated 10 May 2011, http://www.cbc.ca/news/canada/canada-s-military-mission-in-afghanistan-1.777386. See also Angus Reid, http://angus-reidglobal.com/home/.
3 CBC, "Veterans Fighting Service Cuts Felt Disrespected at Fantino Meeting," CBC *News*, last updated 29 January 2014, www.cbc.ca/news/

politics/veterans-fighting-service-cuts-felt-disrespected-at-fantino-meet-
ing-1.2513837.

4 Tanya Navaneelan, "Health at a Glance: Suicide Rates: An Overview"
   (Ottawa, Statistics Canada, 2012), passim. This is not to suggest compla-
   cency regarding veterans' health issues.

5 National Defence and the Canadian Armed Forces, "Fallen Canadians,"
   last modified January 2014, www.forces.gc.ca/en/honours-history-fallen-
   canadians/index.page.

6 National Defence and the Canadian Armed Forces, "Fact Sheet – Canadian Forces' Casualty Statistics (Afghanistan)," 10 June 2013, www.forces.
   gc.ca/en/news/article.page?doc=canadian-forces-casualty-statistics-afghan-
   istan/hie8w9c9. This does not include non-combat injuries (911) and
   deaths (16) during the 2002–09 timeframe; Alison Howell, "Afghanistan's
   Price," *Literary Review of Canada*, November 2011, http://reviewcanada.
   ca/magazine/2011/11/afghanistans-price.

7 "What Would America Fight For? A Nagging Doubt Is Eating Away at the
   World Order – and the Superpower Is Largely Ignoring It," *The Economist*, 3 May 2014, www.economist.com/news/leaders/21601508-nagging-
   doubt-eating-away-world-orderand-superpower-largely-ignoring-it-what;
   Special Inspector General for Afghanistan Reconstruction, "Quarterly
   Report to the United States Congress" (Washington: USGPO, 30 June
   2014), 5, 97.

8 Patrick Porter, "Last Charge of the Knights? Iraq, Afghanistan, and the
   Special Relationship," *International Affairs* 86, no. 2 (March 2010): 355–
   75. See also "Syria Crisis: Cameron Loses Commons Vote on Syria Action,"
   BBC News, 30 August 2013, www.bbc.com/news/uk-politics-23892783.
   Allies may also be more hesitant to contribute to US-led interventions
   because high-profile policy failures, most notably in Iraq, have fuelled perceptions of US decline. The author is grateful to one of the anonymous
   reviewers for pointing this out.

9 *Global Peace Index 2014* (New York: Institute for Economics and Peace, 2014).

10 Randall L. Schweller, "Entropy and the Trajectory of World Politics: Why
   Polarity Has Become Less Meaningful," *Cambridge Review of International
   Affairs* 23, no. 1 (March 2010): passim.

11 Stratfor, "Strategic Forecast 2015," www.stratfor.com/forecast/
   annual-forecast-2015.

12 Thomas L. Friedman, "It's Not Just about Obama," *The New York Times*, 3
   May 2014, SR11.

13 *Global Peace Index 2014*.

14 Schweller, "Entropy."

15 Michael Byers, "The Harper Plan for Unilateral Canadian Disarmament," *National Post*, 8 July 2014, 3.

16 Lee Berthiaume, "Defence Documents Show Cuts Hurting Military Vehicle Maintenance," *Ottawa Citizen*, 10 June 2014, 1.

17 Denitsa Raynova and Ian Kearns, "The Wales Pledge Revisited: A Preliminary Analysis of 2015 Budget Decisions of NATO Member States," London: European Leadership Network, February 2015, 7; Canada, "Fiscal Sustainability of Canada's National Defence Program," Parliamentary Budget Office, March 2015, 15, 18n38.

18 Andrea Janus, "Canada 'Just Can't Get around' Army Cuts, Hillier Says," *CTV News*, 23 September 2013, www.ctvnews.ca/canada/canada-just-can-t-get-around-army-cuts-hillier-says-1.1467584#ixzz30ZZdZeOf.

19 David Perry, "The Growing Gap between Defence Ends and Means: The Disconnect between the Canada First Defence Strategy and the Current Defence Budget" (Ottawa: CDAI, June 2014), 10; Byers, "The Harper Plan," 3.

20 Robert D. Kaplan, "Endless War," *Stratfor*, 1 August 2012, www.stratfor.com/weekly/endless-war#axzz373z3yCoo.

21 "What Would America Fight For?," *The Economist*, 3 May 2014; Lewis MacKenzie, "NATO, the Multiple-Choice Alliance," *Globe and Mail*, 27 March 2014, www.theglobeandmail.com/globe-debate/somnia/article17684203. See also Emile Simpson, *War from the Ground Up: Twenty-first Century Combat as Politics* (Oxford: Oxford University Press, 2013).

22 William S. Lind, "An Officer Corps That Can't Score: How Military Careerism Breeds Habits of Defeat," *The American Conservative*, 17 April 2014, www.theamericanconservative.com/articles/an-officer-corps-that-cant-score.

23 Colonel Ian Hope (PPCLI), in discussions with the author.

24 These have predominantly been policy statements only, in that Canada has produced no formal defence white paper since 1994.

25 US Government, *National Commission on Terrorist Attacks upon the Nation, The 9/11 Commission Report* (Washington: USGPO, 2004), 344.

26 Thomas Homer-Dixon, "What's behind These Fracturing Countries? Stalled Economies," *Globe and Mail*, 11 April 2014, www.theglobeandmail.com/globe-debate/whats-behind-these-fractures-stalled-economies/article17925027. See also Graeme Wood, "What ISIS Really Wants," *The Atlantic*, March 2015, http://www.theatlantic.com/features/archive/2015/02/what-isis-really-wants/384980.

27 Friedman, "It's Not Just about Obama." See also H. Christian Breede's chapter in this volume, particularly his discussion of side payments.

28 Stephen E. Gent, "Strange Bedfellows: The Strategic Dynamics of Major
    Power Military Interventions," *The Journal of Politics* 69, no. 4 (November
    2007); 1089–102.

29 Jennifer Ramos, *Changing Norms through Action* (New York: Oxford Univer-
    sity Press, 2013), passim. This work expands upon the premise that our
    conceptions of human rights have changed the idea of state sovereignty
    being inviolable.

30 Andrew Bacevich, *The New American Militarism: How Americans Are Seduced
    by War* (New York: Oxford University Press, 2013), 25.

31 David Bercuson, "Failing States and Proxy Wars," *Ottawa Citizen*, last
    updated 20 March 2014, http://ottawacitizen.com/opinion/columnists/
    failing-states-and-proxy-wars.

32 Ipsos, "Two in Three (66%) Canadians Support Extension of Canadian
    Forces Mission against ISIS in Iraq," 24 March 2015, www.ipsos-na.com/
    news-polls/pressrelease.aspx?id=6801. See also Stéfanie von Hlatky, *Amer-
    ican Allies in Times of War* (Oxford: Oxford University Press, 2013).

33 Ferry de Kerckhove and George Petrolekas, *Strategic Outlook for Canada –
    A Search for Leadership: 2014*, Vimy Paper no. 7 (Ottawa: Conference of
    Defence Associations, 2014), 2.

34 Hew Strachan, *The Direction of War: Contemporary Strategy in Historical Per-
    spective* (Cambridge: Cambridge University Press, 2013), 99; James Dob-
    bins et al. "The UN's Role in Nation-Building: From Congo to Iraq" (Santa
    Monica, CA: RAND, 2005), xxxv–xxxvii.

35 Robert Kagan, "Superpowers Don't Get to Retire: What Our Tired Country
    Still Owes the World," *The New Republic*, 26 May 2014, http://www.newre-
    public.com/article/117859/allure-normalcy-what-america-still-owes-world.

36 United Nations, "Current Peacekeeping Operations," www.un.org/en/
    peacekeeping/operations/current.shtml.

37 Aidan Hehir, *The Responsibility to Protect: Rhetoric, Reality, and the Future of
    Humanitarian Intervention* (Basingstoke, UK: Palgrave Macmillan, 2012),
    158.

38 Warren Zimmerman, *Origins of Catastrophe: Yugoslavia and the Destroyers*
    (New York: Random House, 1996), 68.

39 Roland Paris, *At War's End: Building Peace after Civil Conflict* (New York:
    Cambridge University Press, 2004), 168–75. Intervening with the multiple
    ambitions of Westernizing, professionalizing, and democratizing may be a
    bridge too far in many instances. Debating this in requisite detail is, how-
    ever, beyond the scope of this chapter.

40 Kagan, "Superpowers Don't Get to Retire"; Michael Ignatieff, *Blood and
    Belonging: Journeys into the New Nationalism* (London: BBC Books, 1993),
    passim.

41 Nils Gilman, "The Twin Insurgency," *The American Interest* 9, no. 9 (July–August 2014): 7–15.

42 Alan J. Kuperman, "The Moral Hazard of Humanitarian Intervention: Lessons from the Balkans," *International Studies Quarterly* 52, no. 1 (March 2008): 49–80, passim.

43 Basil Liddell Hart, *Defence of the West* (London: Morrow 1950), 291–302.

44 Andrej Sitkowski, UN *Peacekeeping: Myth and Reality* (New York: Praeger, 2005), 14–15; Dobbins, "The UN's Role in Nation-Building," xxxv–xxxvi.

6

The Patterns, Implications, and Risks
of American Military Contracting

AARON ETTINGER

In 2014, at the tail end of the 9/11 Wars and the aftershocks of the 2008 recession, the US Department of Defense finally met its match. Neither enemy army nor insurgency could lay low the Pentagon. Rather, it is fiscal restraint in America that has caught up with the world's mightiest military.[1] Institutional reform of such urgency and magnitude is a major undertaking for a public agency as large as the Department of Defense. Other chapters in this volume have discussed the significant inhibitors and enablers of US military capabilities, from improvised explosive devices (see Christopher Barron's chapter) to the technological advances that heralded an ostensible "new American way of war" (see Asa McKercher's chapter). Here, attention turns to military contractors – actors in the Iraq and Afghanistan theatres that have both enabled American war efforts by bringing added capacity, and hindered efforts by exposing problems of control and coordination. In a word, American military contractors have been indispensable to the wars in Iraq and Afghanistan, for better and for worse. Here, attention turns to the new era of military cutbacks in the United States. It draws lessons from military contracting practices over the past five decades and identifies the implications for American military interventions in the near future.

Among the many reforms are personnel changes which include the rebalancing of the Defense Department's contractor workforce. For observers of the public bureaucracy, it is a familiar tune that rings with the tones of institutional streamlining, outsourcing, and the shedding of "non-core" functions. But the 2014 *Quadrennial Defense Review* has signalled a curious direction in contracting. In a reversal of sorts from previous trends in bureaucratic reform, outsourcing is giving way to insourcing. The current disposition is less focused on privatizing or outsourcing peripheral activities. Now the aim is reduce "excessive reliance on contractor support" and developing greater in-house capabilities.[2] This may, however, be wishful thinking. Even in the face of defence budget cuts, the Pentagon's contractor workforce is a component of US capabilities it cannot do without. As a recent analysis from the Congressional Research Service suggests, "[w]ithout contractor support, the US would currently be unable to arm and field an effective fighting force."[3] This chapter extends this observation beyond the fighting force and contingency contracting to the broader security and defence community in the United States.

To appreciate the US military's dependency on contractors it is vital to clarify just what the contractor represents in the assemblage of security actors. And, just as important, it is vital to know where this actor comes from. Here, *contractor* takes on a very broad meaning. It is meant to signify the millions of individuals and thousands of firms that transact with the US defence establishment on a commercial basis. These contracts cover a range of labour from driving cargo through the Khyber Pass, training militaries in sub-Saharan Africa, armed paramilitary security in Baghdad, and running online penetration tests on military computer networks from Northern Virginia. The scope of *contractor* is necessarily broad because of the degree to which the US defence establishment depends on expertise that does not exist in-house, and calls into question the viability of the Pentagon's desire to scale back on its contract workforce. For this chapter, the nomenclature of "private military and/or firm and/or security company" popularized in the current literature on military privatization is too narrowly construed.[4] Its biggest sin is that it focuses on the relatively new corporate military entity that has emerged in the post–Cold War era, and, consequently, has no past tense. This ahistorical terminology elides the fact that contracting during overseas operations, even major interventions, is a long-standing practice for the US Department of Defense – a fact that is often obscured by the unprecedented scale and scope of contracting in Iraq and Afghanistan. But partnership between the US military and the private sector has a rich history which illuminates the long-term determinants and implications of this growing dependency.

HISTORICAL PATTERNS OF
AMERICAN CONTINGENCY CONTRACTING

During the Korean War, "contractors" on the ground were mostly local workers performing hard manual labour for US and UN forces. The troop to contractor ratio in the Korean War is often reported as being about three to one.[5] However, data is not particularly reliable and this estimate probably overestimates the number of contractors. A more likely figure is closer to ten to one, or about 11 per cent of the US total force in Korea.[6] For the Vietnam War, data is more reliable and what exists suggests that the percentage of contractors was approximately the same. Total US military personnel reached its height at 542,400 in January 1969 while the number of contractors is considerably smaller. Based on figures from the two most prominent contractor firms and estimations of smaller firm contingents, the peak figure of contractors reached approximately 70,000 in 1966.[7] Top levels of both contingents suggest troops outnumbered contractors nearly eight to one. On average, between 1963 and 1971 contractors constituted about 10 per cent of the US total force, though this ratio fluctuated depending on US troop commitments. In Vietnam, however, contracting was undertaken on a much larger scale than in Korea, and with a broader scope. Similar to the conflicts in Iraq and Afghanistan four decades later, the US war in Vietnam involved garrisoning large numbers of US troops in countries with very limited infrastructure for over a decade, which required enormous logistical support. Navy Construction Battalions and the Army Corps of Engineers worked collaboratively with major American construction and telecommunications firms to transform the vastly underdeveloped territory below the seventeenth parallel into a theatre that could sustain the presence of a half-million-strong modern military. The type of labour undertaken was contingent on the changing priorities and demands of US political and military operations. By 1965, what had been a limited effort to bolster the technical capabilities of South Vietnam became a full-scale reconstruction and development project to support the expanding war. In South Vietnam, contractors became an indispensable force that made it possible for the United States to "Americanize" the war in Vietnam.[8]

During the post–Cold War period, trends shifted considerably. The US commitment to the Balkans between 1995 and 2000 necessitated a contractor presence that made up about 50 per cent of the US total force. In this instance, the army contracted with more than one hundred firms, the largest of which was a contract with Brown & Root Services (now KBR). BRS performed the vast majority of operations and maintenance, and construction tasks for the US contingent worth $2.168 billion between 1995 and 2000. This included building large portions of base camps in Kosovo, including Camp Bondsteel which was erected in a matter of months and designed to accommodate 5,000 individuals.[9]

Moving to the most recent conflicts, the wars in Iraq and Afghanistan have seen contracting at unprecedented levels. About 55 per cent of the US total force was drawn from the private sector and a broad spectrum of labour. For over a decade, contractors have engaged in construction tasks alongside military training, advisory and armed security functions to support the evolving US missions from stabilization to counter-insurgency and reconstruction.[10] Enumerating these tasks is extremely difficult because the types of work are diverse and constantly evolving, which complicates any typology of contingency contractors. Systematic accounts of contracting in Iraq and Afghanistan are beginning to emerge from official sources, notably the Special Inspectors General for reconstruction in the two countries. What they have found, and what these trends suggest, is that the private sector is deeply integrated into the very composition of the US total force, a reality with significant implications for military interventions in the near future. They are manifold but three are discussed here.

IMPLICATION 1: Long-term contingency operations are extremely expensive and labour-intensive. Relying on contractors is not necessarily cost-effective.

The unexpectedly high costs of contingency contracting in Iraq and Afghanistan illustrate an immediate implication for US military interventions in the forthcoming period of defence budget cuts. Take note of the figures. Between September 2001 and 2014, Congress provided almost $1.6 trillion in budget authority for operations in Afghanistan and Iraq and their related activities.[11] Through 2012, the United States spent approximately $232.2 billion on contractors and, as of 2011, as much as $60 billion has been lost to contracting waste, fraud, and abuse.[12] These figures only reflect what can be measured by auditors using existing contracting data; information that is *not* available may inflate these numbers further. The Special Inspector General for Iraqi Reconstruction (SIGIR) has reported widespread record-keeping deficiencies among US government agencies involved in Iraqi reconstruction. As a result, "the disposition of billions of dollars for projects remains unknown because US government agencies involved in the relief and reconstruction effort did not maintain project information in any uniform or comprehensive manner."[13] Cost considerations are especially salient regarding interventions that involve boots on the ground and elaborate logistical support. This fact is not lost on Pentagon planners. The 2014 *Quadrennial Defense Review* suggests that US forces "will no longer be sized to conduct large-scale prolonged stability operations."[14] The United States was not going to play the nation-building game.

It would seem, then, that the United States would prefer to keep large-scale military interventions to a minimum in the near future, especially when they involve troops on the ground in hostile environments. But, as the Libya intervention in 2011 and the ongoing crisis across Syria and Iraq demonstrate, planning for contingencies entails a high degree of uncertainty for America and its allies. Should another major contingency operation arise, the United States would not be in a sound administrative position to control its contracting costs. The Commission on Wartime Contracting concluded in its 2011 assessment that "the high cost of repeating *ad hoc* arrangements for contract support is unacceptable."[15] Any possible interventions involving protracted stays on the ground will require costly logistical support. In the face of budget cuts, clear policies regarding contracting planning and acquisition oversight are necessary to maintain control over costs. At the same time, the United States shows few signs of deep retrenchment, and will likely continue to pursue a policy of "deep engagement" with the world.[16] This leads to the next implication.

IMPLICATION 2: If the United States aims to maintain a light footprint in future interventions, it will rely on contractors as a complement to uniformed soldiers.

In 2012, 12 per cent of all Department of Defense contract obligations were spent on overseas commands. Though Africa Command (referred to as USAFRICOM) only draws 1 per cent of these obligations, it is an illustrative case of America's light-footprint approach while engaging in continent-wide security and institution-building operations.[17] Established in 2007, the USAFRICOM combatant command operates with an abiding respect for the small footprint. Part of its initial challenge was establishing a presence at a time when US ground forces have been limited by commitments in Iraq and Afghanistan, and of course by the sheer size of the continent.[18] Presently, the imperatives of a small footprint are driven both by economic constraints and a desire to maintain a low profile on the ground.[19] The USAFRICOM regional command only has about 2,000 military and civilian personnel, three-quarters of which are stationed at its headquarters in Germany.[20] Therefore, USAFRICOM functions through multiple US agencies and via contract arrangements with major firms engaging in a broad range of tasks.

The first such contracting mission was initiated, not by the Pentagon, but by the Department of State in 2004, three years prior to the establishment of USAFRICOM. After the fall of Charles Taylor's regime in Liberia, the West African country underwent a thorough restructuring of its security sector, including the armed forces. The US State Department tendered a contract for building the Armed Forces of Liberia (AFL) that was eventually split between the two bidders, DynCorp International and Pacific Architects and Engineers (PAE). A five-point program of security sector reform followed that involved political consultation, demobilizing the existing military, recruiting a new force, training, and deployment.[21] Overall, the Liberian reform project was successful in reconstructing a functioning armed force, though critics have cited the security sector reform project for a lack of transparency, accountability, and limited participation among local actors.[22]

The contracting experience in Liberia is emblematic of United States security assistance in subsequent years.[23] Both the US Departments of Defense and State undertake similar functions on the African continent relating to security sector reform and state building. In 2009, the State Department institutionalized the outsourcing strategy by letting out a five-year $1.5-billion umbrella contract (AFRICAP) for private sector provision of military and security training programs. In the years since, prominent American military contracting firms have undertaken security sector reform projects with state military and civilian police forces across the continent, as well as with the United Nations. A quick overview illustrates the extent of the US military's reach through its contractor auxiliaries. Military Professional Resources Incorporated (MPRI), famous for its intervention in the Serbo-Croatian war in the mid-1990s, provides training for the armed forces of Benin, Ethiopia, Ghana, Kenya,

Mali, Malawi, Nigeria, Rwanda, and Senegal under the auspices
of the State Department's African Contingency Operations Training and Assistance program (ACOTA). Northrop Grumman trains
African peacekeepers under the same program. Not to be left out,
the largest US construction contractor, KBR, services at least three
US military bases in Djibouti, Kenya, and Ethiopia.[24] Contractors
aid in US spy and surveillance missions in Uganda, Congo, South
Sudan, and the Central African Republic.[25] In the Horn of Africa,
private firms engage in anti-piracy consulting for both state agencies
and private shipping companies.[26] And, according to some reports,
contracting extends beyond the Departments of Defense and State
to the CIA.[27] In these cases, the United States maintains a military
and political influence across a vast territory while minimizing
its footprint.

IMPLICATION 3: Light footprints mean heavier reliance on technology to support operations. The broadening commercial base of
technological advancement suggests that Department of Defense is
not necessarily well equipped to take the lead.

Contracting in Vietnam and, in particular, the 9/11 Wars demonstrate that the private sector is a crucial repository of technological expertise for which there is no in-house Pentagon capacity. In
Vietnam, the United States relied upon telecommunications firms
to establish a wireless infrastructure across Southeast Asia in the
same way that the United States required private sector support
for its IT and secure Internet communications in Iraq and Afghanistan.[28] But this dependency extends beyond contingency contracting to the basic twenty-first-century communications infrastructure.
The integration of advanced computer technologies into the critical infrastructure of military operations overseas and at home
requires ongoing collaboration with the private sector.[29] This is particularly relevant in the maintenance of communications network
infrastructure and biometric security systems. In the high-tech communications sector, there is considerable demand for expertise
needed to support both civilian and military IT infrastructure. Militarily, the demand comes from developments in Command, Control, Communications, Computers, Intelligence, Surveillance, and
Reconaissance(C4ISR) programs. This need extends to software
training and development, system modernization and monitoring, information storage, and data security. The issue is especially

pressing given the attention given to cybersecurity. In recent years, prominent cyberattacks initiated by actors in major powers have raised the spectre of a new kind of warfare: Russia's denial-of-service (DOS) attacks on Estonia in 2007, its coordinated cyber-prelude to its kinetic assault on Georgia in 2008, the Stuxnet attack on Iranian nuclear centrifuges discovered in 2010 (likely initiated by the United States and/or Israel), and the coordinated Chinese hacking program uncovered in 2013.[30] These cases underscored the extent to which the cyber domain has become a matter of national security. In-house expertise is no longer enough.

Generally, the capacity to design and maintain the hardware and software has been outsourced to commercial firms that are better situated to keep pace with technological innovations. As former deputy secretary of defense William J. Lynn noted in 2010, it takes the Pentagon eighty-one months, almost seven years, to make a new computer system operational after it is first funded. Given the exponential growth in computing power, by the time systems are delivered, they are already multiple generations behind the most advanced technologies.[31] The impetus comes from the fear of cyberattacks. There is debate as to the actual threat of a "cyber Pearl Harbor, or cyber 9/11" in the words of former secretary of defense Leon Panetta.[32] But the concern is enough for the Pentagon to treat cyberspace as an operational domain, warranting its own command, and resulting in a need to reach deep into the technology sector for expertise. Big businesses like Booz Allen Hamilton as well as independent start-ups have turned computer-system security and hacking into a lucrative business.[33] Underscoring the dependency of the US security establishment on contractors is that of the 1.5 million people with top-secret clearances, more than one-third are private contractors, and their background checks are often undertaken by other subcontractors.[34]

The robotics sector represents another area of defence production and manufacturing that is heavily dependent on the private sector. The technological leaps of the so-called Revolution in Military Affairs exceeded what the US military could feasibly maintain in-house. Thus, much of these responsibilities have been devolved to contractor representatives trained on specialized equipment. Take, for instance, the emblematic weapon of the 9/11 Wars – the unmanned aerial vehicle (UAV). The use of UAVs in the air and on land has increased considerably over the past thirteen years.

Beginning with only a handful at the outset of the Afghanistan war, the military now has about 8,000 UAVs and 12,000 ground robots at its disposal.[35] The contractor role in robotics requires close collaboration with suppliers in the private sector, not only in acquisition but in maintenance. Historically, life-cycle and other technical maintenance of vehicles could be managed by army mechanics, with some assistance from civilian contractors, as was the case in most US wars in the twentieth century.[36] Presently, specific weapons technologies are so advanced that they require specialized expertise for their maintenance that outstrip the capabilities of the typical military technicians.

Indeed, the role of the private sector in robotics is only symptomatic of the increasing influence of commercial developments on military technology. Public-private partnerships involve traditional contractors like Lockheed Martin and unexpected apparel companies like Under Armour and Adidas, to produce advanced body suits for soldiers.[37] Recent years have also witnessed entry of the private sector into space travel both by policy design and by entrepreneurial ambition. In 2013, the International Space Station (ISS) received a delivery of supplies from the private firm SpaceX as part of a $1.6-billion contract with NASA to make twelve supply runs.[38] These are only isolated examples, but they underscore the increasing dependence of the US military and related security agencies in the technological field. In the past, the Defense Advanced Research Project Agency (DARPA) was at the fore of technological research and development. But the broadening commercial base of technological development has brought the private sector into a closer collaborative, and sometimes competitive, relationship with the public agency.

These three implications represent three different areas of contracting and no doubt, the list is far more extensive than what can be provided here. Wartime contracting in Iraq and Afghanistan entails a different set of considerations than does the kind of contracting underway in Africa. By the same token, research, development, and manufacturing turns to the private sector in ways that have tremendous potential for innovation, but with its own considerations about capacity. Indeed, the potential for innovation – organizational and technological – is enormous, but there are considerable risks to take into account.

RISKS

Contracting out services has been debated in academic and policy literature for decades.[39] While there are many dimensions of the privatization debate, three considerations are addressed in terms of financial cost, capacity, and control.

Financial Cost

The first question about contracting is simple: is it cheaper than doing it in-house? The theory of outsourcing would certainly suggest so, especially when it comes to the federal government where labour costs include large overhead expenditures. That is the theory. On the ground, cost savings is an empirical matter. When measured against full-time equivalents in the federal government basis, contracted labour in Iraq and Afghanistan did, indeed, lead to cost savings. The 2011 Congressional Commission on Wartime Contracting evaluated the costs of contracting out contingency operations tasks and found that heavy reliance on local nationals and third-country nationals did lead to considerable cost savings. Labour from developing countries is more cost-effective when compared to US federal employees, military personnel, or private US citizens. This is particularly true in the logistics and base support sector where much of the work is low- or semi-skilled and easily filled with migrant labour – often with exploitative results.[40] In all other sectors, the commission made two conclusions. The first is that contractors are more cost-effective than military personnel in longer-term contingency operations when all living costs are taken into consideration. The second is that American nationals contracted by the United States are comparably cost-effective with US federal employees in similar skill or occupation categories. In short, unskilled labour from the developing world presents huge cost savings, and privately sourced skilled labour from the United States is comparable to full-time equivalent federal employees. Tellingly, though, the commission concedes that the relative advantage of contractors over federal employees rests on "factors other than labor cost."[41] Here is where theory meets reality.

"Factors other than labour cost" are the known unknowns of wartime contracting. Take, for example, the obvious security costs.

In Iraq, private security for reconstruction personnel and projects increased a typical project by as much as 22 per cent. For capacity-building projects, bodyguard duties for coalition advisers drove security costs up anywhere from 24 to 53 per cent. Often, the security costs were paid out of funds that would have been invested in the project itself, thereby limiting the scope of projects or increasing the overall billing costs.[42] The other obvious "factors other than labour cost" come from losses associated with contracting malpractice. As the Commission on Wartime Contracting estimated, some $31 to $60 billion was lost to contracting waste, fraud, and abuse in the first decade of war in Iraq and Afghanistan.[43] These losses, which have no doubt climbed in the years since, have come about because of woefully insufficient contracting protocols and oversight that had steadily eroded in the 1990s and early 2000s.[44] In its final report, SIGIR found that the volume of contracting overwhelmed the ability of the military's acquisition oversight staff. SIGIR found that statements of work were not sufficiently detailed, invoices were not checked thoroughly, and opportunities for fraud and theft proliferated along with the size of the reconstruction. Though contract management practices became more effective over time, "the US government lacked the right regulations and sufficient personnel to support a large-scale stabilization and reconstruction program."[45] In short, outsourcing to cut labour costs works on paper, but those "factors other than labour cost" belie the neat deductions of economic theorization.

Capacity

There are two concerns regarding capacity. The first concern with contracting out tasks is the loss of in-house capacity to perform that work. In some sectors, the concern is obvious. Outsourcing the supply runs to space stations, as mentioned earlier, means losing certain capacities in space flight. The increasing reliance on manufacturers' technicians to maintain complex machinery represents another area of skilled expertise that is lost to private actors. But where capacity losses are less obvious, but still striking, are in areas where the government and private sector compete for scarce expertise. Take, for example, the computer security sector where there is a considerable concern with the loss of proprietary skills to the private sector. For the labour force of computer hackers, private network-security firms offer much more permissive and lucrative workplaces than the tightly constrained American defence establishment.[46] The kind of reliance on advanced computer technologies discussed above places a premium on personnel retention. Competition for expertise between the public and private sectors not only compromises in-house capacity but may also drive up the personnel costs. (This is to say nothing of major security breaches like the one effected by Edward Snowden in 2013.) Loss of capacity is also a concern in areas where technical knowledge is considered proprietary and therefore, zero-sum. The private security industry has, in the past decade, developed vast expertise in post-conflict reconstruction. The trouble for public agencies is that the technical expertise involved is not necessarily transferred, creating an asymmetry of expertise between public and private. As Sean McFate suggests in his recent book *The Modern Mercenary: Private Armies and What They Mean for World Order,* this could lead to circumstances where policy decision making depends on proprietary knowledge residing exclusively in the private sector. As a consequence, certain expertise may not only be "lost" by governments but the price of reacquiring may be driven up if the demand is great enough.[47]

The second concern is about lessons learned. To be sure, outsourcing entails a certain in-house capacity loss, but not all capacity is necessarily forsaken. The contracting experience can lead to increased bureaucratic capacity in managing a contractor workforce. However, this only applies if and practical experience is properly institutionalized. The question is this: has the United States improved its institutional capacity to undertake contingency contracting as a result of the past thirteen years of experience? Thus far, the answer is no. The United States has yet to leverage its contracting experiences into institutional capacity to manage a vast contingency contractor workforce. According to the SIGIR's final report, the United States faces considerable bureaucratic challenges institutionalizing the lessons of contingency contracting in Iraq and Afghanistan. While individuals in the public sector have developed a decade or more of experience, there is still no integrated means of institutionalizing this experience. Astoundingly, given the systematic mismanagement of design and build projects in Iraq and Afghanistan, still no integrated data system exits for tracking construction projects for contingency operations.[48] At the time of writing, the SIGIR reports that the United States is in no better position to prepare for the next stabilization operation than it was in 2003 at the outset of the Iraq invasion.

Control

For over a decade in Iraq and Afghanistan, half of the US footprint was contractor, meaning that as many as a quarter million people were subjected to multiple and sometimes unclear lines of control. The concept of control itself is tricky to assess. Control of whom, by whom, and based on what criteria? Monetary losses are an obvious empirical measure, but the parameters of control extend beyond costs. In her excellent study of privatization and the control of force, Deborah Avant identifies three interlocking mechanisms of control: functional, political, and social.[49] Functional control is control over what kinds of capabilities will be present in an armed service. This mode of control speaks directly to the capacity losses and gains associated with outsourcing. Political control is control over who gets to decide about the deployment of arms and services. Of the many shortcomings of contingency contracting during the 9/11 Wars was the unclear legal and regulatory regime that governed US contractors. As the years progressed, the United States clarified the operating environment with a patchwork of laws and regulation which include changes to the Uniform Code of Military Justice and the Military Extraterritorial Jurisdiction Act to bring contractors into a recognized legal regime, as well as amendments to the annual National Defense Authorization Acts since 2008 which have instituted tighter rules for contingency contracting.[50] Still though, legal commenters note that the extension of law and regulation to military contractors in the United States has not kept pace with the industry's development and that the US regulatory regime remains incomplete and scattered across multiple levels of legislative authority.[51] Social control is the degree to which the contracted activities are integrated with prevailing values. In a democratic society, these can only be established in the public square. If a democratic society finds that the benefits and risks of widespread military contracting fall within the prevailing social values of the day, then the ongoing dependency on contracting may be deemed socially acceptable. This is especially salient in the United States where the broader political economy continues to lean toward privatization and outsourcing, and is entering a period of military austerity.

Social control also includes the darkest side of wartime contracting – the human toll of war and the role of casualties in public debate. Throughout the 9/11 Wars, US contractors were not included in the overall casualty count for soldiers. Observers have noted that the underreporting of contractor deaths obscure the human cost of war. This is significant because it comes at the cost of social control, measured in terms of transparency and the impoverishment of public debate. Contractor casualties have been relatively hidden from the public view in the United States. As of December 2014, there have been 6,839 US troops killed in Iraq and Afghanistan (4,487 and 2,352 respectively). If contractor deaths were included, the totals would include at least the 3,632 contractor deaths reported to the US Department of Labor, an increase of 51 per cent.[52] How this would influence public decision making is uncertain and the conclusion to this volume explores this issue, but social control is not well-served when information remains obscured. As the chapters by Peter Tikuisis and H. Christian Breede in this volume show, the prospect of casualties and the history of their impact in past engagements are a major component of the conditions for going to war.

CONCLUSION

Military contracting since 2001 has revealed the wartime role of the private sector to be both prominent and consequential. Historical trends suggest that contractors are crucial repositories of technical and personnel resources for overseas military operations. In this sense, the private sector is an indispensable part of US intervention capacity and the capabilities of other countries.[53] The trend of contracting out certain tasks can have benefits in an era of tighter defence budgets. This is not to say that contractors are the cheaper option, but they offer defence departments the ability to hedge against cuts by procuring capabilities quickly to fill gaps in case of deployment.

If this is the case, then gaining control over its contracted workforce is vital for the newly chastened Department of Defense, particularly in light of fourteen years of contracting malpractice and poor oversight. Illustrated here are only three implications of the deep integration of contractors into the US total force. Despite the Pentagon's recent claims to re-establish greater in-house capabilities, reducing the alleged excessive reliance on contractor support may prove to be more difficult than it seems. For the foreseeable future, contracting will remain a crucial part of US contingency operations and its broader military capabilities.

NOTES

1 Thom Shanker and Helene Cooper, "Pentagon Plans to Shrink Army to
   Pre–World War II Level," *New York Times*, 23 February 2014.

2 US Department of Defense, *Quadrennial Defense Review*, Washington, DC
   (2014), 67.

3 Moshe Schwartz and Wendy Ginsberg, *Department of Defense: Trends in Overseas Contract Obligations*, Congressional Research Service (2014), 1.

4 The foundational terminological statement comes from P.W. Singer, *Corporate Warriors: The Rise of the Privatized Military Industry* (Ithaca, NY: Cornell
   University Press, 2003), 88–100. For a helpful survey of typologies, see
   Molly Dunigan, "The Future of US Military Contracting: Current Trends
   and Future Implications," *International Journal* 69, no. 4 (2014): 510–24.

5 Congressional Budget Office, *Contractors' Support of US Operations in Iraq*,
   Washington, DC (2008), 13; William W. Epley, "Civilian Support of Field
   Armies," *Army Logistician* 22 (1990): 30–5.

6 This figure is an estimate based on historical documentation of theatre-
   wide personnel among US and UN forces in Korea in 1952. See James A.
   Huston, *Guns and Butter, Powder and Rice: US Army Logistics in the Korean
   War* (Selinsgrove, PA: Susquehanna University Press, 1989), 377.

7 Adrian G. Traas, *Engineers at War* (Washington, DC: Center of Military History, 2010); Richard Tregaskis, *Southeast Asia: Building the Bases –
   The History of Construction in Southeast Asia* (Washington, DC: Department
   of the Navy, 1975); Joseph M. Heiser Jr, *Logistic Support, Vietnam Studies*
   (Washington DC: Department of the Army, 1974).

8 James M. Carter, *Inventing Vietnam: The United States and State Building,
   1954–68* (Cambridge, UK: Cambridge University Press, 2008), 149–80.

9 Government Accountability Office, *Contingency Operations: Army Should Do
   More to Control Contract Cost in the Balkans*, GAO 00–225 (2000), 9.

10 US Commission on Wartime Contracting in Iraq and Afghanistan,
   Transforming Wartime Contracting: Controlling Costs, Reducing Risks,
   Washington, DC (2011); US CENTCOM, "Quarterly Contractor Census
   Reports," 2014, http://www.acq.osd.mil/log/PS/CENTCOM_reports.html.

11 US Congressional Budget Office, *The Budget and Economic Outlook: 2014 to
   2024*. Washington, DC (2014), 68.

12 US Commission on Wartime Contracting, *Transforming Wartime Contract-
   ing*, 5; Moshe Schwartz and Jennifer Church, *Department of Defense's Use of
   Contractors to Support Military Operations: Background, Analysis, and Issues for
   Congress*, Congressional Research Service (2013), 8.

13 Special Inspector General for Iraq Reconstruction, *Learning from Iraq: A Final Report from the Special Inspector General for Iraq Reconstruction* (Washington DC: Government Printing Office, 2013), 73.

14 US Department of Defense, *Quadrennial Defense Review*, 19.

15 US Commission on Wartime Contracting, *Transforming Wartime Contracting*, 19.

16 Stephen G. Brooks, G. John Ikenberry, and William C. Wohlforth, "Don't Come Home, America: The Case against Retrenchment," *International Security* 37, no. 3 (2012–13): 7–51.

17 Schwartz and Ginsberg, *Department of Defense Trends in Overseas Contract Obligations*, 7.

18 Lauren Ploch, *Africa Command: US Strategic Interests and the Role of the US Military in Africa*, Congressional Research Service (2011), 2, 11.

19 Nick Turse, "The Pivot to Africa: The Startling Size, Scope, and Growth of US Military Operations on the African Continent," *TomDispatch*, 5 September 2013, http://www.tomdispatch.com/blog/175743/.

20 AFRICOM, "About the Command," accessed 26 March 2014, http://www.africom.mil/about-the-command.

21 Sean McFate, *Building Better Armies: An Insider's Account of Liberia* (Carlisle Barracks, PA: Strategic Studies Institute and US Army War College Press, 2012).

22 Morten Bøås and Karianne Stig, "Security Sector Reform in Liberia: An Uneven Partnership without Local Ownership," *Journal of Intervention and Statebuilding* 4, no. 3 (2010): 285–303.

23 Kwesi Aning, Thomas Jaye, and Samuel Atuobi, "The Role of Private Military Companies in US-Africa Policy," *Review of International Political Economy* 35, no. 3 (2010): 613–28.

24 David Isenberg, "Africa: The Mother of All PMC," *CATO Institute*, 22 March 2010.

25 Craig Whitlock, "Contractors Run US Spying Missions in Africa," *Washington Post*, 14 June 2012.

26 Scott Fitzsimmons, "Privatizing the Struggle against Somali Piracy," *Small Wars & Insurgencies* 24, no. 1 (2013): 84–102; Christopher Spearin, "Private Military and Security Companies v. International Naval Endeavours v. Somali Pirates," *Journal of International Criminal Justice* 10, no. 4 (2012): 823–7.

27 Mark Mazzetti and Eric Schmitt, "Private Army Formed to Fight Somali Pirates Leaves Troubled Legacy," *New York Times*, 4 October 2012, http://www.nytimes.com/2012/10/05/world/africa/private-army-leaves-troubled-legacy-in-somalia.html?_r=0.

28 For electronic communications support in Vietnam see Thomas Matthew
    Rienzi, *Communications Electronics 1962–1970, Vietnam Studies* (Washington
    DC: Department of the Army, 1972); for data on communications support
    contractors in Iraq and Afghanistan see US Commission on Wartime Con-
    tracting, *Transforming Wartime Contracting*, 198–207.
29 William J. Lynn III, "The Pentagon's Cyberstrategy, One Year Later:
    Defending against the Next Cyberattack," *Foreign Affairs*, 28 Septem-
    ber 2011, https://www.foreignaffairs.com/articles/2011-09-28/
    pentagons-cyberstrategy-one-year-later.
30 Yong-Soo Eun and Judith Sita Aßmann, "Cyberwar: Taking Stock of
    Security and Warfare in the Digital Age," *International Studies Perspectives*,
    9 May 2014, 1–18, http://onlinelibrary.wiley.com/doi/10.1111/
    insp.12073/abstract; David Sanger, David Barboza, and Nicole Perlroth,
    "Chinese Army Unit Is Seen as Tied to Hacking against US," *New York
    Times*, 18 February 2013, http://www.nytimes.com/2013/02/19/tech-
    nology/chinas-army-is-seen-as-tied-to-hacking-against-us.html; Adam P.
    Liff, "Cyberwar: A New 'Absolute Weapon'? The Proliferation of Cyber-
    warfare Capabilities and Interstate War," *Journal of Strategic Studies* 35, no.
    3 (2012): 401–28.
31 William J. Lynn III, "Defending a New Domain: The Pentagon's Cyber-
    strategy," *Foreign Affairs* 89, no. 5 (2010): 107.
32 Lynn III, "The Pentagon's Cyberstrategy."
33 Nicole Perlroth and David E. Sanger, "Nations Buying as Hackers Sell
    Flaws in Computer Code," *New York Times*, 13 July 2013, http://www.
    nytimes.com/2013/07/14/world/europe/nations-buying-as-hackers-sell-
    computer-flaws.html.
34 David E. Sanger and Nicole Perlroth, "After Profits, Defense Firm Faces
    Pitfalls of Cybersecurity," *New York Times*, 15 June 2013, http://www.
    nytimes.com/2013/06/16/us/after-profits-defense-contractor-faces-the-
    pitfalls-of-cybersecurity.html. See also Brian Fung, "5.1 Million Americans
    Have Security Clearances," Washington Post, 24 March 2014, https://
    www.washingtonpost.com/news/the-switch/wp/2014/03/24/5-1-million-
    americans-have-security-clearances-thats-more-than-the-entire-population-
    of-norway/.
35 Peter W. Singer, "The Predator Comes Home: A Primer on Domestic
    Drones, Their Huge Business Opportunities, and Their Deep Political,
    Moral and Legal Challenges," *Brookings Institution*. 8 March 2013, http://
    www.brookings.edu/research/papers/2013/03/08-drones-singer.
36 Epley, "Civilian Support of Field Armies," 30–3.
37 Sharon Weinberger, "Iron Man to Batman: The Future of Sol-
    dier Suits," *BBC*, 21 January 2013, http://www.bbc.com/future/
    story/20130121-batman-meets-iron-man-in-combat.

38 "And This Time It Means Business," *The Economist*, 8 October 2012, http://www.economist.com/node/21564523; Kenneth Chang, "Private Sector Edges Deeper in Space," *New York Times*, 14 May 2012, http://www.nytimes.com/2012/05/15/science/space/contracts-help-private-sector-edge-deeper-into-space.html.

39 John D. Donahue, *The Privatization Decision: Public Ends, Private Means* (New York: Basic Books, 1989); Harvey Feigenbaum, Jeffrey Henig, and Chris Hamnett, *Shrinking the State: The Political Underpinnings of Privatization* (Cambridge, UK: Cambridge University Press, 1999); Kevin R. Kosar, *Privatization and the Federal Government: An Introduction*, Congressional Research Service, Washington, DC (2006).

40 Sarah Stillman, "The Invisible Army: For Foreign Workers on US Bases in Iraq and Afghanistan, War Can Be Hell," *New Yorker*, 6 June 2011, http://www.newyorker.com/magazine/2011/06/06/the-invisible-army.

41 US Commission on Wartime Contracting, *Transforming Wartime Contracting*, 235.

42 Special Inspector General for Iraqi Reconstruction, *Hard Lessons: The Iraq Reconstruction Experience* (Washington, DC: Government Printing Office, 2009), 233.

43 US Commission on Wartime Contracting, *Transforming Wartime Contracting*, 1.

44 Commission on Army Acquisition and Program Management in Expeditionary Operations, *Urgent Reform Required: Army Expeditionary Contracting* (Washington, DC: Government Printing Office, 2007), 30.

45 SIGIR, *Learning from Iraq*, 51.

46 David Kushner, "The Geeks on the Front Lines," *Rolling Stone*, September 2013, http://www.rollingstone.com/feature/the-geeks-on-the-frontlines#i.obfdgo3hocowrr.

47 Sean McFate, *The Modern Mercenary: Private Armies and What They Mean for World Order* (Oxford: Oxford University Press, 2014).

48 SIGIR, *Learning from Iraq*, 121.

49 Deborah D. Avant, *The Market for Force: The Consequences of Privatizing Security* (Cambridge: Cambridge University Press, 2005), 40–5.

50 Aaron Ettinger, "Neoliberalism and the Rise of the Private Military Industry," *International Journal* 66, no. 3 (2011): 731–52.

51 Kristine Huskey and Scott Sullivan, "United States: Law and Policy Governing Private Military Contractors after 9/11," in *Multilevel Regulation of Military and Security Contractors: The Interplay between International, European and Domestic Norms*, eds. C. Bakker and M. Sossai (Oxford: Hart Publishing Inc., 2012).

52 For US troop casualties, see Ian S. Livingston and Michael O'Hanlon, "Iraq Index: Tracking Variables of Reconstruction and Security in

Post-Saddam Iraq," Washington, DC: Brookings Institute, 31 January 2012; Michael E. O'Hanlon, and Ian Livingston, "Afghanistan Index: Tracking Variables of Reconstruction and Security in Post-9/11 Afghanistan," Washington, DC: Brookings Institute, 10 February 2015. Data updated bimonthly; for contractor casualties, see US Department of Labor, "Office of Workers' Compensation Programs (OWCP)," 2015, http://www.dol. gov/owcp/dlhwc/dbaallemployer.htm. Figure is current as of 31 March 2015. Data updated biannually.

53 Molly Dunigan and Ulrich Petersohn, eds., *The Markets for Force Privatization of Security across World Regions* (Philadelphia: University of Pennsylvania Press, 2015).

PART THREE

The Allied Experience

7

Measuring Success:
A Canadian Perspective of Red Teaming
Operations in Afghanistan[1]

PAUL DICKSON, ANTON MINKOV,
AND HEATHER HRYCHUK

What does victory look like? How could we tell if we were winning? How should we measure progress? No questions were more central to the conduct of the international coalition's Afghanistan campaigns – whether counter-insurgency (COIN), counterterrorism (CT) or nation building and stability – or better highlight a critical challenge facing states in twenty-first-century conflicts. Crises across the globe continue to prompt demands for military intervention, but the post-intervention status of Afghanistan and Iraq loom over every policy-maker's calculations over whether to provide aid and what kind. The experiences in those countries suggest that for Western democracies, commitments must be tied to clear end states – or end dates – but how to best identify those remains elusive, despite a considerable effort, then and now. To address these questions, military and political commanders in Afghanistan accessed a range of military as well as public and private civilian analytical and intelligence support. This chapter is based on the work and observations of three Defence Research and Development Canada's Centre for Operational Research and Analysis strategic analysts deployed from 2011 to 2013 in support of the commander of the International Security Assistance Force (COMISAF) Red Team at HQ ISAF in Kabul. The team provided analysis and recommendations for senior ISAF military and civilian decision makers, working with, and drawing on, the multiple staff and analytical organizations responsible for the direction and execution of the campaign. From the coalition headquarters' perspective, the Red Team's assessment shows how successive ISAF commanders and their staffs executed their missions and implemented the coalition strategy and the concurrent COIN and CT campaigns (including nation and capacity building). The assessment also sheds some light on the challenges of commanding and pursuing conflicting objectives within a coalition environment. It does not directly address the issue of whether and why future interventions will occur; rather, it speaks to the complexity of evaluating them against stated ends and thus some critical considerations shaping future coalition efforts and decisions for military interventions.

The Red Team was one of three headquarters analytical groups providing the commander, ISAF/US Forces-Afghanistan (USFOR-A), the deputy chief of staff, intelligence (DCOS CJ2)/ Director of Intelligence, USFOR-A and other senior commanders with in-depth analytical products to support decision making and avoid strategic surprise. The establishment of the Red Team was part of the evolving analytical assessment architecture that reflected refined ideas for executing the operational concepts and strategy. Arguably, it was clear by 2008 that the international intervention, originating in the US-led Operation Enduring Freedom (OEF), was insufficient. OEF's attempts to deliver security concurrent with reconstruction were fragmented and uncoordinated, as were its efforts to rebuild and stabilize the Afghan government and economy. They could not meet the challenges posed by the insurgency and the corrupt government considered by many Afghans to represent one faction among many competing for power, as well as a stagnant economy, and a robust narcotics trade. ISAF and USFOR-A conducted separate, and sometimes contradictory, operations. The ISAF operations and goals fractured along national lines, differences hardened by national caveats on rules of engagement as well as genuine differences in capabilities and operational approaches.[2]

Many ISAF-contributing nations reached this conclusion separately, but Barack Obama's 2009 election prompted a serious adjustment of the intervention's scale and scope.[3] In March 2009 and again in December 2009, following much internal debate, the new president revealed a shift in strategy predicated on creating the conditions to withdraw coalition forces and transition to

Afghan-led security. Obama's "AfPak" strategy reduced the scope of American ambitions to "disrupt, dismantle, and defeat Al Qaeda in Afghanistan and Pakistan and to prevent their return to either country in the future." To achieve this aim, he announced an increase in US forces, a civilian surge, and a goal of taking the fight to the insurgency while growing Afghan security forces and engaging Pakistan.[4] The emphasis of Western intervention shifted from combat to support, but in order to create those conditions it would execute two missions: the coalition counter-insurgency mission and the US-led counterterrorism mission, both proving security to enable a third mission, United Nations Assistance Mission in Afghanistan, a UN effort devoted to political and economic development.[5]

THE EVOLUTION OF COIN IN AFGHANISTAN

In 2009, General Stanley McChrystal was appointed as Commander ISAF (COMISAF) with a specific mandate to execute this latest US version of COIN, and, over the course of the next two years, the COMISAF was provided with the resources – military, civilian, and financial – to undertake it.[6] In general, the US counter-insurgency doctrine that emerged from its experience in Iraq prescribed several inter-related lines of operation: combat operations, civil security, development of essential services, governance capacity, and economic development, with the primary focus on securing the safety (and support) of the population.[7] McChrystal's report on the COIN campaign stressed the centrality of the population, as well as an effective assessment architecture to measure the effects of the strategy, assess progress toward key objectives, and make necessary adjustments.[8] He was replaced by General David Petraeus in 2010. Petraeus refined the approach, shifting to "enemy-centric" counter-insurgency, focused on fracturing the insurgency through kinetic operations as well as reintegration programs.[9] He also established the Combined Joint Interagency Task Force (CJIATF)-Shafafiyat (Pashto for "transparency") to foster a common understanding of the corruption problem in Afghanistan and to coordinate ISAF anti-corruption efforts.[10]

During 2009–13, the resources devoted to the campaign in Afghanistan also changed materially. The international military commitment reached its apex in 2011, with US forces surging from 32,800 at the end of 2008 to approximately 100,000 in June 2011, including special operations forces (SOF) increments to OEF.

ISAF-contributing nations' deployments were approximately 42,500 around the same time, peaking in April 2012 at an estimated 44,900. The Afghan National Security Forces (ANSF) grew, on paper, to a mandated ceiling of 352,000.[11] American government civilian support to governance and development tripled, focusing on developing Afghan government and economic capacity, a gap that other countries had also tried to address.[12]

Command and control were also restructured. In 2008, in an attempt to create unity of command and mitigate the incoherent approaches to operations, the United States appointed COMISAF General David D. McKiernan as commander, USFOR-A to ensure synchronization of US and ISAF forces as well as proper coordination of COIN operations and ANSF capacity-building efforts.[13] An ISAF Joint Command (IJC) was stood up to act as an operational level headquarters. The NATO Training Mission–Afghanistan (NTM-A) was established to manage ANSF generation and institutional capacity. A sixth regional command, Regional Command-Southwest (RC-SW), was stood up to address the excessive span of control and the operational tempo in Regional Command-South (RC-S). New structures were also established to emphasize key elements of the USFOR-A CT effort. The CJIATF-435 succeeded the US command Joint Task Force 435 (JTF 435) in 2010 and managed detention operations and rule of law. This created three levels of command in-theatre. HQ ISAF reported to Joint Forces Command (JFC) Brunssum and USFOR-A to the United States Central Command (UNCENTcom). The COMISAF had command responsibility over the operational level commanders of IJC, the NTM-A, and SOF. The tactical level regional commands (RCS) reported to IJC.

Coalition efforts followed US COIN parameters to greater or lesser extents, but differences in scale and emphasis mattered. Not all agreed with COIN theory and the need to shift away from the combat mission.[14] There was ongoing debate about whether COIN was a strategy, operational approach or concept, or a substitute for them.[15] There was also disagreement within ISAF as well as within national contingents about how COIN should be executed, resulting from serious disagreements about the nature of the conflict, and what was driving it.[16] Multiple "factions" within HQ ISAF promoted an emphasis on one aspect of the campaign instead of another, and the apportionment of regional commands by nationality diffused this effort even further. Because nations had responsibility for discrete regions, execution varied across the country.[17] These distinctions in concepts, combined with real constraints imposed by national caveats on combat and varying capabilities, exacerbated the challenge of understanding progress and success.

HOW THE CAMPAIGN WAS ANALYZED AND ASSESSED

As others have argued, COIN proved very analysis- and intelligence-intensive.[18] COIN doctrine had emphasized the importance of ongoing analysis and assessment. It defined assessment as the "continuing monitoring and evaluation of the current situation and progress of an operation [against established criteria]." The US COIN manual provided modest insights into what indicators should be used, but drew on the Iraqi experience to distinguish between "measures of performance" and "measures of effectiveness." Performance measures addressed task accomplishment against intent ("Are we doing things right?"), while effectiveness measures addressed change against expectations ("Are we doing the right things?").[19]

Analysis and assessments evolved in response to these demands in structure, in focus and in method. There were attempts to distinguish the role of analysis from campaign and, later, strategic assessment.[20] From early 2009, a new campaign analysis architecture was established to address the shortfalls highlighted later that year by McChrystal and as part of the effort to bring coherence to the campaign assessments. Over eight years of the campaign, individual contributing nations had developed their own assessment models and methods resulting in, by one analyst's estimate, more than twenty different campaign assessments.[21] The stand-up of the Afghan Assessment Group (AAG) at HQ ISAF in early 2009 was recognition that analysis was an essential element of counter-insurgency. It was also the first step toward a centralized strategic and operational assessment process. McChrystal refined the analytical architecture, expanding the AAG's mandate to include quantitative assessments, and changed the reporting structure, minimizing charts and graphs, and calling for more interpretative reports. He also established a COIN Advisory and Assistance Team (CAAT) to operationalize commander's intent in the ongoing counter-insurgency campaign and to support the development and integration of COIN efforts across the country.[22] Data and qualitative assessments were organized along three lines of operation (LOO) that reflected McChrystal's population-centric COIN: protecting the population, building the ANSF and increasing the capacity of the Afghan government.

McChrystal also introduced a reporting structure that, in an attempt to ensure a holistic perspective to overcome the stovepipes of the LOO analytical bins, used the RCS to implement a District Assessment Model to measure and report on security, governance, and development. The unit of measure was considered appropriate, but the colour-coded reporting method was considered too limited to be useful. There were also ongoing concerns that the assessment methods led to impressionistic evaluations, with too great an emphasis on performance rather than progress, and analysis by analogy, with commanders drawing on their experiences in Iraq.[23] The reporting system was also hampered by the reality that US leadership, at least, had little real understanding of the complexity of the country, and they realized it.[24] There were ongoing questions surrounding the type and reliability of the data and whether the appropriate metrics – or observable indicators – were being used.[25] And what did it all mean? Even when behaviours were identified, what did they signify? McChrystal leaned heavily on outside experts to identify metrics and assess their significance.[26] He also pressed, unsuccessfully, to have the narrative assessments unclassified, and subject to scrutiny by academics, journalists, and experts from a variety of private think tanks.

When Petraeus assumed command in 2010, he changed the assessment philosophy to match his approach to Afghan COIN and CT. He established sets of objectives based on identifiable and measurable effects. He further refined campaign assessment, changing the focus to quantitative data to measure the interim effects of his policy. To some observers, the emphasis on effects came at the expense of understanding outcomes, even if it gave the illusion of progress.[27] The introduction of an element of ambiguity, resulting from the limited data and poor metrics, proved to have a political benefit beyond that envisioned by many critics: no clear indication of success or failure held out the possibility of success, and therefore the continuation of the surge, and the fight. Observers of the political infighting surrounding the scale and timing of the surge suggest that this ambiguity worked in favour of those who hoped to keep US troop levels high for as a long as possible.[28] This ambiguity also highlighted another important element of the COIN strategy (and strategy in general) that would emerge as a core metric: perceptions of who was winning were as important as the reality on the ground. Real results were necessary, but not sufficient.

General John Allen's assumption of command in July 2011 did not alter the trajectory of a campaign already transitioned to capacity building, although he reprioritized efforts to focus on security forces. However, the start of the drawdown of the US surge that same month and subsequent announcements over the next year of formal timelines for the transition to Afghan-led security, and the consequent debates over the scale and timing of troop withdrawals all increased the complexity of assessing the campaign as well as the variables to be considered.[29] There was increased pressure to understand how the campaigns were progressing relative to established timelines, decreasing resources and ever-changing threats to success. There was a growing appetite and need for analysis and data even as the number of analysts, staff and intelligence gatherers declined. The political context for the end of the ISAF mission was in place by the spring of 2012.[30] The decision to declare an end to the mission reshaped the idea and the evaluation of progress. Victory was not simply a function of transitioning security to the Afghans but a successful transition itself. Identifying conditions for the transition exacerbated the challenges of measuring success.[31]

Within a few months of assuming command, Allen changed the assessment architecture. Most of his initial concerns centred on the explanatory power of the assessment and reporting methods, and their limited utility to facilitate discussion among senior leaders or provide clarity on the areas where changes could and should be made. The shift in emphasis was on trying to explain behaviours rather than simply identifying them, a complicated analytical task itself. The AAG initiated a review with the aim of creating a system of assessment that was both holistic and comprehensive.[32] To address the former, the group developed two levels of assessment: strategic and campaign. The former was the more innovative of the two, built as it was on strategic questions designed to ensure NATO and US policy and strategic goals were being met. The latter was a refinement on existing metrics, with the notable introduction of "regional relations," and one that would drive much effort in terms of policy and analysis at the headquarters. These changes prompted a rebalance between quantitative and qualitative analysis to inform the assessment process. From an analytical perspective, this manifested itself in a number of ways.

District assessments evolved into "deep-dive" evaluations, stressing the value of context to interpret the quantitative measures, which were increasingly important as transition to Afghan leadership became the primary target. These were facilitated by an increased emphasis on quantitative assessment methods that shed light on trends such as time-series analysis, but required data acquired over time, baseline data, and (in some cases) a threshold to assess progress.[33] There was no consistent or comprehensive capture of the required data before 2009.

The new COMISAF also tried to introduce a more systematic approach to coordinating the analytical efforts across the headquarters, as well as enhancing the capacity to provide contextual and qualitative analysis. The renewal of the mission of the Red Team (originally stood up in 2011) was one example. Its mandate was decision-support through alternative analysis and the questioning of assumptions, which was distinct from traditional Red Team or Red Force analysis that was based on emulating the enemy or threat. Alternative analysis red teaming applies a range of methods to offer decision makers qualitative and contextual analysis. The COMISAF Red Team was also built to provide a range of perspectives as a multinational team of military and civilian analysts. The products (papers and briefs) provided alternative and strategic perspectives and recommendations on key issues (as identified by the COMISAF and J2), examining underlying assumptions; seams; adversary motivations; regional dynamics; and social, cultural, and economic factors surrounding issues.[34] Allen also changed the remit of the CAAT (renamed the COMISAF Advisory and Assistance Team) with a new mission to provide directed observations and reporting to the COMISAF on strategic priority areas. In practice, the CAAT focused on the development of Security Force Advisory Teams, the aim of which was to advise, mentor, and train Afghan security forces at the unit level.[35] The third team charged with providing context and assessments was the Commander's Action Group (CAG) a small multinational staff working directly to support the COMISAF.[36]

There was overlap in the remits of each team, and those remits were fluid, influenced by crisis and the immediate requirements of the COMISAF (in the case of the Red Team, of the priorities of the deputy chief of staff intelligence). In 2012, an equilibrium was established that assigned the CAG more immediate and short-term assessments, and the CAAT-specific tasks related to campaign execution.

The Red Team focused on contextual and narrative analysis. There were other groups of analysts evaluating similar topics and issues. The CJ2 Intelligence officers provided "deep dives" and daily assessments. Some analysts worked to support their national contingents; others worked for other layers of command, notably the IJC and the RCS. Desk officers in the various divisions also produced analysis and assessments. The senior civilian representative (SCR) had his own analytical pools. Commanders also brought their own advisers or brought in outside experts and specialists. There was no shortage of analysis undertaken, representing a wide range of opinions and conclusions, and of varied quality and impact. The cacophony of analysis created a need for a few trusted pools of analysts, as well as prioritized efforts, a goal articulated by the COMISAF and his deputies in CJ2 Intelligence.

Allen left unchanged Petraeus's focus on effects rather than outcomes. The operational plan listed tasks, but not objectives, reflecting the challenge of objectively determining when "security" was achieved or when governance was "good." Given the challenge of describing the various aspects of effectiveness in absolutes, defining proper indicators and explaining them became the focus of analysis. Under General Allen, there was an increased effort to define what success meant from an Afghan perspective, to provide both campaign and strategic assessments, and to explain behaviour in order to both more effectively address it, and to prioritize the coalition's effort. Understanding the issue of corruption provides a good example. CJIATF took a legalistic approach to the issue. However, in 2012, General Allen directed that some of the underlying assumptions surrounding the approach be examined, with the focus on reconceptualizing patronage and corruption, and trying to understand corruption in terms of it being legitimate or illegitimate rather than legal or illegal. Treating all levels of corruption the same failed to account for the role of "functional" corruption in Afghan society, particularly in the absence of well-paid employment and social services.[37] As an example, too often the legal system apprehended local officials, while leaving senior government leaders who were "capturing" the state untouched, further degrading faith in the rule of law and good governance.

Marine General Joseph Dunford assumed command in February 2013. He established headquarters priorities as managing the ISAF drawdown and the transition to the post-2014 Resolute Support mission.[38] The change of command, which included a new DCOS CJ2, also brought about a change in decision-making culture and a new analytical support paradigm. The new leadership favoured greater interaction to formal analytical products. The Red Team's analytical contributions gradually shifted from papers to briefings only, as well as direct support to staff and operational planning. The production list remained, however, with the papers becoming increasingly shorter and reactive to short-term priorities.

Much of this reflected the conviction that the time for deepening ISAF understanding of Afghanistan was over, and, with decreasing data collection and analytical resources, effort would be better expended focusing on more immediate transition-related issues. Ironically, this had the effect of breaking down some stovepipes in the analytical architecture. For example, the "limited-distribution" restriction on Red Team papers was removed and the papers were accessible across the headquarters, still classified but not sensitive.

RED TEAM PRODUCTION INSIGHTS

Through 2011 and 2012, analysis focused on prioritization in an effort to determine where best to put limited resources. Much of the focus for the team – and the headquarters' staff – was on rationalizing command and control.[39] This was a contentious issue, highlighting the relative costs of maintaining unity at the expense of efficiency. Priority setting became an issue when examining options for merging or revising HQ's tasks and functions. While the idea of reducing the number of general and flag officer positions and functions for efficiency appealed to some, others argued that the political considerations of the number of general officers employed and national representation were of paramount concern. And the division was not always along national lines. Later in 2012, when the operational level was examined for efficiencies, the sequence of rationalizing the various HQs became a contentious issue between the American and coalition general officers, with COMISAF effectively moderating. This was in part due to the complicated nature of the mission itself, but was exacerbated by the dual command structure. This was further complicated in the multinational environment where national interests and national conceptions or interpretations differed. For example, national conceptions of command structures did not always align, and often provoked contentious discussion. It did allow COMISAF to receive a variety of views before making a decision – ensuring he was as informed of all possible repercussions for the coalition.

Hedging and factionalism were also key areas of effort for the Red Team during the first half of 2013, reflecting growing concerns about Afghan responses to the end of the mission. Hedging – in this context meaning the provision of qualified support to a number of options to reduce risk – was identified as a major threat to the transition to Afghan security. There was the potential to lose the best-educated and wealthiest segments of society, and it sent the wrong signal to the international community, which was asked to make some commitments post-2014. Conversely, COMISAF characterized these activities as direct evidence of uncertainty regarding the future, but increasingly believed that the short-term solution was political.[40] Hedging became shorthand in media and even headquarters' discourse to suggest Afghans' lack of faith in their country's future following the withdrawal of coalition forces. However, the concept was not well understood, nor measured. Subsequent studies of the concept and regional case studies helped to clarify it.[41]

Hedging studies were a good example of the progress made in taking a more nuanced approach to measuring and understanding Afghan attitudes as well as an example of how national interpretations of factionalism challenged the underlying assumptions of COIN. Opinions on factions and the threat of factionalism varied across the coalition, differences that were highlighted with the appointment of a new deputy commander, British Lieutenant General Sir Nicholas Carter in October 2012. Carter was not convinced the insurgency was the main, or only, existential threat to the government of the Islamic Republic of Afghanistan (GIROA).[42] Drawing on his recent experience Afghanistan as commander Regional Command-South in 2009–10, and reflecting the British interpretation of COIN, he believed the conflict was not binary between the GIROA and the insurgency, but one with multiple and overlapping factions and fractures, a view shared by many but difficult to address militarily. There were also many divisions within the insurgency, and varying degrees of ideological and religious motivation.[43] From that perspective, the insurgency's destruction was not necessarily central to the mission nor even realistic in all parts of the country. In essence, Carter wanted instead to elevate challenges such as hedging, concerns about regional powerbrokers and ethnic and tribal divisions to ISAF priorities to threats of the first order because they challenged national stability and the state's monopoly on the use of force. He promoted analysis and assessments framing the issue as one of competing factions.[44] He also implemented a strategy to convince the GIROA that factions and factionalism were existential threats, and that the GIROA itself was, unfortunately, perceived as one faction among many. Carter's initiatives shaped debate across the headquarters, displacing some analysis of the campaign.[45]

Indeed, how to engage the insurgents proved a challenge throughout this period. Obama identified the need to engage in a political dialogue with the Taliban, if not other insurgent groups. The animating theory behind this goal was that the insurgents represented a part of the body politic. This was incrementally realized through 2012 as the headquarters examined insurgent responses to the campaign as well as the announcements to end the mission. For example, an assessment as to whether the insurgency might stop operations in response to the ISAF 2014 end of mission challenged and informed commanders' perceptions of potential insurgency leadership response. Fundamental assumptions about the utility of trying to divide the Taliban while concurrently trying to negotiate were also addressed.[46]

Campaign priorities were, of course, subject to changes in insurgent tactics and the strategic situation. For example, through 2012, the "insider threat" posed a significant threat to the unity of the coalition at a time when member nation-states – considering timetables for troop withdrawals – were weary of the conflict and particularly sensitive to casualties. Between January 2008 and August 2014, attacks by ANSF against ISAF soldiers (known as "green on blue") killed 143 ISAF personnel and wounded another 183. Incidents peaked in 2012, when forty-four attacks killed 61 (out of a total 402 coalition dead) and wounded another 81.[47] Through 2012, significant analytical and staff resources were devoted to identifying causes, and explaining behaviours as well as recommending mitigation strategies. This issue was further complicated by the Afghan narrative that the "foreign elements" were responsible for the attacks, a result of the stated Afghan political leadership's preference for the coalition to equip and train it for conventional conflicts against regional threats, rather than for counter-insurgency operations.[48]

Over the course of 2012–13, the increased focus on Afghanistan's geostrategic situation was also evident in the growing demand for analysis of regional relationships, their potential impact on

Afghanistan, and what, if anything, ISAF or USFOR-A could do to influence those relationships. While Obama had specifically directed that engagement with Pakistan become a US priority, it was under Allen that ISAF HQ turned to regional relations in real terms and relative to other priorities. There were deep differences of opinion on responses and engagement. Even security issues that were clearly within ISAF's mandate were problematic. One of the main issues through 2012 was the border, both the growing number of incidents of cross-border artillery fire between Pakistan and Afghanistan as well as the question of regulation and interdiction activities. The issues were contentious. Concepts of corruption and patronage proved to be complicating factors in coalition efforts to improve control of the border, particularly given patronage networks that extended from border guards to government officials. Red Team and SCR analysis, among others, suggested that, among many factors in enforcing border regulations, these complicated patron-client relationships needed to be understood as a political as well as a legal issue. It took time to fully understand the historic affiliations, the dynamics of political and economic relationships, and balances of power within them, as well as the respective roles of individuals in the context of the broader national political settlement. The shape of proposed border strategies in general remained a divisive issue between military and civilian leadership.[49]

Cross-border "fire" (exchanges of gunfire between ANSF and Pakistani forces) were equally complicated. COMISAF staffed analysis on the pros and cons of a public statement as well as an exploration of other options in response to fires in northeast Afghanistan. This reflected divisions between ISAF and Afghan political and military leadership as well as an issue where Allen's command of USFOR-A was in potential conflict with his command of coalition forces. The issue continued to unsettle senior decision makers through 2013 as they were drawn into supporting Afghan-Pakistani relations over the Durand Line, a border that Afghans refuse to recognize.[50]

Iran-Afghanistan relations were another troublesome issue. ISAF leadership and Western policy analysts in general perceived Iran's objectives in the region as malign; therefore, the focus of Iran's engagement in Afghanistan was often assessed through the prism of its support for the Taliban and other activities that may have presented a direct threat to the military campaign, or were damaging the relations between ISAF and the GIROA.[51] Iranian leadership considered ISAF a direct threat to its security, especially after 2003, when the US invasion in Iraq placed US troops on Iran's borders. Consequently, Iran initiated a dual strategy of securing its eastern border by supporting reconstruction and economic activities in the traditionally Iranian sphere of influence in western Afghanistan, reinforcing linkages with the Shia Hazara population, and, at the same time, seemingly assisting subversive activities against ISAF troops to prevent success of the mission.[52] The COMISAF directed his analysts to focus on evidence of the latter. Red Team analysis attempted to address what some at headquarters considered an evolution of Iranian interests and offered more comprehensive evaluation in view of the changing regional environment, in particular the Syrian conflict, and the broader Iranian objectives in Afghanistan, not simply those threatening ISAF efforts.[53] Whether views at the headquarters changed is unclear, but the UK embassy requested a meeting to discuss the assessment, suggesting some national divisions over Iran.

The support of deeper analysis also allowed for more nuanced approaches to assessments of Afghanistan's neighbouring countries as a group rather than individually. Such an approach was critical to assess the regional impact on the mission. For example, the Red Team focused on estimating the impact of joint policies in Russia's and Iran's overlapping areas of interest and positions of influence in Afghanistan, such as the security environment, the energy sector, foreign trade, and others.[54]

Analysis of Pakistan, technically considered a major US ally in the region and a recipient of significant military and economic aid from Washington, was another challenge. Pakistan played a double-sided game since the Taliban was potentially one of its instruments in post-ISAF Afghanistan and did little to prevent the insurgents from using its territory as a safe heaven. From 2009, the US administration began to consider the Afghan-Pakistani border area as a single theatre of operation and introduced the term *AfPak*.[55] Given the new strategic focus on Pakistan's role in solving the Afghan quagmire, Pakistan was increasingly prominently in HQ ISAF analytical efforts. It is notable that as late as 2013, HQ ISAF formulated its AfPak strategy by asking for assessments of Pakistan's views toward Afghanistan,[56] avoiding the wider regional context, particularly the role of India in Islamabad's policy toward Afghanistan.[57] The growing focus on regional dynamics included Russia and China, reflecting a belated acceptance of the complexity of the region but also the challenges of analyzing and addressing the full range of strategic and operational issues with limited resources.[58]

The mission drawdown deadline had implications not only for ISAF but for the Afghan political environment as well. President Hamid Karzai portrayed the deadline as abandonment and sought to increase his own legitimacy in the eyes of the Afghan public by building a perception of political influence over ISAF. In addition to increased anti-American rhetoric, his seemingly antagonistic behaviour and actions threatened to derail essential mission elements and negotiations surrounding the Bilateral Security Agreement. Managing relations with the Afghan government became entangled with mission planning and analysis.[59] Another key element of the success of the drawdown was the smooth transition of power after the 2014 presidential elections; fears of unexpected circumstances were abundant.[60] Red Team analysis focused on how, or if, ISAF could support the Afghan election process.

CONCLUSION:
CONSIDERATIONS FOR FUTURE OPERATIONS

What do the insights of the Red Team production and experience suggest about future Western interventions and missions? In general, the lessons of the period under review suggest that information and the ability to identify, gather, and analyze systematically to produce useful assessments are critical for strategy development as well as campaign planning, assessment, and evolution. At the same time, campaign analysis and assessment are not capabilities that can be built at the last minute. Evidence-based analysis should be used to make sense of a complex mission as early as possible. Context matters; so too does the concept being used to understand the problem. Metrics will change as operations and commanders change, but decision makers need to establish the means to gather useful data, and produce and use analysis as part of the stand-up of any mission. Analysis and concepts affect how the conflict will be interpreted, operations conducted, and resources prioritized.

The capability to properly identify and understand the measures of successes – and recognize failure – became a critical enabler in the Afghan COIN operation. Where success was not measured in ground gained, casualties inflicted, or regime change, then nuanced campaign analysis and assessments of a range of indicators were essential to decision makers. However, organizations measure what their leaders tell them to report on. Thus, one key way for a leadership team to shift an organization's focus was to change reporting requirements and the associated measures of performance and effectiveness. These changes also provided insights into the leader's intent and the execution of his concept. Looking at the execution can also provide insights into the distance between goals and reality in allied operations.

Under McChrystal and his successors, unity of command was nominally achieved, but it was messy and inefficient, although, arguably, it prevented a run for the exits by coalition partners. This came at the cost of unity of effort: national representatives had different perspectives on the utility of policy and execution and how best to measure effects. Unity of command is likely to continue to be an issue in future coalition operations, but this analysis suggests that achieving unity of effort is by far the more challenging. ISAF behaviour – that is unity of effort – needs to be understood first and foremost as a balancing act between individual ISAF participants, and those who represented the ISAF headquarters and the responsibility for the execution of the theatre strategy and the operational concepts and missions. ISAF command culture was a work in progress, and the issue was often whether the imperatives of maintaining the coalition outweighed the pursuit of unity of effort. The demands of the analytical architecture provided some consistency in terms of shared ideas on execution, but as emphasis and effort changed, so too did measures and metrics. Balancing the needs of the coalition (primarily NATO, but also various bilateral relations such as US-Australia) with those of the campaigns was at times detrimental to achieving the unity of effort required to set and reach reasonable goals.

The introduction of a counter-insurgency framework was meant to clarify the nature of the problem, in order to achieve the coalition aims; but, as the analytical program suggested, there was always confusion as to what COIN was and how it should be executed. Approaches varied not only among contributing nations, but also between different schools of thought within the HQ ISAF, thus making the understanding of progress and success very difficult. In that context, the challenge and strategic assessment functions provided by the Red Team were important. While the team's work was only one small portion of the overall analytical effort, it provided an important service to the commander by providing analysis that was not subject to revision by the chain of command or aligned with functional staffs. The Red Team provided, in theory, objective advice that could be used in conjunction with other staff analyses to ensure the COMISAF was making the most informed decision possible.

The period under analysis was also marked by the challenges of high turnover among military and civilian personnel, with the concurrent loss of corporate memory, continuity and expertise. The decreasing numbers of staff and analysts exacerbated the impact of the high turnover as the effort wound down. There was also a consistent shortfall on the civilian side, which created a vacuum that military staff at HQ ISAF filled, a trend illustrated by the range of topics under study. The civilian effort was never sufficient to achieve coalition goals for capacity building, a challenge for any government considering interventions of this nature in the future.

Maintaining the momentum of lengthy campaigns will always be a challenge, and exacerbated by some mix of the factors described above. In this case, there was no easy means to analyze progress, and determine where the weight of effort should be made, or whether some aspects of the campaign were more successful than others, a characteristic that, from a historical perspective, is not unusual. The coalition only slowly groped its way toward understanding the limits of COIN in general, and specifically as executed by a very diverse coalition. In the end, setting a hard target for the transition to an Afghan-led process was one of the few objective goals, and arguably created conditions and a focus that had been missing.

NOTES

1 The opinions expressed in this article are those of the authors and do not represent, or otherwise reflect, any official opinion or position of the government of Canada, or any of its departments and agencies.

2 See, for example, David P. Auerswald and Stephen M. Saideman, *NATO in Afghanistan: Fighting Together, Fighting Alone* (Princeton, NJ: Princeton University Press, 2014).

3 See, for example, Independent Panel on Canada's Future Role in Afghanistan, *Final Report* (Ottawa: Minister of Public Works and Government Services, 2008); Sultan Barakat, *A Strategic Conflict Assessment of Afghanistan* (York, UK: University of York, 2008), a report commissioned by the Afghan and British governments; HQ ISAF, General Stanley McChrystal, *COMISAF's Initial Assessment: Initial United States Forces – Afghanistan (USFOR-A) Assessment*, 26 June 2009; Appendice of Matthew C. Brand, *General McChrystal's Strategic Assessment Evaluating the Operating Environment in*

Afghanistan in the Summer of 2009 (Air Force Research Institute, Maxwell Air Force Base, Alabama: Air University Press, 2011), http://www.au.af. mil/au/aupress/digital/pdf/paper/ap_brand_mcchrystals_assessment. pdf; Robert M. Gates, *Duty: Memoirs of a Secretary at War* (New York: Knopf, 2014), 341–59. Gates provides a useful perspective on the debates surrounding the changes to Afghanistan campaign.

4 "Remarks by the President in Address to the Nation on the Way Forward in Afghanistan and Pakistan," The White House, Office of the Press Secretary (1 December 2009), https://www.whitehouse.gov/the-press-office/news-conference-president-obama-4042009.

5 USFOR-A was initially tasked with two missions: direct the Combined Security Transition Command-Afghanistan to focus on force generation and institutional and ministerial development and, second, to transfer OEF units to Operations Control COMISAF, thereby placing them on the ISAF Combined Joint Statement of Requirements – see "Command and Control and Command Relationships," Brand, *Appendix: Initial Assessment*, B-2. In March 2010, the Pentagon announced its intention to integrate nearly all of the remaining 20,000 US troops operating in Afghanistan under OEF into ISAF. Only small detachments of US Special Forces and a detention unit remain outside of the NATO command structure.

6 Hy Rothstein, "Chapter 4: America's Longest War," in *Afghan Endgames: Strategy and Policy Choices for America's Longest War*, eds. Hy Rothstein and John Arquilla (Washington, DC: Georgetown University Press, 2012), 59–81; Brand, *Appendix: Initial Assessment*, 2-20-21.

7 The US Army and Marine Corps *Counterinsurgency Manual FM 3-24* (Chicago: University of Chicago Press, 2007); see, for example, Celeste Ward Gventer, David Martin Jones, and M.L.R. Smith, eds., *The New Counter-Insurgency Era in Critical Perspective* (Hampshire, UK: Palgrave Macmillan, 2014).

8 Fred Kaplan, *The Insurgents: David Petraeus and the Plot to Change the American Way of War* (New York: Simon and Schuster, 2013), 305–8; Brand, *Appendix: Initial Assessment*, Section 1.

9 He established an HQ ISAF Force-Reintegration Cell for Afghan-led reintegration and reconciliations programs. Islamic Republic of Afghanistan, National Security Council, *Peace and Reintegration Program*, program document, July 2010; COMISAF/CDR USFOR-A, HQ ISAF, "COMISAF's Counterinsurgency (COIN) Contracting Guidance," 8 September 2010.

10 COMISAF/CDR USFOR-A, HQ ISAF, "COMISAF's Counter-Insurgency Guidance," memo, 1 Aug 2010, http://www.isaf.nato.int/images/stories/File/COMISAF/COMISAF_COIN_Guidance_01Aug10_.doc; US Department of National Defense, *Report to Congress: Report on Progress toward Security and*

Stability in Afghanistan, November 2010, 11–17; Kaplan, *The Insurgents*, 342–44; Paul Dixon, "The British Approach to Counter-Insurgency," in *The British Approach to Counter-Insurgency: From Malaya and Northern Ireland to Iraq and Afghanistan*, ed. Paul Dixon (London: Palgrave MacMillan, 2012), 40–2.

11 NATO ISAF "'Placemat' Troop Numbers and Contributions," Placemats for 2009, 2010, 2011, 2012; Brookings Afghanistan Index: Troop and Security Forces in Afghanistan (2001–2012), http://www.brookings.edu/about/programs/foreign-policy/afghanistan-index, index last accessed 15 July 2014; US Department of National Defense, *Report to Congress: Report on Progress toward Security and Stability in Afghanistan*, December 2012, 13–14.

12 Canada's Strategic Advisory Team was one example of many. By most accounts, the civilian surge failed, although there have been few serious assessments. See Toby Dodge, "Domestic Politics and State-Building," in *Afghanistan: 2015 and Beyond*, eds. Toby Dodge and Nicholas Redman (London: Routledge, 2011), 69–96. See also Rajiv Chanrasekaran, *Little America: The War within the War for Afghanistan* (New York: Alfred A. Knopf, 2012) for a harsher journalistic investigation and assessment of the civilian surge.

13 This issue of streamlining command and control was raised in the *Progress toward Security and Stability in Afghanistan Report to Congress* in accordance with the 2008 National Defense Authorization Act (Section 1230, Public Law 110-181), January 2009, 27, http://www.defense.gov/pubs/OCTOBER_1230_FINAL.pdf. For a discussion of these issues, see Ian Hope, *Unity of Command in Afghanistan: A Forsaken Principle of War* (Carlisle Barracks, PA: Army War College, 2008).

14 See, for example, Chanrasekaran, *Little America*, 152–65, and his account of Colonel Harry Tunnel, commanding officer of the Fifth Brigade of the US Second Infantry Division deployed in and around Kandahar from August 2009; David H. Ucko and Robert C. Egnell, "Options for Avoiding Counterinsurgencies," *Parameters* 44, no. 1 (Spring 2014): 11–22.

15 See for example, Emile Simpson, *War from the Ground Up: Twenty-First Century Combat as Politics* (New York: Oxford University Press, 2013); Colin S. Gray, "Concept Failure? COIN, Counterinsurgency, and Strategic Theory," *PRISM* 3, no. 3 (2012): 17–32.

16 See, for example, Simpson, *War from the Ground Up*, 5–14.

17 For example, see Ministry of Defence (MOD), *British Army Field Manual*, vol. 1, part 10, *Countering Insurgency*, Army Code 71876, Chapter 4 (October 2009).

18 See contention of Walter L. Perry and John Gordon, *Analytic Support to Intelligence in Counterinsurgencies* (Washington, DC: RAND Corporation, 2010); observers had been suggesting the centrality of analysis, information, and intelligence to successful prosecution of "wars among the peoples" for a decade. See, for example, Colonel Thomas X. Hammes, *The Sling and the Stone: On War in the 21st Century* (St. Paul, MN: Zenith Press, 2004); General Rupert Smith, *The Utility of Force: The Art of War in the Modern World* (New York: Vintage, 2008), 377–85.

19 *FM 3-24*, 188–91.

20 Analysis and assessment are distinct in form, even if they can both perform the same function. Analysis is a focused process that uses an identified method. Assessment is a decision-support function that might *or might not* include one or more analytic processes and methods. An assessment can include analysis, and the latter can serve as the assessment. For example, a military commander can provide a campaign assessment based on personal reading of the data with no formal analysis, or they can incorporate a time-series analysis of similar data over time, which requires the focused application of a method. The latter could serve as the assessment, or could be one of a series of analytical studies that inform an assessment of the campaign. See Ben Connable, Walter L. Perry, Abby Doll, Natasha Lander, and Dan Madden, *Modeling, Simulation, and Operations Analysis in Afghanistan and Iraq Operational Vignettes, Lessons Learned, and a Survey of Selected Efforts* (Washington, DC: RAND Corporation, 2014), 5–9.

21 Jonathan Schroden, "Why Operations Assessments Fail: It's Not Just the Metrics," *Naval War College Review* 64, no. 4 (Autumn 2011), 89–102.

22 No author (CAAT), Power Point Brief to NATO HQ, Brussels, "ISAF COIN Advisory & Assistance Team (CAAT)," 29 October 2009, slides 2–4.

23 Schroden, "Why Operations Assessments Fail," 89–102; Kaplan, *The Insurgents*, 345; for issues related to analysis by analogy see Richard E. Neustadt and Ernest R. May, *Thinking in Time: The Uses of History for Decision Makers* (New York: The Free Press, 1996), 34–57.

24 McChrystal titled the chapter of his memoirs covering the summer and autumn 2009 "Understand." General Stanley McChrystal (US Army, Retired), *My Share of the Task: A Memoir*, rev. ed. (New York: Penguin, 2013); "An Interview with Lieutenant General Mike Flynn," *PRISM* 4, no. 4 (2014): 181–9.

25 On data, see Etienne Vincent, Philip Eles, and Boris Vasiliev, "Opinion Polling in Support of Counterinsurgency," *The Cornwallis Group XIV: Analysis of Societal Conflict and Counter-Insurgency* (Cornwallis, Nova Scotia, 2010), 1–25. On both, see William Upshur, Jonathan

Roginski, and David Kilcullen, "Recognizing Systems in Afghanistan: Lessons Learned and New Approaches to Operational Assessments," *PRISM* 3, no. 3 (2012): 87–104; S. Downes-Martin, "Operations Assessment in Afghanistan is Broken: What Is to Be Done?," *Naval War College Review* (Autumn 2011): 103–25; see also Ben Connable, *Embracing the Fog of War: Assessment and Metrics in Counterinsurgency* (Santa Monica, CA: RAND Corporation, 2012); Schroden, "Why Operations Assessments Fail," 89–102.

26 Primary among those shaping the COIN debate was David Kilcullen, an Australian officer who was instrumental in promoting COIN, and then shaping the debate about metrics. His standard brief, "United States Counter-insurgency: An Australian View," was considered the catalyst for a US reconsideration of the campaign. See Kilcullen, *Counterinsurgency* (New York: Oxford University Press, 2010).

27 Kaplan, *The Insurgents*, 344–5; Schroden, "Operations Assessment at ISAF: Changing Paradigms," in *Innovation in Operations Assessment Recent Developments in Measuring Results in Conflict Environments*, eds. Andrew Williams, James Bexfield, Fabrizio Fitzgerald Farina, and Johannes de Nijs (Norfolk, VA: Headquarters Supreme Allied Commander Transformation, 2013), 43–4.

28 Kaplan, *The Insurgents*, 294–348; Gates, *Duty*, 478–502.

29 In December 2010, following a lengthy assessment of the war, Obama announced that the United States would start withdrawing troops from Afghanistan in July 2011, however, there were no specifics as to the potential size or pace of withdrawal.

30 In April 2012, NATO finalized agreements to wind down the war in Afghanistan by formalizing commitments to move the Afghans gradually into a lead combat role, to maintain a military presence in Afghanistan beyond 2014, and to finance the Afghan security forces.

31 Chicago Summit Declaration on Afghanistan, Issued by the Heads of State and Government of Afghanistan and Nations contributing to the NATO-led International Security Assistance Force (ISAF) 21 May 2014.

32 Jonathan Schroden, Rebecca Thomasson, Randy Foster, Mark Lukens, and Richard Bell, "A New Paradigm for Assessment in Counterinsurgency," *Military Operations Research* 18, no. 3 (2013): 5–6.

33 Connable, *Embracing the Fog of War*, 205; Schroden, "Operations Assessment at ISAF," 39–67; Schroden et al., "A New Paradigm," 5–20.

34 Matthew A. Lauder, Phil Eles, and Katherine Banko, "The Glaucus Factor: Red Teaming as a Means to Nurture Foresight," *The Canadian Army Journal* 14, no. 1 (2012): 45–59; see for example North Atlantic Treaty Organization, *Alternative Analysis Handbook*, 13 June 2012; NATO, TSC FEF-0040/

TT-8108/Ser: NU 0018, *Bi-Strategic Command Concept for Alternative Analysis*, 23 April 2012.

35   PowerPoint Brief "ISAF COIN Advisory & Assistance Team (CAAT)," slides 5–6.

36   The CAG was formerly known as the Commander's Initiative Group (CIG). In 2011, it had acted as a support staff preparing files and briefing books for COMISAF, but its role was expanded in 2012 to include some analysis.

37   Discussion with, COMISAF General John Allen on brief "Reconceptualizing Corruption and Patronage," 13 August 2012; Paul Dickson interview with Carl Forsberg, analyst with CJIATF–Shafafiyat, 10 June 2012; Analysts who worked exclusively on this issue believe this is a key lesson for future interventions, see Tim Sullivan and Carl Forsberg, "Confronting the Threat of Corruption and Organized Crime in Afghanistan: Implications for Future Armed Conflict," *PRISM* 4, no. 4 (2014): 157–73.

38   United States Senate, Statement of General Joseph F. Dunford Commander US Forces-Afghanistan before the Senate Armed Services Committee on the Situation in Afghanistan, 12 March 2014.

39   Papers produced during the period included Ross Boyd, Heather Hrychuk, and Ben Jensen, "Optimizing Campaign Management" Red Team Paper, 16 November 2011; Kevin Ellson and Heather Hrychuk, "Downsizing HQ ISAF: Reducing the Footprint but Maximizing the Effect," Red Team Paper, 1 March 2012; Heather Hrychuk, Neil Chuka, Don Neill, and Captain (N) Heidi Berg, "No Peace to Keep: Implications of a Shifting UN Mandate," Red Team Paper, 17 April 2012; and Squadron Leader Steve Ponting, "Combining HQ ISAF, IJC and NTM-A: The Way Ahead," Red Team Paper, December 2012.

40   General John Allen (retired), "General Allen Speaks about the Day the Afghan Campaign Almost Ended," *Foreign Policy*, 21 February 2014, http://foreignpolicy.com/2013/02/21/allen-speaks-about-the-day-the-afghanistan-campaign-almost-ended-kurt-campbell-making-moves-panetta-working-it-at-nato-how-hagel-might-seek-revenge-retired-af-brass-find-an-alternative-to-seque/.

41   Paul Dickson, Liz Abbott, and Tom O'Neill, "Understanding the Impact of Hedging," Red Team Paper, 27 November 2012; Will Hall, John Ivory, and Paul Dickson, "Hedging and Uncertainty in RC-North," Red Team Paper, 2 January 2013; see, for example, the COMISAF, "Commander ISAF's Afghanistan Update, Winter 2014," *ISAF* (Winter 2013–14).

42   Maeva Bambuck interview with Lieutenant General O. Bavinchove in "Les talibans n'ont plus le soutien des Afghans," *Le figaro*, 9 September 2012, http://www.lefigaro.fr/international/2012/09/17/01003-20120917ART-FIG00574-les-talibans-ont-perdu-le-soutien-des-afghans.php.

43 See Robert Johnson, *The Afghan Way of War: How and Why They Fight*
    (Oxford: Oxford University Press, 2012).

44 Carter's approach and views highlighted distinctions between coalition
    approaches to COIN. See Jonathan Owen, "'British Army Chief Risked
    Soldiers' Lives,' Says US Colonel," *The Independent*, 25 November 2012,
    http://www.independent.co.uk/news/uk/home-news/british-army-chief-
    risked-soldiers-lives-says-us-colonel-8348397.html; Emma Graham Harri-
    son, interview with Carter, "'We Should Have Talked to the Taliban,' says
    top British officer in Afghanistan," *The Guardian*, 28 June 2013, http://
    www.theguardian.com/world/2013/jun/28/talks-taliban-british-officer-
    afghanistan; Abdullah Sharif, Round table with Red Team, 8 February
    2013; see also Chandraserkaren, *Little America*, 145–6.

45 Red Team (multiple authors),"The Threat to GIROA," Red Team Paper,
    January 2013. Translated into Dari for distribution to GIROA.

46 Red Team group authorship, "Taliban Strategy: Alternative Courses of
    Action," Red Team Paper, 18 November 2012; and "Should We Divide the
    Taliban?" Red Team Paper, 18 February 2013.

47 This violence generated a new term, *green on blue*, from the US military
    colour designation for friendly and US forces (the enemy is typically
    red). More recently these attacks were referred to as "the insider threat"
    or "insider attacks," in part because most of the attacks are carried out
    against Afghan security forces ("green on green"). Statistics drawn from
    Bill Roggio and Lisa Lundquist, "Green-on-Blue Attacks in Afghanistan:
    The Data," *The Long War Journal*, last updated 5 August 2014, http://www.
    longwarjournal.org/archives/2012/08/green-on-blue_attack.php. Cas-
    ualty figures vary. The Brooking Institute Index claims ISAF fatalities were
    399 for 2012. The discrepancy is explained by the inclusion of private
    security personnel in the US figures – see Ian S. Livingston and Michael
    O'Hanlon, *Afghanistan Index, Also Including Selected Data on Pakistan* (Wash-
    ington, DC: Brookings Institute, 2013).

48 Roggio and Lundquist, "Green-on-Blue Attacks in Afghanistan."

49 Discussion with Red Team by NATO Senior Civilian Representative Ambas-
    sador Simon Gass, July 2012; Paul Dickson and Captain (N) Heidi Berg,
    "Comprehensive Cross-Border Strategy Responses," Red Team Paper, July
    2012; on patron-client relations see, for example, James Scott, "Patron-
    Client Politics and Political Change in Southeast Asia," *The American Polit-
    ical Science Review*, no. 1 (March 1972): 91–113.

50 The Durand Line is the name given the boundary between Afghan-
    istan and Pakistan, established in 1893 by treaty negotiated between the
    Afghan Amir and British representative for British India (the Raj), Sir
    Mortimer Durand, While the Durand Line has international recognition,

it is unrecognized by Afghanistan, and remains a source of contention, splitting as it does several tribal areas, notably Pashtun and Baloch. Will Hall, Anton Minkov, and John Ivory, "Afghanistan, Pakistan, and the Durand Line," Red Team Paper, April 2013.

51 See for example, Thom Shanker, Eric Schmitt, and Alissa J. Rubin, "U.S. Sees Iran in Bids to Stir Unrest in Afghanistan," *New York Times*, 4 April 2012, http://www.nytimes.com/2012/04/05/world/asia/irans-efforts-to-stir-afghan-violence-provoke-concern.html?ref=todayspaper. Discussions in June 2012 with Ambassador Gass, seconded from British foreign service, indicated divisions in views of Iran's intentions. For COMISAF assessments of Iran, see Department of Defence, *Report on Progress toward Security and Stability in Afghanistan*, December 2012, 18.

52 The duality of the Iranian approach to Afghanistan can also be explained with a divergence of opinions between its political and military leaders, see Marlène Laruelle, "Iran's Regional Quagmire," *FRIDE Policy Brief* 135 (September 2012): 4.

53 Anton Minkov, "Reconsidering Iranian Engagement in Afghanistan," Red Team Paper, April 2013.

54 Anton Minkov, "Russia-Iran Cooperation in Afghanistan: Myth or Reality," Red Team Paper, July 2013.

55 Remarks by the President in Address to the Nation on the Way Forward in Afghanistan and Pakistan, December 2009, http://www.whitehouse.gov/the-press-office/remarks-president-address-nation-way-forward-afghanistan-and-pakistan (accessed June 2014).

56 Squadron Leader Nick Hall, "Pakistan's Strategic Goals in Afghanistan," Red Team Paper, April 2013.

57 One of the weaknesses of the AfPak strategy was it failed to appreciate the larger regional context for Pakistan, namely the role of India in formulating Islamabad's policy toward Afghanistan – see for example, Stephen Cohen, "Failure in AfPak: How the U.S. Got It Wrong," *The National Interest*, 15 July 2011, http://nationalinterest.org/commentary/failure-afpak-how-the-us-got-it-wrong-5613; the Red Team Paper "Indian Military Aid to Afghanistan" tried to address this gap in analysis.

58 Richard Cappelli, "Impact of Iranian Elections on Afghanistan," Red Team Paper, May 2013; and Jonathan Prue, "Can the SCO and CSTO help NATO in Afghanistan," Red Team Paper, January 2013.

59 "Karzai's Evolving Reconciliation Strategy," Red Team Paper, 8 March 2012; and "Supporting Karzai's Sovereignty Narrative, While Protecting the Mission," Red Team Paper, 23 March 2013.

60 Valarie Rabideau, "How Karzai Can Derail the Elections," Red Team Paper, March 2013.

8

Going South? Europe's African "Pivot"*

JAN VON DER FELSEN

In early 2013, France quickly and effectively responded to a crisis in northern Mali, and repelled the Islamist rebel groups that were threatening to overthrow the rest of the country and destabilize western Africa. Exacerbated tensions between Sudan and its seceded neighbour South Sudan, along with tribal rivalries and continued ethnic atrocities in Darfur, impend the overspill of refugees, instability, and war into neighbouring hotspots such as Chad, the Central African Republic, the Democratic Republic of Congo, Uganda, and Ethiopia. In April 2014, the terrorist organization Boko Haram abducted more than 270 schoolgirls and conducted devastating raids on villagers in Nigeria, Africa's most populated country. International public outrage followed, but no effective action other than the exchange of intelligence between neighbouring states and others like France, Great Britain, or the United States stemmed from it.

Africa has certainly gained more attention within the last couple of years both in public awareness and in the propagation and execution of foreign policy by Western organizations and individual states. Notwithstanding the increasing threat the Ukrainian crisis is posing to the European Union (EU) and the North Atlantic Treaty Organization (NATO), both organizations clearly have begun

---

*Disclaimer: The views expressed in this text are those of the author and do not reflect the official policy or position of the German federal government or the federal Ministry of Defence.

to advocate for recognition of the threat to the south. General Martin E. Dempsey, then chairman of the US Joint Chiefs of Staff, clearly addressed the challenge in May 2014: "And yet the issues that are emanating into the NATO southern flank from the Middle East and North Africa could quite profoundly change life inside of Europe, not only Southern Europe, but well into Central and Northern Europe."[1] In short, Africa has an overwhelming impact on European security, and the European defence community is beginning to acknowledge this.

Throughout 2014 the full range of foreign policy options has been used at a surprisingly new and heightened level of intensity, to include increased diplomatic initiatives, the provision of financial and logistical support to the African Union, sanctioning of regimes and individuals, as well as military involvement and more robust interventions. Yet, their effectiveness and resolution need to stand the test of time. But time is a dwindling resource for the evolving continent.

The security risks stemming from African insecurity currently shape and reprioritize the focus of European partners and allies, and will eventually require an indispensable international response involving the United States and Canada. This chapter discusses security concerns for Africa that involve migratory effects into Europe, the spread of violence and war, and the obvious danger of mass killings and genocide. Highlighting the impending risks and challenges for Europe will therefore omit a more concrete look at the United Nations (UN) or the African Union (AU). Instead, the chapter will offer a closer look at the postures of NATO and the EU at an organizational level, and France and Germany at an individual state level, in their efforts to solve conflicts and crises in Africa.[2] A special focus will be on Germany's noticeable shift toward more decisive and substantive (military) engagements that should be perceived as being more concrete and reliable by partner nations and organizations alike.

THE STATUS QUO

During and shortly after the Cold War, the world looked at Africa only when international aid organizations had managed to rally enough media support to "make the case" and draw public attention toward devastating droughts and the resulting effects on the population, such as hunger, disease, and death. HIV was considered a continental problem. Wars were omnipresent but saw no obvious intervention – the situation in most African states in the aftermath of the continent's "decolonization" appeared to be too confusing for anyone to become seriously involved. Besides, access to Africa's plethora of resources was taken for granted, even though during the Cold War proxy wars had to be financed and sometimes fought, and Chinese influence kept growing ever since. The world, including the UN, had made its peace with Africa, until the overwhelming and horrifying massacres in Rwanda in 1994.

Since then, views on Africa have significantly changed; the perceived signals of insecurity are more frequent and telling. The 2011 Arab Spring briefly opened a window of opportunity for more democracy (and security) in northern Africa, only to dismiss Egypt into an uncertain future under a renewed military rule, and see Libya drift into chaos and anarchic violence more quickly. Frequent acts of piracy off the Horn of Africa and in the Gulf of Guinea make not only the news but also Hollywood movie fodder. Exacerbated tensions between Sudan and its seceded neighbour South Sudan, along with tribal rivalries and continued ethnic atrocities in Darfur, causes instability, war, and refugee overspill, in neighbouring hotspots such as Chad, the Central African Republic, the Democratic Republic of Congo, Uganda, and Ethiopia. Terrorist groups have increased their presence and influence in the Maghrib (al Qaeda), Somalia (al Shabaab) and Nigeria (Boko Haram), already exercising influential local and cross-boundary terror, to include allegiance pledges to the Islamic State (IS). These groups' offering of training and human resources would unleash the ugly face of international terrorism, again.

Finally, the effects of wars, ethnic atrocities, hunger, terror, and economic hopelessness are no longer contained in Africa alone. The daily exodus of desperate, mostly young people from the central African region,[3] risking life and limb when climbing the fences surrounding the Spanish exclave of Melilla in Morocco, or aboard unsafe and overloaded boats en route to the Italian island of Lampedusa, produces enough successful immigrants to reach Europe in high numbers and devastating conditions to set off public and political reactions. The current mass exodus of Syrian and Afghan people takes away awareness from the continuous flow of African migrants.

The UN and the AU are increasingly engaged in pursuing peace and stability for Africa, and what might have started as smaller

missions in 2003 have grown into full-scale military operations with
relatively high numbers of troops and some level of robustness.[4]
While there are obvious positive effects caused by this more or less
coordinated approach,[5] the AU's capabilities are far from sufficient
to cope with the magnitude of the problems. Smaller, sub-regional
or national initiatives are but a drop of water on a hot stone. Other
international actors – organizations like NATO and the EU, or individual states like France and Germany – have started to take on some
responsibility for African security. The motives, extent, magnitude,
and resolution for their involvement differ significantly and will be
analyzed in turn.

THE BIG COUSIN OF SECURITY BUILDING IN AFRICA: NATO

NATO's "eagerness" and resolution for any involvement in African
matters is, of course, driven by its members' intentions. Its ongoing
anti-piracy operation off the Horn of Africa[6] has effectively contributed to international efforts for maintaining safe passage of maritime vessels through the Gulf of Aden and into the Indian Ocean.
But this success only came with an uncomfortably high price tag.
NATO's European members were torn between contributing their
scarce maritime capabilities to either NATO or the EU's similar Operation Atalanta. This organizational "rivalry" made NATO's regular
force planning processes a repetitive and painstaking puzzle. Yet,
the conduct of the operation allowed NATO to explore some new
and surprising partnerships at sea when NATO vessels at least coordinated their operations with vessels from non-traditional partner countries like China, Russia, India, Pakistan, or Iran.[7] Despite
remarkable successes, the threat remains. Imprisoned by circum-
stance, the alliance's defence ministers decided to extend the mission until the end of 2016.[8]

A strong push by the United States, Great Britain, and France
resulted in a hasty and controversial but nevertheless successfully
portrayed conduct of the 2011 Operation Unified Protector (OUP).
In an effort to protect the Libyan population from a looming raid by
pro-Gadhafi forces on the city of Benghazi and other rebel strongholds, NATO leaped into this operation without a clear political goal.
Even worse, while NATO was struggling hard in finding the right
arguments for getting involved in the first place, an apparent rift

ran through the heart of the alliance's unity, when half of its member states decided to withhold active participation in military operations. NATO's interpretation of the United Nations Security Council's (UNSC) relevant resolutions[9] is subject to international discourse, judicial proceedings, and academic research. The alliance also needed to steer clear from appearing overly biased toward the rebel groups. More than this, with its ISAF mission continuing in Afghanistan and the Iraq War just having ended,[10] NATO had to avoid giving the impression that OUP was "just another war" of the West against an Islamic state. Although a strong signal for consensus with the AU could never be portrayed, the significant contributions offered by Qatar, the United Arab Emirates (UAE), Jordan, and Morocco helped in effectively brushing off that stigma. In the aftermath of Gadhafi's defeat, NATO did not play a strong role in re-establishing Libya. At the beginning of 2014, the political situation within Libya and its immediate neighbourhood was far from secure. While in the short term, military operations were concluded (and publically portrayed) as a success, the long-term political and economic viability of this now volatile country was far from being achieved. Even more so, in May 2014 then secretary general Anders Fogh Rasmussen had to admit that "instability and [the] lack of security in Libya" were hindering NATO's efforts in responding to a Libyan request for assistance in developing their security sector.[11]

In the long run, NATO tends to project tangible security efforts mainly through the provision of military air- and sealift capabilities, as well as training support. This concept had been applied during an early assistance mission for the AU in Sudan,[12] and still is being carried out in support of the AU mission in Somalia. The final signing of a technical agreement on 8 May 2014 formalizes the status of the NATO liaison office to the AU Headquarters in Addis Ababa and thus can be seen as visible instantiation of this relationship.[13]

Outside this rather political and strategic relationship with the AU, NATO maintains a regional partnership network in the form of the Mediterranean Dialogue.[14] Other unilateral co-operation is being conducted at varying levels with states such as Libya, Djibouti, Egypt, and Mauritania.[15] The overall goal of NATO's actions is founded on its "commitment to projecting stability in its neighbourhood."[16] Through the provision of expert and trainer support to the establishment of an African Standby Force (ASF), NATO seeks to further support the AU's increasing independence in terms of combat troops and command-and-control capabilities. Rather than being called to the stage whenever deemed necessary by a small number of its members, or having to fear picking an open-ended mission, NATO will support any initiative aimed at developing an African peacekeeping capability. NATO employs an indirect approach by enabling other regional alliances to conduct their own military engagements. This not only leverages local expertise but also allows NATO to address real security concerns at an acceptable cost.

THE CONCERNED NEIGHBOUR: THE EUROPEAN UNION

The EU struggles under endless discussions about ambition and mechanisms of its own foreign and security policy. More so, political timidity, conflicting national interests, and declining national defence budgets pose an additional burden on the EU's general lack of sufficient military capabilities. On the contrary, pictures of overloaded boats and disturbing news about drowned refugees in the Mediterranean Sea, hundreds of young Africans trying to climb a fence to Melilla, starving babies, and the sudden outbreak of Ebola add to the public pressure on the EU to act. The EU understood that resulting from its "continental neighbourhood" with Africa, topics like international terrorism, migration and economic development needed to be addressed at their roots – in Africa.

Nevertheless, the EU acts in unison with the AU, based on a commonly agreed Africa-EU Strategy.[17] At the two continents' most recent summit, the EU and African delegates more than once emphasized the interdependence as well as their shared objective of addressing common challenges: "Peace and Security are essential prerequisites for development and prosperity."[18] The resulting *Roadmap 2014–2017* lists "peace and security" at the top of its priority areas with an equivocal emphasis on strengthening "the operationalisation of the African Peace and Security Architecture (APSA)" through training and capacity building, as well as on the "[coordinated] planning and conduct of conflict prevention and peace support activities."[19]

Supporting the AU in assuring peace and stability is in the EU's own interest and thus has resulted in small-scale but long-lasting successful military and civilian missions like in Guinea-Bissau[20] and Chad,[21] and more recently in Mali and the Central African Republic.[22] These missions have seen more and more fruitful coordination and even co-operation with AU troops and organizations. The EU and its missions seem to enjoy a good reputation in African states. But make no mistake, the EU's, or more so its member states', willingness to engage in full-scale, costly, and bloody wars in Africa (such as in South Sudan) is more than limited. The idea of sending European soldiers into dirty battles against some warlord's private army of child soldiers and drug-induced teens is not a convincing one. Thus the *Roadmap* provides more concreteness for the capacity building of African forces rather than for coordinated military measures.[23] Here, the EU's indirect approach is evident.

Beyond creating enough willingness, the EU would also need to overcome a more severe dilemma in terms of trying to execute a common European security policy. While the EU was certainly able to agree in analyzing the Mali conflict in late 2012, it lacked the decisiveness for any quick and potent reaction. Maintaining sovereignty and/or national contemplations almost always factor in on EU decision making.[24] Moreover, with initiatives like NATO's Smart Defence, Framework Nation Concept (FNC) and multinational (rather than European) brigades, and the EU's Pooling and Sharing (P&S) initiatives, critics warn of the looming danger of "renationalized politics."[25] Again, the EU's political ambition seems to fail the "reality check" when faced with current and evolving crises and conflicts.

FRANCE'S RESPONSIBILITY TO PROTECT

Current French involvement in Africa can partially be explained by relating it to France's colonial past. Yet, France seems to have overcome the mid-1990s mantra of failing badly in Rwanda and other war-torn states of that time.[26] The political perception of Africa as becoming "an engine of global growth and [making] a strong contribution to European prosperity"[27] opens an alternative explanation. Following its very own national and economic interests and international, European benefit, France is stepping in readily in order to answer to the "political and humanitarian challenge [...] on Europe's doorstep."[28] In doing so, France is allocating significant political and financial effort, as well as military engagement to the African "hotspots": the Maghrib, and even more, the Sahel. France is also clearly taking the political lead. Responding to the April 2014 abduction of more than 270 school girls in Nigeria by the terrorist organization Boko Haram, French President François

Hollande initiated an anti-terror summit, held in Paris on 17 May 2014. Leaders from Nigeria, Chad, Cameroon, Niger, and Benin, as well as representatives from the United States, Great Britain, and the EU put forward an action plan for much better regional coordination, border security, and the exchange of intelligence.[29] The agreement stopped short of immediate, significant military actions, but resulted in the rapid deployment of US, French and British intelligence experts to that region.

Within the EU, France stands out as the driving force for enhancing security and stability in Africa through military training of local and AU forces, and/or the use of military intervention. The *French White Paper on Defence and National Security 2013* outlines the "support for [the] establishment of a collective security architecture in Africa [as] a priority of France's cooperation and development policy."[30] Eight defence partnership agreements and sixteen technical co-operation agreements are currently being used, thus also providing France's armed forces with a forward deployment capability "for anticipation and reaction."[31]

More frequent and more robust deployments of French armed forces can be observed nowadays in the Central African Republic and Mali. The latter might as well be seen as a blueprint for the reasoning for French interventions in Africa: an internal crisis to any given state would give way to criminal trafficking, and in its wake foster terrorist groups, "threatening to transform the whole of this sub-region into a hotbed of international terrorism."[32] While favourably under French leadership, France's missions[33] are carried out using bilateral alliances (such as German support to Opération Serval in Mali) and – with increasing demand – trailed by EU-sanctioned training missions (such as the EU Training Mission in Mali, EUTM Mali).

Beyond partnering with other European states, France has secured itself a strong ally in a joint endeavour to fight al Qaeda in northern Africa: US and French Presidents Obama and Hollande affirmed the "deepening partnership" which is "nowhere [...] on more vivid display than in Africa" as "a model for international cooperation."[34] However, France certainly sees Africa as a "collective European priority, in that our American and Canadian allies expect us to assume an essential share of our responsibilities in regions where they consider themselves to be less directly concerned."[35]

GERMANY: A GLOBAL PLAYER?

In early 2014, a new wind started to blow out of the German ministry of defence – as well as through its corridors. With the swearing-in of Germany's first-ever female minister of defence, Ursula von der Leyen, expectations were high – and were served well initially. Among other, rather surprising, and closely monitored initiatives, the minister broke in on the German public with unusual but not at all uncoordinated statements on Germany's potential new role in worldwide security politics. During the fiftieth Munich Security Conference in early 2014, Germany's top-ranking political figures equivocally sounded the horn for a more visible instantiation of their country's foreign policy. Federal President Joachim Gauck once again[36] reminded his compatriots that "Germany should make a more substantial contribution, and it should make it earlier and more decisively if it is to be a good partner."[37] This strong but rather general statement found a more Africa-focused elaboration when he referred to the UN concept for Responsibility to Protect, "[transferring] to the international community the responsibility to protect the people of a given country from such atrocities when their own government fails to assume that responsibility."[38] Foreign Minister Frank-Walter Steinmeier seconded the president in proposing Germany's obligation "for [an] earlier, more decisive and more substantive engagement in the foreign and security policy sphere," and suggested "practical assistance, also of a military nature, [...] to help stabilise fragile states in Africa, Mali in particular."[39]

Defence Minister von der Leyen's statements, however were more ambivalent. While drawing special emphasis toward a more active German role in current and future international missions in Africa, she also echoed the government's "party line" of not sending German combat troops to Central Africa.[40] So it came as no surprise when she maintained her ambivalence in Munich: this more active role would not necessarily involve sending the Bundeswehr, Germany's armed forces. Instead, financial, logistical and other support were considered as equally important as deploying troops, and should be aimed at enabling "reliable [African] partners on the ground," using "a comprehensive way through training, advice, assistance and if necessary also equipment aid."[41] After all, "the primary goal ought to be finding African solutions to African problems."[42]

In a logical extension to this barrage of announcements, on 21 May 2014 the German federal government released its policy guidelines for Africa. Building on an earlier version from 2011, the new guidelines are unsurprisingly well in synch with the results of the EU-Africa Summit of April 2014. In short, any action in Africa, carried out under EU framework or with single European partners, would be under the UN's roof, in support of and at eye-level[43] with a more capable (but notoriously under-resourced) AU. The guidelines balance the potential and perceived stability of Africa with the existing challenges and fragility of the continent's individual states.[44] Africa's neighbourhood status with Europe is seen as privilege and obligation. The privileges of shared interests and bilateral economic development are contrasted by the obligation to fend off corruption, organized crime, trafficking, and terrorism. Crises and the results of conflicts in Africa are more than likely to hit back on Europe and Germany.[45] Like France, Germany is also undertaking an indirect approach to security engagements in Africa.

Expectations for a much stronger role for Germany in Africa are high, and are voiced by African and Western partners and allies alike. Yet, the German government underlines a natural responsibility and increasing capability of African states, the AU, and other regional organizations for ensuring stability and security in Africa. In addition, countries such as China, India, Turkey, Brazil, Japan, and the United States are described as having strategic interests in Africa that need to be understood and taken into account, when assuring the EU's influence and access.[46]

Germany, together with France, is the most prominent protagonist within the EU to promote security and stability in Africa in order to ensure improved security for Europe. Despite strong French national interests and German self-restraint, these two special partners' activities and alliances are traditionally well synchronized, promoting a strong European position. Both governments declared unanimously that they would increase efforts to boost EU's Common Security and Defence Policy (CSDP) in general and with a special focus on Africa.[47] In more practical terms, Germany's pledge for increased military and logistical support for France's operations in Africa became most apparent in the two nations' decision to deploy units of the Franco-German Brigade to Mali in the fall of 2014.[48]

Officers and soldiers of the Bundeswehr find themselves deployed in small-scale contingents within UN or EU missions, mostly in a staff, monitoring, or training role.[49] Each of the missions had been mandated by the parliament, the Bundestag; but the number of personnel deployed never even came close to the numbers allowed for. The larger French operations in Mali and the Central African Republic found additional limited, but politically important logistical support by the Bundeswehr.

Of course, Germany is aware of its international responsibility to play a more decisive and substantial role in ensuring peace and security in Africa and beyond. The 2011 *Defence Policy Guidelines* state: "In each individual case, there must be a clear answer to the question of whether German interests and the related fulfillment of international responsibility require and justify an operation and what the consequences of non-action would be."[50] President Gauck expanded on this policy at the 2014 Munich Security Conference: "Germany will never support any purely military solution, but will approach issues with political judiciousness and explore all possible diplomatic options. However, when the last resort – sending in the Bundeswehr – comes to be discussed, Germany should not say 'no' on principle. Nor should it say 'yes' unthinkingly."[51] Nevertheless, the move toward a much stronger German response to any given crisis has yet to unfold. Political ambivalence and public uncertainty are not enough to support a shift in German security policy as envisioned by the president. And thus it comes to no surprise that the fifteen pages of the government's policy guidelines for Africa show a high degree of leverage for other measures: strengthening and promoting the regional security architecture, improving jurisdiction and individual rights, addressing migratory roots and effects, boosting economy and agriculture, granting access to better education, among many others.[52] When it comes to the successful prevention of crises and the effective reaction to conflicts, the paramount goal is to strengthen African autonomy through training, counselling, and the provision of military equipment.[53] Beyond this, the German government only "stands ready to become engaged directly in the making of peace and security in the wake of a serious crisis."[54] An all-encompassing, interagency approach within the framework of a collective, international crisis management process, and sanctioned under international law, remains a major prerequisite.[55] In other words, "German policy is based on a comprehensive understanding of security."[56]

CONCLUSION

This discussion was certainly not about national (military) capabilities, but political necessities and commitment. It addresses the second puzzle posed in the introduction, which asked how regional security concerns and alliance priorities are reconciled, with a focus on European powers. This chapter shows that in Europe, there is an increased, yet multi-faceted approach toward a joint security policy for and in Africa. Such a focus on Europe's southern flank is to be seen as important as any reaction to the increasing tensions on Europe's eastern flank following Russia's annexation of Crimea. Naturally we may notice a split between European countries, which are closer to Russia vis-à-vis those on the western and southern flanks. The latter are pivoting to (EU-mandated) actions in Africa while the former are focused squarely on the Ukraine crisis and looking to NATO for reassurance.

Europe's heightened interest in Africa is due to the continents' geographical proximity and the impact that Africa's deteriorating security status will have on Europe. But considering the sheer magnitude and complexity of the various security issues, African security becomes a much higher priority for many states and international organizations. The question remains that whether in times of fiscal austerity and public war-weariness, the international resolve and unity observed during the thirteen-year ISAF mission in Afghanistan can be preserved for Africa; hence the emphasis on an indirect approach to security engagement in Africa. In addition to the security imperatives, many European countries might also view EU-led military interventions in Africa as more politically palatable than a NATO- or US-led mission. This seems to be the case for Germany.

Undoubtedly, the AU should have the first say when it comes to assuring security in Africa. "African solutions to African problems,"[57] or pursuing the AU's vision of "[an] integrated, prosperous and peaceful Africa, driven by its own citizens."[58] Still, nationally and economically driven interests cannot always be declined. The EU has a natural stake in assuring peace and stability in neighbouring Africa, whereas NATO is observing attentively. Both organizations

can and should play an essential role in providing military assets
and training to the AU for enhancing its capabilities as quickly as
possible. A long-lasting "robust" intervention of either organization
should only be a last resort and mandated by the UN, or, in case of a
deadlock in the UN Security Council, at least happen in unison with,
and on invitation by the AU.

France has renewed national claims but under a different parame-
ter. While the positives of French vigour and speed (as it was the case
in Mali) cannot be talked away, the side effect of potentially "rena-
tionalizing" the EU's foreign and security policy even further should
be monitored quite carefully and weighed against a waning confes-
sion for European unity. Germany, on the other hand, might finally
find itself drawn into reinvigorating a more reliable and more concrete attitude toward promoting security in the world. Africa seems
to be the region of choice to start this process under much different – and maybe more favourable – conditions than in Afghanistan.
Still, Germany's military actions are cautious and well-conceived.[59]

NOTES

1 US Department of Defense, "NATO Defense Chiefs to Discuss Russia,
   Afghanistan," 20 May 2014, http://archive.defense.gov/news/newsarti-
   cle.aspx?id=122290.
2 Great Britain, while unarguably the third major power within the European context next to France and Germany, and the driving force within
   NATO on its side of the Trans-Atlantic Alliance, usually would require a
   similar level of consideration on its influence on (foreign policy) decision making in both bodies. However, beyond the strong push toward
   an involvement in Libya in 2011, my research did not reveal enough evidence that would warrant a comparable analysis of British stakes in Africa.
3 For mid-2014, UNHCR estimated almost 3.9 million refugees and people
   in refugee-like situations originating from Africa. See UNHCR, "UNHCR
   Mid-Year Trends 2014," *United Nations High Commissioner for Refugees*, 7
   January 2015, 17.
4 Ansorg and Haaß observe an operational shift from monitoring toward
   peacekeeping missions, as well as an increased role played by African
   states in supplying troops for such missions in Africa. See Nadine Ansorg
   and Felix Haaß, "Multilaterale Friedenssicherung in Afrika," *GIGA Focus*
   6/2013: 1, 7.

5 In April 2014, the UN Security Council mandated a new mission MINUSCA
   with 10,000 troops to relieve the African Union's 6,000 troops in the Central African Republic in fall 2014. See United Nations Security Council,
   "United Nations Official Document," Resolution 2149 (2014): 7.

6 Operation Ocean Shield was approved 17 August 2009, but began as
   Operation Allied Provider in 2008 and Operation Allied Protector in
   2009. See NATO, last updated 26 March 2015, http://www.nato.int/cps/
   en/natohq/topics_48815.htm.

7 NATO, "Address by Admiral Giampaolo di Paola, Chairman of the Military
   Committee at Young Pakistani Parliamentarians visiting NATO HQ," NATO,
   13 July 2010, last updated 24 January 2011, http://www.nato.int/cps/en/
   natohq/opinions_69909.htm.

8 NATO, "NATO Defence Ministers Decide to Extend NATO's Counter-pir-
   acy Mission until 2016," NATO, 4 June 2014, last updated 4 June 2014,
   http://www.nato.int/cps/en/natolive/news_110867.htm.

9 UNSCR 1970 (Arms Embargo) and UNSCR 1973 (No-fly Zone).

10 NATO's very own training mission in Iraq (NTM-I) officially came to an end
   on 31 December 2011.

11 NATO, "Monthly Press Conference by NATO Secretary General Anders
   Fogh Rasmussen," NATO, 19 May 2014, last updated 20 May 2014, http://
   www.nato.int/cps/en/natolive/opinions_109980.htm.

12 African Union Mission in Sudan (AMIS) ran from June 2005 to 31 December 2007.

13 NATO, "NATO and the African Union boost their cooperation," NATO,
   8 May 2014, last updated 13 May 2014, http://www.nato.int/cps/en/
   natolive/news_109824.htm.

14 Algeria, Egypt, Mauritania, Morocco, Tunisia, as well as Israel and Jordan.

15 NATO, "The Secretary General's Annual Report 2013," 27 January 2014: 9.

16 Ibid.

17 Council of the European Union, "The Africa-EU Strategic Partnership: A
   Joint Africa-EU Strategy," 9 December 2007.

18 Council of the European Union, "Fourth EU-Africa Summit – Declaration," 2–3 April 2014: 2.

19 Council of the European Union, "Fourth EU-Africa Summit – Roadmap
   2014–2017," 2–3 April 2014: 3.

20 EU mission in support of the Security Sector Reform in Guinea-Bissau (EU
   SSR Guinea-Bissau), 2008–2010.

21 EUFOR Tchad/RCA in eastern Chad and the northeast of the Central African Republic, 2008–2009.

22 In addition to civilian missions in Mali, Niger, and Djibouti, the EU currently conducts military operations/missions in RD Congo and Somalia.
   See: http://www.eeas.europa.eu/csdp/missions-and-operations/.

23 Council of the EU, "Roadmap 2014–2017," 3.

24 Rolf Clement, "Europäische Sicherheitspolitik – Perspektiven und Hemnisse," *Der Mittler-Brief*, Nr. 4/2013: 1–2.

25 Ibid., 8.

26 Youssouf Diallo, "Sicherheitspolitik in Afrika," *Reader Sicherheitspolitik*, 03/2014: 7.

27 Ministère de la Defénse, "French White Paper on Defence and National Security 2013," July 2013: 39.

28 Ibid.

29 Présidence de la République française, "Paris Summit for Security in Nigeria – Conclusions," 17 May 2014, http://www.elysee.fr/declarations/article/paris-summit-for-security-in-nigeria-conclusions/.

30 Ministère de la Defénse, "French White Paper on Defence," 54.

31 Ibid.

32 Ibid.

33 For a current breakdown of French deployments see: Ministère de la Defénse, "Carte des opérations extérieures," http://www.defense.gouv.fr/operations/rubriques_complementaires/carte-des-operations-exterieures.

34 Barack Obama and François Hollande, "Obama and Hollande: France and the U.S. Enjoy a Renewed Alliance," *Washington Post*, 10 February 2014, https://www.washingtonpost.com/opinions/obama-and-hollande-france-and-the-us-enjoy-a-renewed-alliance/2014/02/09/039ffd34-91af-11e3-b46a-5a3d0d2130da_story.html.

35 Ministère de la Defénse, "French White Paper on Defence," 55.

36 See also: Joachim Gauck, "Speech by Federal President Joachim Gauck to Mark the Day of German Unity," Bundespräsidialamt, 3 October 2013, http://www.bundespraesident.de/SharedDocs/Downloads/DE/Reden/2013/10/131003-Tag-Deutsche-Einheit-englische-Uebersetzung.pdf.

37 Joachim Gauck, "Germany's Role in the World: Reflections on Responsibility, Norms and Alliances," Bundespräsidialamt, 31 January 2014, 4, http://www.bundespraesident.de/SharedDocs/Downloads/DE/Reden/2014/01/140131-Muenchner-Sicherheitskonferenz-Englisch.pdf.

38 Ibid., 6.

39 Frank-Walter Steinmeier, "Speech by Foreign Minister Frank-Walter Steinmeier at the 50th Munich Security Conference," Federal Foreign Office, 1 February 2014, http://www.auswaertiges-amt.de/EN/Infoservice/Presse/Reden/2014/140201-BM_MüSiKo.html.

40 Ursula von der Leyen, interview in *ARD Bericht aus Berlin*, 26 January 2014, https://www.youtube.com/watch?v=rMUHqX8a1rQ.

41 Ursula von der Leyen, "Speech by the Federal Minister of Defense on the Occasion of the 50th Munich Security Conference," Bundesministerium der Verteidigung, 31 January 2014, 6, https://bw2.link/PTlwP.

42 Ursula von der Leyen and Jean-Yves Le Drian, "Afrikas friedliche
    Entwicklung liegt in unserem ureigensten Interesse," *Frankfurter All-
    gemeine Zeitung*, 2 April 2014, http://www.faz.net/-hpo-7nyhv.
43 Die Bundesregierung, "Afrikapolitische Leitlinien der Bundesregier-
    ung," 21 May 2014: 1.
44 Ibid., 2.
45 Ibid., 2–3.
46 Ibid., 3–4.
47 Deutsch-französisches Internetportal, "Erklärung des Rates des
    Deutsch-französischen Verteidigungs-und Sicherheitsrats (DFVSR)
    vom 19. Februar 2014," 19 February 2014, http://www.deutschland-
    frankreich.diplo.de/Erklarung-des-Rates-des-Deutsch,8795.html.
48 Ibid.
49 For a current breakdown of Bundeswehr deployments see:
    Bundeswehr, "Einsatzzahlen – Die Stärke der deutschen Einsatzkon-
    tingente," https://bw2.link/sTISt.
50 German Ministry of Defence, "Defence Policy Guidelines," 27 May
    2011: 4.
51 Gauck, "Germany's role in the world," 5.
52 Die Bundesregierung, "Afrikapolitische Leitlinien," 4–12.
53 Ibid., 14.
54 Ibid., 15.
55 Ibid.
56 Ekkehard Brose, "Recalibrating German Security Policy three years
    after Libya," German Institute for International and Security Affairs
    (SWP), 17 March 2014, http://www.swp-berlin.org/en/publications/
    point-of-view/recalibrating-german-security-policy-three-years-after-
    libya.html.
57 Diallo, "Sicherheitspolitik in Afrika," 6.
58 African Union, "Vision and Mission – Vision of the African Union,"
    http://www.au.int/en/about/vision.
59 In October 2015, various German media reported on government
    plans for an increased military contribution of some additional
    500 to 700 soldiers to the UN's MINUSMA mission in Mali, includ-
    ing a mandate for actions in the more hostile northern region of
    that country, which would begin in early 2016 and support the
    Dutch contingent. See "Von der Leyen will Mali-Einsatz Anfang
    2016 erweitern," *Zeit Online*, 18 October 2015, http://www.zeit.de/
    politik/deutschland/2015-10/von-der-leyen-mali-bundeswehr.

PART FOUR

The Canadian Experience

9

Canadian Involvement
in the Middle East[1]

ALI DIZBONI AND PETER GIZEWSKI

Historically, the Middle East has not ranked high as a Canadian foreign policy priority. In fact, throughout the Cold War, involvement in the region was moderate at best – with the majority of military involvement largely focused on peacekeeping. In this regard, not only did Canada play an instrumental role in Suez in 1956 – the United Nation's (UN) first peacekeeping mission – but Canada was also a willing and active contributor of military forces to all six such missions involving Israel and the Arab states.

Continuing and growing turmoil in the region since the Cold War's end nonetheless witnessed a rise in Canada's military involvement within the region – and a marked expansion of such involvement to include combat operations. Not only has this included a peacekeeping role in missions such as Operation Gladius (the UN disengagement and observer force on the border between Israel and Syria), Operation Calumet (the Multinational Force and Observers in the Sinai Peninsula) and with the US security coordinator to build capacity in the Palestinian Authority known as Operation Proteus, but participation also in allied air campaigns against Iraq in the Persian Gulf War (1991), Libya (2011), sea-based counterterrorism operations in the Arabian Peninsula and Persian Gulf (Operation Artemis),[2] and most recently, with Canada's operations against the Islamic State (IS) in Iraq (Operation Impact). Beyond this, Canada's recently concluded military involvement in Afghanistan (2002–14) stands as the longest combat mission that the Canadian forces have performed to date.

The shape of future Canadian military involvement in the region is more uncertain. Even in light of the rise of IS, Canada's highly active military role in the Middle East may still eschew certain forms of intervention and favour others. Faced with declining defence budgets, war-weariness on the parts of the government and Canadian public, and a growing focus on trade and foreign investment as central planks of Canadian foreign relations, the continuation of significant Canadian military involvement in the region may strike some as unlikely. And the fact that Canadian – and indeed North American – dependence on Middle Eastern oil is on the wane suggests that the region has less geopolitical consequence.[3] In short, both domestic constraints and changing international realities suggest that future Canadian military presence in the Middle East may be marginal, with little to do with what is actually happening on the ground, focused rather on maintaining relationships with allied states. The nature of Canada's and the West's response to IS suggests support for this reasoning. Significant numbers of combat troops on the ground have not been an option; rather, air strikes and special operations forces have been the tools of choice.

Yet while such forces may indeed prompt some lessening of Canada's *current* appetite for involvement in the region, any claim that possibilities for future Canadian military involvement are at an end, or that such involvement will likely be marginal would be premature. Indeed, this overstates the declining significance of the region to the West. It understates Canada's willingness to undertake commitments abroad – at times even in the face of seeming constraints on defence decision making and Canada's military capabilities. And it ignores the fact that military commitments need not be large to deliver significant benefits. In fact, elaborating these points suggests that while the Middle East may not stand out as a priority for future Canadian military involvement – the region *is no less likely* to represent the focus of Canadian military operations than will many other regions of the world.

THE MIDDLE EAST: DOWN BUT NOT OUT

While the Middle East has long been viewed as a region crucial to Western strategic interests, signs that it may be becoming less so have been on the rise. In areas such as trade and commerce, energy, and security, a number of developments indicate that the region may well fade somewhat as a major location of Western interest and involvement in the years ahead.

With regard to trade and commerce, opportunities within the region have generally been marginal, and show few signs of substantial improvement in the years ahead. Perhaps most notably, the importance of the region in terms of future opportunities for Western trade and commerce pales in comparison to those available in Asia and Latin America not to mention with the European Union (EU).[4] On the energy front, recent discoveries of new oil resources in the Mediterranean and other regions – along with growing energy independence in North America as a result of new extraction technologies – indicate a marked decrease in global market reliance on Middle Eastern oil in future.[5] Moreover, political stability within the region remains a concern. In this regard, growing challenges from regional powers and *rogue states* elsewhere (such as Russia, North Korea, or China), and a rise in extremism in Africa, not only suggest some relative decline in the region's threat potential vis-à-vis the West, but the need to focus attention elsewhere. So too does a growing shift in the focus of Muslim wars from anti-West to intra-Muslim conflicts.

Signs that such considerations are having some impact on Western thinking are already evident. US policies drastically scaling back troop levels in Afghanistan and Iraq, as well as the Obama administration's recent announcement of its intention to focus greater attention on the Asia-Pacific region in its future foreign relations are perhaps most noteworthy. And other nations – including Canada – have indicated an intent to pursue a similar course as well.[6]

Yet while suggestive, any claim that Western interests or military involvement in the region will fade *any time soon* would not be fully convincing. In fact, any such assertion is premature. Not only would this tend to exaggerate the region's decline but also the extent to which it will continue to generate significant impacts beyond it – including in Western Europe and North America. The Canadian announcement of Operation Impact (the deployment of forces against IS in Iraq) in September 2014 bears this out.

In the case of energy, while new finds and extraction technologies may have the *long-term* potential to rival or even sideline the key position of the Middle East as the major supplier of oil, their capacity to threaten the dominance of the region as a source of *high-quality* oil and gas in the *near term* remains marginal. Indeed, notwithstanding such developments, exports of Middle Eastern oil continue to exceed by far those of current as well as potential competitors both in quality and quantity and are likely to do so over the next decade. Nor are available supplies from elsewhere even remotely capable of meeting the growing energy demands of Asian and other booming economies.[7] Beyond this, the economic and environmental viability of exploration and new extraction methods are far from assured. In the case of fracking, not only is the process technology intensive but runs serious environmental and ecological risks – risks that generate considerable public opposition and political controversy.[8] Moreover, demand for oil-based products beyond just gas and heating oil remain. Plastics, in particular, will ensure some demand for oil in the coming decades even as new sources of energy capture come online. In short, with new sources of supply still unclear, near-term challenges to Middle East dominance as a crucial source of oil and gas for Western and rising economies in the developing world remain more latent than real. Accordingly, the significance of the region as a reliable (i.e., proven) energy source will continue to remain substantial for some time to come.

Meanwhile, the region is as unstable as ever. Old crises associated with the problem of fragile nation-states, and Israeli-Arab conflicts persist. And new dangers continue to emerge. With the Arab Spring giving way to an Arab Winter, instabilities have not only re-emerged but deepened – threatening a breakup in the so-called regional order. Authoritarianism is on a steady march. Syria, Yemen, Iraq, and Libya are on the verge of collapse, monarchies in the Persian Gulf are ever-more repressive, and the Egyptian revolution has ended in military rule following a *coup d'état* against the Islamist government. Beyond this, prospects for Israeli-Palestinian peace are ever-more remote.

These conflicts, most of them occurring by proxy, provide breeding grounds for radicalization and terrorism. Religious radicalism is of particular concern, as groups such as IS in Iraq, Jabhat al-Nusra in Syria, Islamist militias in Libya, al Qaeda militants in Yemen, and the Shia uprising in Bahrain pose growing threats to existing regimes as well as regional and even international stability.

In the case of IS – not only is the organization's regional influence growing but its presence in Western nations is as well.[9] Arguably more dangerous than other extremist Islamist groups, IS is expansionist, highly motivated, well resourced, and well equipped to seize and hold territory. Moreover, its anti-Israeli and anti-Western ideology is well-known. Indeed, while the immediate agenda of IS aims at the elimination of Persian *Shia* influence in the Arab world, its stated long-term goal is the destruction of Israel and the fall of US Arab allies. So much so, that it has elicited a strong Western – as well as regional – response. Indeed, while a significant ground combat role has been avoided, such a response has included special operations forces and warplanes. H. Christian Breede's chapter in this volume offers some insight on the possible rationale surrounding the military means chosen.

Beyond this lie lingering issues concerning weapons of mass destruction (WMD). The recent use of chemical weapons in Syria, lingering state fragility in nuclear-armed Pakistan and Iran's nuclear ambitions all raise regional and international concerns over the future integrity of existing non-proliferation arrangements, as well as longer-term worries over prospects of a regional arms race, turmoil, and even war. Indeed, while progress in limiting Iran's nuclear program is undoubtedly possible, prospects for a successful and enduring agreement are not assured.[10]

The prospects for instability and conflict are legion, and potential impacts could be considerable – both within the region and elsewhere. In this regard, territory under IS control not only ensures greater local influence but offers new sanctuaries for training and the financing of operatives with an international agenda. The tide of Salafi purist extremism in Syria, Yemen, Bahrain, and Iraq (surrounding Saudi Arabia and sheikdoms) threatens Persian Gulf monarchies – and with them an area responsible for roughly 60 per cent of international oil exports. Meanwhile, perceptions of Iranian nuclear ambitions continue to raise dangers of an arms race, a regional war, and the loss of blood and treasure that any such war would involve.

The potential dangers to Western interests – including those of North America – could be significant. Not only could such dangers take the form of a disruption of energy flows due to inter- and intrastate regional conflict, but threats to nationals as well as to Western bases and intelligence assets within the region. Beyond this lie prospects of a flow of refugees, the infiltration of radical groups and ideologies into Western societies, and the possibility of armed attacks on Western soil (as witnessed in Ottawa 22 October 2014, in Paris 7 January 2015, and in Copenhagen 14 February 2015). Accordingly, both the need and the incentive for future Western involvement within the Middle East either in response to armed conflict or as a means of stabilizing the region and thereby reducing or preventing its occurrence remains considerable.

CANADIAN MILITARY INVOLVEMENT:
THE "DECADE OF DARKNESS" REVISITED?

Given past practice, Canadian support for such operations is not out of character. As a strong advocate and defender of a predictable, rules-based international order, a faithful ally both within NATO and to Israel, and as a nation with a strong commitment to human rights and human security, Canada would undoubtedly retain some interest in the promotion of peace and stability throughout the region – on strategic and humanitarian grounds. In fact, Canadian military involvement within the region has been heavily predicated on such rationales – and has included Canadian Armed Forces (CAF) participation in a range of operations aimed at their realization (such as peacekeeping, stability and reconstruction, capacity building, anti-terrorism and combat operations).[11]

Canada is a strong supporter of the Middle East peace process, an active participant in the multilateral process and a significant contributor to assistance programs in the region. Under Operation Proteus, for instance, Canadian forces assist in capacity-building efforts in aid of the Palestinian Authority Security Forces (PASF) under Task Force Jerusalem, a mission that helps the PASF develop logistics capabilities; supports the construction of security infrastructure for the Palestinian Authority; and facilitates co-operation between the Palestinian Authority and the Canadian government on issues that are not usually of military interest, such as borders and crossings, and movement and access.[12] Members of the Royal Canadian Mounted Police (RCMP) train and professionalize Palestinian police forces as part of Proteus and the EU Coordinating Office for Palestinian Police Support (EUPOL COPPS).[13] And under Operation Artemis, the Royal Canadian Navy has engaged with twenty-nine other countries since 2001 in counterterrorism operations aimed at securing the Middle East's maritime environment by patrolling the Arabian Sea and Persian Gulf.[14] In September 2014, Canada engaged with its allies as part of the Middle East Stabilization Force (MESF) with Operation Impact. This mission involves an air task force of six CF-188 multi-role fighter jets (ended in February 2016), two CP-140 Aurora surveillance planes, and a CC-150 Polaris air-to-air refueller. The mission also includes special operations forces who continue as advisers in Iraq along with a service-support systems in Kuwait for the air task force. All told, some six hundred soldiers are serving in Kuwait, Iraq, and in the skies over Syria as part of this mission.[15]

Still, the extent to which Canada would in fact have the will and the capacity to actively engage in future military missions within the region is another matter. After more than a decade of combat operations in Afghanistan, and in the wake of a global economic recession, Ottawa's appetite for expeditionary operations is not strong. Nor – some might contend – is it likely that the Canadian public would offer any significant support for missions within this or in fact any other region in the near future.

Indeed, recent commentary suggests that Canada's military operation in Afghanistan has not only resulted in public disillusionment regarding the utility of the operation itself, but quite possibly in foreign intervention more generally. In essence, Afghanistan may well have ensured the creation of Canada's own version of the US "Vietnam syndrome," whereby Ottawa avoids any major military undertaking abroad altogether (barring any major military attacks on Canada or its allies). From this standpoint, while future Canadian governments might well offer diplomatic and *rhetorical* support for ongoing and future Western interventions, providing *concrete* contributions to military operations in the Middle East, beyond a handful of aircraft and advisers, may well be a bridge too far.

To be sure, such arguments and realities cannot be ignored, particularly in the current context. Not only is mission fatigue evident among political leaders and the public but in defence circles as well – with a number of Canadian military leaders expressing the need for a strategic pause given the high pace and tempo of operations over the past decade. Growing fiscal restraint has also been apparent, with some commentators claiming that the impacts of current government cuts to defence equal – if not exceed – those which occurred in the early to mid-1990s during the CAF's so-called decade of darkness.[16] As Breede notes in this volume, the fiscal perfect storm of economic growth and budget surpluses has passed.

Yet the extent to which such factors serve to constrain military deployments should not be exaggerated. Public opinion generally has a limited impact on foreign policy decision making. This is especially so when a government enjoys a solid 38 to 41 per cent popular support and majority status. In fact, foreign- and defence-policy issues have rarely been decisive factors in Canadian electoral politics. Notably, if social fatigue was truly a major concern in decisions regarding Canadian military operations abroad, it is unlikely that Canada's military involvement in Afghanistan would have been extended beyond 2009. Yet circumstances surrounding passage of the motion in Parliament show little evidence of the government's willingness to abort the mission or, for that matter, of a united "no" vote from opposition parties. However, recent evidence suggests[17] that Canadians in general, and the Conservative government in particular, did in fact tire of the war eventually.

In short, and notwithstanding public opinion, general fatigue, or party politics, domestic political considerations may take a back seat in favour of international commitments when it comes to Canada's decisions on international operations – a fact made abundantly clear by Canada's actions following its stated decision to forgo participation in the US-led military operations in Iraq. Indeed, as Benjamin Zyla and Joel J. Sokolsky note

> in spite of Chrétien's "no," Canada indirectly supported the US by sending thirty-one exchange officers to serve with American and British ground forces … Canadian ships sailed to the Persian Gulf in support of enforcing UN sanctions against Iraq. Ironically, despite Ottawa's loud protestations that it was unwilling to join the "coalition of willing," Canada made a larger contribution than some who did join.[18]

Nor is there much evidence indicating that the challenges encountered in past missions serve to deter Ottawa's willingness to undertake future military operations. Notably, Canada's participation in Afghanistan occurred despite considerable evidence from CAF experiences in the Balkans and from the US-led intervention in Iraq that nation building was no easy task. Subsequent Canadian participation in NATO's Libya operation and the US-led coalition against IS occurred despite the challenges of Afghanistan.

As for the constraining effect of declining budgets, evidence is weak. While fiscal austerity has undoubtedly impacted the level (and quality) of capabilities available for missions undertaken in the past, there is little evidence indicating that tight budgets have significantly constrained governments from committing Canadian forces to participate in such missions when such commitments were viewed as necessary. Indeed, available data actually indicate a negative correlation between major military operations undertaken by Canada and the size of Canada's defence budget (as a percentage of gross domestic product [GDP]) – with the bulk of Canadian operations occurring during the CAFs "decade of darkness" (the very period in which defence budgets were at their lowest). As Christian Leuprecht and Joel J. Sokolsky argue in this volume, not only did Canada contribute more troops and resources to missions during this period than a number of other NATO countries, but it devoted more resources to military missions abroad than it had in earlier periods when defence budgets were more favourable.

Admittedly, it may still be argued that such contributions were generally modest in terms of sheer numbers of forces involved. Yet judging the significance of military contributions based on numbers alone can be unwise. Not only does such a view undermine the precise nature and quality of support provided, but says little concerning the specific objectives of the missions themselves. In this regard, contributions aimed at host-nation capacity building so as to reduce prospects of conflict occurring may be highly effective yet relatively modest in comparison to those devoted to combat operations employed in a losing cause.

In short, and notwithstanding the fact that such forces will undoubtedly condition future Canadian military operations, they are unlikely to fully determine their location, their conduct or their importance. In the final analysis, while public opinion, past challenges, and cost considerations may play some role in determining the extent to which the CAF will be used abroad, it is likely that Canada's willingness to undertake future military operations – not only in the Middle East but elsewhere – will be determined primarily by the specifics of the situations encountered as well as the context in which they arise. As always, fiscal realities may curtail the extent of involvement, but not necessarily involvement itself.

To the extent that this is the case, the prospects for future Canadian participation in military operations in the Middle East cannot be discounted. At the very least, Canadian participation in military operations within the region would appear *no less* likely than CAF participation in expeditionary operations elsewhere. And the fact that the region continues to be a source of concern internationally can only heighten such possibilities.

CANADA'S FUTURE INVOLVEMENT: SOME POSSIBILITIES

In fact, as it currently stands, ongoing trends indicate that prospects for instability and armed conflict in the Middle East will remain substantial. A civil war in Bahrain, a takeover of power in Pakistan by Wahhabi extremists,[19] or recurring challenges in constraining Iran's nuclear capability suggest just some of the possibilities. And in view of the fact that the security and economic implications of the region both for the West as well as other nations continue to be inextricably linked, the potential for Western military involvement in the region will likely remain alive for some time to come.

Given Canada's standing as a faithful ally to the United States, NATO, and Israel, as well as its commitment to human security and a stable, rules-based international order, Western involvement in the region could well include Canada. The fact that Canada's economic interests in the region are growing (most notably in the Gulf States) only heightens such possibilities.[20]

The precise purpose and form of future Canadian military operations within the region remains unclear; however, given current and near-future realities, a continuation of missions akin to those currently underway is likely. To this end, Canada would focus on offering military contributions to peacekeeping and peacemaking/building operations within the region. It will continue to play a supporting role in capacity-building efforts (such as military training, support for developing better governance in whole of government-type operations, and stabilization and reconstruction). And it will also be on call to offer humanitarian assistance and disaster relief in the event that the wide range of demographic, environmental, and social pressures, which will continue to plague the region, lead to humanitarian crisis.[21]

Notable as well is the prospect that future missions may well be more complex than those undertaken during earlier periods – particularly in light of ongoing changes in the political, social and economic character of the region and the expanded range of actors and issues that such missions will have to take into account (such as the rise in number and importance of non-state actors). They will require an ability to effectively practice a more comprehensive approach to operations.[22] And, they may also require that military interventions undertaken are more robust. Indeed, given existing threats within the region, they may well involve the possibility for *some* armed combat, but likely not on the scale witnessed in Afghanistan.

To the extent that Ottawa has the ability to choose its role, involvement in combat operations will likely remain strictly limited. Far better – and less costly – will be to engage in efforts geared toward easing tensions within the region and strengthening governance and civil society than to engage in armed conflict. However, should major armed conflict occur once again – and key Canadian allies are involved – it is possible that Canada may be compelled to contribute in a combat capacity. As noted, potential scenarios leading to such conflict are plentiful and Western stakes in the region remain high. In such a case, while the preferred – and indeed likely – Canadian contribution may be relatively modest in size and duration, particularly when compared to Canada's mission in Afghanistan, the significance of the region, the logic of armed conflict, and Canada's role as ally may make a combat role hard to avoid.[23]

CONCLUSION

Accurately forecasting the future course of events is clearly difficult, if not impossible. Nevertheless, careful examination of past history and ongoing trends does allow one to make some reasonably educated generalizations concerning the broad contours of future developments. In the case of the Middle East and Canada's future military role, examination of the region itself as well as Canada's past record of expeditionary operations yields several observations.

First, while certain trends suggest that the strategic importance of the Middle East to the West may indeed be lessening, such decline must not be exaggerated. Notwithstanding recent developments in the fields of energy exploration and extraction technologies, the region is likely to retain its importance as a proven and reliable source of high-quality oil for the near future. This, along with its status as home to key Western allies and its continued potential to generate instability and armed conflict – within the region itself and elsewhere – will continue to ensure its place as an important security concern for some time to come. Accordingly, not only are future Western security operations within the region possible, they are also likely.

Second, the extent to which Canada will lend its military forces to support such efforts in future is admittedly unclear. Yet as we have argued, any suggestion that participation in future military operations in the Middle East will *not* occur is not convincing. Not only does such a claim fly in the face of clear and varied Canadian military contributions to the region in the past, but also to the fact that Canada maintains recurring and current missions in the Golan Heights, the Sinai, and Palestine. Beyond this, it ignores the fact that conditions within the region continue to require concerted efforts aimed at fostering peace and stability among its inhabitants. Viewed from this perspective, the region *is no less likely* to prompt Canadian interest and participation in military operations than many others.

Third and finally, fiscal realities, lessons derived from past military missions, and general war-weariness within the nation itself may well work to constrain somewhat the size and character of any future Canadian military operations within the region – particularly in the near term and particularly in terms of ground combat. Yet such factors are unlikely to prevent the conduct of such operations should the Canadian government judge them as necessary. Perhaps most importantly, such forces would not necessarily preclude Canada from making an effective, meaningful contribution to peace and stability in what will doubtless continue to be a significant and still highly volatile region in the years ahead.

NOTES

1 For the purposes of this chapter the term is used in a broad sense to cover those nations associated with the "Greater" or "New" Middle East. Defined as the region stretching from Pakistan-Afghanistan to North Africa, the term *Greater Middle East* reflects the notable degree of homogeneity in politics and history present within the region itself – a fact that works to ensure that developments in one area have clear and often significant impacts elsewhere.

2 See National Defence and the Canadian Armed Forces, "Current Operations," http://forces.gc.ca/en/operations/current.page.

3 Notably, Canada has moved from an oil-importing country to an exporting one and therefore does not rely on Middle East markets for energy provisions. According to Gordon Laxer, for instance, "Canada produces 3.23 million barrels/day of oil and consumes 1.8 million barrels daily." Gordon Laxer, "Superpower, Middle Power or Satellite? Canadian Energy and Environmental Policy," in *Canada's Foreign and Security Policy: Soft and*

Hard Strategies of a Middle Power, eds. Nick Hynek and David Bosold (Don Mills, ON: Oxford University Press, 2010), 157.

4 In fact, Canada, like the United States, has already shifted the focus of its foreign policy and trade from Africa and the Middle East to Asia and South America. See Foreign Affairs, Trade, and Development Canada, "Global Markets Action Plan," last modified 11 September 2015, accessed 13 August 2014, www.international.gc.ca/global-markets-marches-mondi-aux/index.aspx?lang=eng.

5 According to Edward L. Morse, global head of commodities research at Citi, the shale revolution in oil and gas promises "a paradigm shift in thinking about hydrocarbons." Indeed, he notes that US adoption of such technologies has resulted in a 60 per cent increase in oil production since 2008, climbing from 3 million barrels a day to more than 8 million barrels a day, and that the United States will exceed its old record of 10 million barrels a day in a couple of years. By that point, Morse argues that the United States will overtake Russia and Saudi Arabia to become the world's largest oil producer. See Edward L. Morse, "Welcome to the Revolution: Why Shale is the Next Shale," *Foreign Affairs* 93, no. 3, (May–June 2014): 3–7.

6 As an example, see James Manicom, "Canada's Role in the Asia-Pacific Rebalance: Prospects for Cooperation," *Asia Policy* 18 (2014): 111–30.

7 Beyond this lies the fact that excessive reliance on particular energy suppliers often carries risks – a fact underlined in the recent Russia-NATO conflict over Ukraine and Europe's growing sense of vulnerability to energy coercion given its dependence on Russian oil and gas.

8 See Fred Krupp, "Don't Just Drill Baby – Drill Carefully: How to Make Fracking Safer for the Environment," *Foreign Affairs* 93, no. 3 (May–June 2014): 15– 20.

9 Thus far, IS recruits for the civil war in Syria have been considerable – exceeding by far those joining the Afghan war against the Soviets in the 1980s. The number of jihadists from Europe and North America is estimated at 3,000 and 100 respectively. Also operating in Iraq, IS has 10,000 fighters of whom 500 are from the United Kingdom. Like the Afghan case, the return of these lonely veterans to their European home countries is likely to raise a host of security issues.

10 For a balanced examination of the key issues, see Robert Einhorn, "Debating the Iran Nuclear Deal: A Former American Negotiator Outlines the Battleground Issues," *Brookings Review,* August 2015, http://www.brookings.edu/research/reports2/2015/08/iran-nuclear-deal-battleground-issues-einhorn.

11 Notably, some view recent Canadian security policy – both within this
region and elsewhere – as reflective of a more realist, hard-power orientation; a fact owing much to the 11 September 2001 terrorist bombings of
the World Trade Center and events surrounding it. According to Patrick
James, for instance, such events have worked to generate a fundamental
shift in Canada's security orientation – in effect moving Ottawa away from
a predominantly liberal internationalist security stance emphasizing soft
power toward one far more firmly grounded in hard-nosed *realpolitik* and
national interest. Once considered a "peacekeeping nation," Canada post-
9/11 has become a country far more willing and able to use force and
engage in armed combat in pursuit of its goals. Such assertions gain support not only given Canada's participation in the war in Afghanistan but
also in its growing commitment to a range of border security and continental defence initiatives with the United States, its steady upgrading of the
military capability of the Canadian Forces, its increasingly assertive stance
on Arctic sovereignty and security, and its active involvement with other
NATO allies in the bombing and eventual overthrow of the Gadhafi regime
in Libya. See Patrick James, *Canada and Conflict* (Don Mills, ON: Oxford
University Press, 2012).

12 For a complete description, see National Defence and Canadian Armed
Forces, "Operation Proteus," last modified 27 November 2014, accessed
12 August 2014, http://www.forces.gc.ca/en/operations-abroad-current/
op-proteus.page.

13 One can see the description of those operations on the RCMP and the
National Defence websites. See Royal Canadian Mounted Police, "Current
Operations," last modified 17 July 2015, accessed 12 August 2014, http://
www.rcmp-grc.gc.ca/po-mp/missions-curr-cour-eng.htm; and National
Defence and Canadian Armed Forces, "Operation Proteus."

14 See National Defence and Canadian Armed Forces, "Operation ARTE-
MIS," last modified 21 May 2015, accessed 12 August 2014, http://www.
forces.gc.ca/en/operations-abroad-current/op-artemis.page, and "Operation Proteus."

15 See National Defence and Canadian Armed Forces, "Operation Impact,"
last modified 24 August 2015, accessed 28 October 2014, http://www.
forces.gc.ca/en/operations-abroad-current/op-impact.page.

16 According to Michael Byers, while the Liberal government under
Jean Chrétien reduced defence spending to 1.2 per cent of GDP following the Cold War's end, defence spending under the Harper government stood at 1 per cent of GDP – a level roughly equivalent
to that of Belgium, Latvia, and Slovakia. See Michael Byers, "The

Harper Plan for Unilateral Canadian Disarmament," *National Post,*
8 July 2014, http://fullcomment.nationalpost.com/2014/07/08/
michael-byers-the-harper-plan-for-unilateral-canadian-disarmament/.

17 H.C. Breede, "Defining Success: Canada in Afghanistan 2006–2014,"
American Review of Canadian Studies 44, no. 4 (2014): 483–501.

18 Benjamin Zyla and Joel J. Sokolsky, "Canada in the Atlantic Alliance in
the Post–Cold War Era: More NATO than NATO," in *Canada's Foreign and
Security Policy: Soft and Hard Strategies of a Middle Power,* ed. Nick Hynek and
David Bosold (Don Mills, ON: Oxford University Press, 2010), 244.

19 For example, Ahmad Rasheed, a leading expert on Pakistan, maintains
that short of difficult, necessary, and quick changes in the army, Pakistan
may well slip into chaos in the years ahead. See Ahmad Rasheed, review
of *The Wrong Enemy: America in Afghanistan, 2001–2014,* by Carlotta Gall,
New York Review of Books, 5 June 2014, http://www.nybooks.com/articles/
archives/2014/jun/05/pakistan-worse-than-we-knew/.

20 Bessma Momani, Padraig Landy, and Agata Antkiewicz, "Canada's Economic Interests in the Middle East," Canadian-Arab Institute, policy
brief, April 2013, http://www.canadianarabinstitute.org/publications/
policy-briefs/canadas-economic-interests-middle-east/.

21 Other contributors to this book emphasize that Canadian participation in humanitarian operations may well be a growing trend. As Rachel
Lea Heide maintains, humanitarian operations will be a significant part
of future CAF international engagements. In this regard, both predictable and unforeseeable forces (such as climate change, resource scarcity,
unstable geography) and social disasters (such as intrastate clashes, demographic pressures, and the failure of urban structures) may work to trigger
Canadian responses.

22 For a survey of Canadian thought on the comprehensive approach, see
Michael Rostek and Peter Gizewski, eds., *Security Operations in the 21st Cen-
tury: Canadian Perspective on the Comprehensive Approach* (Montreal: McGill-
Queen's University Press, 2011).

23 Canada's recent mission against IS offers a particularly salient case in
point. The mission also illustrates that war fatigue on the part of the Canadian public may be less enduring than often assumed. In an exclusive
Global News/Ipsos Reid poll, 73 per cent of respondents said they strongly
(31 per cent) or somewhat (41 per cent) agree that "everything possible"
needs to be done to stop IS from establishing its self-declared caliphate –
and that includes putting Canadian boots on the ground. See Nick
Logan, "Majority of Canadians Support Use of Troops to Stop ISIS: Poll,"
Global News, 31 December 2014, http://globalnews.ca/news/1750470/

majority-of-canadians-support-use-of-troops-to-stop-isis-poll/. Other polls
report that a majority of Canadians not only favoured extending the mission but widening it to Syria should circumstances warrant. See Nick
Logan, "Majority of Canadians Favour Extending Anti-ISIS Mission: Poll,"
Global News, 23 March 2015, http://globalnews.ca/news/1897768/major-
ity-of-canadians-favour-extending-anti-isis-mission-poll/. See also Mark
Kennedy, "Parliament Votes 149–129 to Widen Canada's Mission against
ISIS and Extend It for a Year," *National Post*, 31 March 2015, http://
news.nationalpost.com/news/canada/canadian-politics/parliament-
votes-149-129-to-widen-canadas-mission-against-isis-to-syria-and-extend-it-
for-a-year.

10

Defence Policy
"Walmart Style": Canadian Lessons
in "Not-So-Grand" Grand Strategy[1]

CHRISTIAN LEUPRECHT AND JOEL J. SOKOLSKY

After years of historically relatively large increases Canada, along-side America and its allies, is tightening the defence purse. Since 2010 alone, reductions have been in the order of 10 per cent with force reallocations amounting to another 3 per cent.[2] Despite a change in government in 2015, there is no indication that this downward trajectory is likely to reverse anytime soon. In its 2014 budget, the then Conservative government announced a three-year deferment of more than $3 billion in major equipment purchases.[3] As rising costs and long delays of military procurements became a looming political liability, the government also moved to reduce the military's role in defence acquisitions in favour of greater civilian bureaucratic oversight of major defence projects.[4] Although these cutbacks are returning Canada to an historic norm when it comes to defence spending, they have touched off a lively discussion in the Canadian foreign and defence policy literature on the subject of whether Canada does and/or should have a "grand strategy."[5] For some critics, Ottawa has consistently underinvested in its military to the detriment of the country's vital national interests and its standing in the world.[6] In its 2014 *Strategic Outlook for Canada* the Canadian Defence Associations Institute (CDAI) criticized Prime Minister Stephen Harper for not having "articulated a broad vision for Canada on the international stage and, as a consequence, Canada's credibility in the world has suffered." Although calling for "more teeth and less tail in Canada's national defence, the lack of a clear definition of what the Government wants from its armed forces makes it difficult to define a strategy and underpin it with the right equipment, resources, and training and to plan joint services operations." In this "post-Afghanistan amnesia," Canada, the CDAI claims, is often "a non-player in times of crisis."[7]

Alleged failure to articulate a clear strategy backed up by commensurate defence expenditures has been the staple of discussions about Canadian defence policy for decades. In this sense, neither the former Harper nor the successor Trudeau government are suffering from "amnesia" but, as argued below, are actually recovering its memory of defence policies past. Those charged with formulating Canada's defence policy have consistently, except in times of war and pressing international crisis, concluded that the country's vital national interests and a modicum of global influence do not correlate with profligate spending on the armed forces. Advocates for a better made-in-Canada grand strategy contend that this happy situation may be the result of simple geography. Structurally (as neoclassical realists might say) Canada does not face existential threats and, therefore, has little incentive to spend on defence in peacetime. And more spendthrift countries' (principally the United States) investment in their own armed forces to advance their national interests generates security externalities of which Canada takes advantage, making Canada a "free rider," shamelessly benefiting from the wiser – if more costly – grand strategy of its bigger peer(s).[8]

For Paul Kennedy, grand strategy conceived myopically as military capacity is misinformed; grand strategy must instead be understood as state capacity more broadly conceived:

> The crux of grand strategy lies therefore in policy, that is, in the capacity of the nation's leaders to bring together all of the elements, both military and non-military, for the preservation and enhancement of the nation's long term (that is in wartime and peacetime) best interests ... it operates at various levels, political, strategic, operational, tactical, all interacting with each other to advance (or retard) the primary aim.[9]

Judged by international standards, even restricting the scope conditions to the major Western liberal free-market democracies, Canada is secure from armed attack, has an economy and a citizenry that continue to enjoy prosperity even amid worldwide economic upheaval, and is so stable internally as to be out-and-out boring to residents and (infrequent) foreign observers alike. Yet, one of the latter, John Fund, writing in the conservative American journal *National Review*, praised Canada for its recent economic acumen. Since 1995, "our more socialist and, consequently, our [heretofore] poorer neighbor to the north," had put its fiscal house in order, achieved a higher per capita income than the United States and created a more business-favourable corporate tax structure. As Fund admonished both Republicans and Democrats, "Canada proves that a country can climb out of a deep fiscal hole within a remarkably small number of years and build a prosperous society while it retains large welfare-state programs."[10] And Brookings Institution in Washington, DC, recently mused about the American Dream having moved to Canada.[11] Either Canadian society is already (and has long been) the beneficiary of an effective grand strategy, or it is an example of the great things that can be achieved without one; especially one that does not pledge copious amounts of national treasure to military power.

Canada does actually have a grand strategy; it is just not all that "grand." Yet, it is firmly entrenched in "realism" both with regard to exogenous (international) and endogenous (domestic) constraints. Concerning the military elements of grand strategy and the benefits that may flow from it, Canada – like so many North Atlantic Treaty Organization (NATO) allies – is actually more of an "easy rider" than a "free rider" – understood as bandwagoning as a function of (opportunistic) followership as opposed to acquiescence[12] – yet is so not by default, but by deliberate, adroit, and largely successful choices. In retail-shopping terms, Canada has no need for an upscale Saks Fifth Avenue level of grand strategy when it has fared well with Walmart. Dollar stores peddle cheap off-label knock-offs; Walmart shoppers look for deals on name brands. Specifically, the department store analogy is meant to capture Canadian politicians' (albeit not the generals') overall approach to defence expenditures: a predilection for window-shopping, deferred procurements, shopping for defence goods without breaking the bank, yet enough practical utility and superficial style to keep the country secure, prosperous, and stable.

This chapter examines how Canada has struggled to calibrate its "easy riding," Walmart-shopping, yet wholly realistic grand strategy. In addition to explaining the underlying realism of Canada's

"Walmart" approach to defence policy, this chapter also suggests that the lessons from Canada's "not-so-grand" strategy resonate beyond Canada. This is not because of its admittedly unique geostrategic situation, but because throughout the West politicians and bureaucrats charged with formulating and implementing so-called grand strategy may well be, implicitly, gravitating toward the approach long honed by Canada: easy riding – not free-riding – on the coattails of US military power while seeking to reduce the fiscal burden to maintain military establishments. However, the chapter concludes on a word of caution: Canadian lessons notwithstanding, given the uncertainties of the international geostrategic environment, defaulting to Walmart may not be the most realistic way to get the best bargain for dwindling defence dollars.

CANADIAN STRATEGIC CULTURE: EXPEDITIONARY EXPEDIENCY

Canada's grand strategy has rested on two seemingly contradictory dimensions of its strategic culture. The first is that Canada has historically embraced an expeditionary approach when it comes to defence policy and the posture and deployment of Canadian military power. "From Paardeberg to Panjwai," as eminent historians David Bercuson and J.L. Granatstein have written, "Canadian governments [...] have believed that one of the key missions of the Canadian military is to deploy abroad."[13] These deployments have served the national interest because, in imperial wars, world wars, the Cold War and myriad limited conflicts that have characterized the post–Cold War and post-9/11 period, Canada has contributed extremely useful and highly regarded forces to the efforts of allies to contain global threats and lesser challenges posed by regional instability to the security and stability of the West and, therefore, to Canada. As such, Canada's national interest was served.

But in addition to meeting a common threat, forces have been dispatched overseas to send a message and, by so doing, to guarantee Ottawa "a seat at the table" along with a sense of status and prestige.[14] This expeditionary strategic culture allowed Canada – which was never regarded, nor saw itself, as a great power – to nonetheless

show larger nations (e.g., Britain and the United States), international organizations, such as the United Nations, or allied nations such as the members of NATO that Canada is ready and able to put a shoulder to the wheel when military forces are needed to defend allies, deter aggression, or keep or enforce the peace. In other words, Canada has been willing to do its share of the hard, dirty work. Doing so wins Canada diplomatic recognition, political acceptance, entrée into arrangements, treaties, and alliances that are important to Canada and Canadians, and a voice on how future international policies will be pursued. Were Canada not to take part in such missions abroad, friends and enemies alike would have concluded long ago that Canada is of no consequence, does not deserve to be heard and ought not to be accorded any favours in bilateral or multilateral negotiations over matters of consequence.[15]

In sardonic terms: "the main and overriding motive for the maintenance of Canadian military establishment since the Second World War has had little to do with our national security as such [...] it has had everything to do with underpinning our diplomatic and negotiating position vis-à-vis various international organizations and other countries."[16] These operations assured Canada an international profile which, safely situated between two oceans and adjoining a decidedly benign and friendly hegemon, it would otherwise not have had. In this sense, Canada has been no different than other countries which, to greater and lesser degrees, employ their armed forces as an instrument to do their military, diplomatic and policing bidding.[17] Yet, recognition, influence, and acceptance, are means to assuring security and prosperity, not ends in and of themselves. They are inherently chimerical, transitory, and difficult to pin down and turn into real assets.[18] In a world dominated by super and great powers, where small powers can stir up trouble regardless of whether Canada is at the table or not, how does Ottawa know when its expeditionary expenditures of treasure – and sometimes blood – are worth the price?

Moreover, it is virtually impossible to establish an actual causal link between any metrics of meaningful global influence and Canadian military contributions to operations overseas. The best that can be said is that Canadian expeditionary deployments have contributed to the peace and security of the West, and, therefore, have benefited Canadians. Although Canada might have been conspicuous by its absence, it has not always been conspicuous by its presence, especially in the higher geostrategic stratospheres where great powers deliberate on the fate of the world and try (with mixed success) to manage regional conflicts and restore a degree of stability and civility. Canadian leaders, skillful and worldly practitioners of the ancient political art of the possible, rarely speak the language of *realpolitik*. Wont to explain Canada's foreign and defence policies by resorting the seemingly selfless (and domestically appealing) rhetoric of liberal internationalism, they labour under few illusions about how much concrete influence could be bought by the dispatch of forces overseas in peace and in war. Thus, along with an expeditionary orientation, Canadian strategic culture has always included a second important characteristic, predilection for expediency. A careful trade-off between costs and benefits had to accompany individual deployments, and defence policy in general. To Robert S. McNamara's famous question, "How much is enough?" Ottawa would, for the most part, retort: "How much is *just* enough?" The answer, bearing in mind the entirely reasonable yet unavoidably imprecise objective of securing a seat at the diplomatic table or multilateral military headquarters, was expediency, an essential part of Canadian strategic culture. This approach to allied commitments "guaranteed that Canada will always prefer to undertake less of an effort than its great-power partners want it to, but not so little as to be eliminated altogether from their strategic decision making."[19]

CANADA'S WALMART APPROACH: JUST ENOUGH

The nature of the post–Second World War "threats" that Canada faced and character of the country's external defence commitments afforded its leaders the luxury of spending less on defence in the pursuit of recognition than allies – and a small but vocal "defence lobby" – would have preferred. The overwhelming threat was a Soviet strategic nuclear attack. While Canada could and did contribute to warning of an air and missile strike through the binational North American Aerospace Defence (NORAD) Command, there was little either Washington or Ottawa could do in the way of active defence. All bets were on the American offensive strategic nuclear deterrent, which was extended to Western Europe courtesy of NATO.

The alliance sought to maintain a conventional capability, to which Canada contributed, but the politics of NATO meant that no contribution, however trivial, would be turned away. Thus, over the

Table 10.1

Canadian defence expenditures as a percentage of GDP

1960–61	1966–67	1970–71	1975–76	1980–81	1985–86	1990–91	1995–96	2000–01	2005–06	2010–11	2012–13
4.2	2.6	2.1	1.8	1.7	1.7	1.6	1.2	0.9	1.1	1.3	1.3

Note: For the full-time series, see Statistics Canada, Fiscal Reference Tables, table 8. https://www.fin.gc.ca/frt-trf/2013/frt-trf-1302-eng.asp#tbl7. Due to a break in the series following the introduction of full accrual accounting, data from 1983–84 onward are not directly comparable with earlier years.

Source: Statistics Canada, Fiscal Reference Tables, table 8, https://www.fin.gc.ca/frt-trf/2013/frt-trf-1302-eng.asp#tbl7

course of the Cold War, Canada was able to draw down its physical presence in Europe and still remain a member in good standing. When it came to the Atlantic Alliance, Ottawa's goals were to keep Canada in allied councils, keep defence spending down, and keep criticism from the right and left out of the public discourse on defence policy.[20] Beyond the Atlantic triangle and apart from the Korean War, Canada did not dispatch or maintain forces. Ottawa did become active in United Nations (UN) peacekeeping operations, but these were sporadic and did not represent a major portion of the defence burden. Indeed, except for the very early years of the Cold War – and even then to a certain extent – Ottawa had a great deal of discretion when it came to size, posture, and especially foreign deployment of Canadian forces. As summed up by James Eayrs at the time, "We would be as safe from attack by any conceivable aggressor with no armed forces at all, as with the armed forces we now have, or any combination of armed forces we may care to have."[21] Or, as the minister of defence put it in 1971, "There is no obvious level for defence expenditures in Canada"[22] – precisely because grand strategy transcends military capacity. Table 10.1 proves the point.

Peacekeeping operations undertaken by Canada during the Cold War were widely mythologized as Canada's altruistic commitment to the global community and international peace. In fact, as Sean Maloney has argued, it was Cold War by other means.[23] It was not in Canada's interest for the superpowers to go to war: either a nuclear war that posed a genuine existential threat, or a war that might antagonize anglo-franco relations and thus jeopardize national unity.[24] Canada also had another reason to instrumentalize peace-keeping for strategic purposes: although supportive of an American-led collective Western defence effort, Canada lacked the financial means and inclination to keep pace with the defence spending of its larger allies in the effort to maintain the nuclear peace. As defence budgets atrophied from their early Cold War heights, peacekeeping was but a manifestation of support for national interest that proved to be a cheap supplement to Canada's allied obligations and a man-ifestation of Canada's overall commitment to Western collective defence while also showing support for broader collective security through the United Nations.[25]

The discretion around classic peacekeeping of the Cold War period was a domestically popular activity for Canada's Walmart grand strategy. It contributed to the search for a distinctively Canadian identity and, by providing an (allegedly) "non-American" alternative contribution to collective defence, reinforced the axiom (or myth) that Canada was an honest broker in the world: "Amer-icans make war, Canadians make peace."[26] Canada's "romance" with peacekeeping coincided with the push for unification. After an initial surge in defence spending early on in the Cold War, the Canadian Army's "big war" aspirations were drawing the attention of defence-spendthrift Canadian politicians.[27] Ministers and their civilian bureaucrats sought to save money and assert civilian con-trol by unifying the three services – the Royal Canadian Navy (RCN), the Royal Canadian Air Force (RCAF) and the Army – into a single entity.[28] Now, "Canada's world-wide intervention force was literally all dressed up with nowhere to go [...] Canada had a structurally unified defence force without a mission to match."[29] Unification was designed to break entrenched service cultures and interests, keep Canada in the game, and at the table, but without having to ante up any more than necessary in the hopes of creating a US-style expe-ditionary Marine Corps – of sorts. As grand strategy, this worked splendidly. Washington's and Brussels' reservations notwithstand-ing, Ottawa remained an active participant in NATO military com-mands and political councils and the NORAD agreement continued to be renewed.

Reassured that strategic payoff was not directly related to the size and structure of its military, Ottawa could count on being welcomed in allied strategic organizations, and with the advent of Soviet-American détente in the late 1960s, Pierre Trudeau's Liberal government championed a nationalist retrenchment that jettisoned Pearsonian middle-power liberal internationalist enthusiasm, fore-shadowed by a policy more closely linked to domestic priorities, with greater emphasis on projecting "Canadian" national interests abroad: "Canada, like other states, must act according to how it perceives its aims and interests. External activities should be directly related to national policies pursued within Canada, and serve the same objectives," read Trudeau's *Foreign Policy for Canadians.*

In 1969, the defence budget was frozen and troop strength reduced from 98,000 to 82,000. Between 1968 and 1971, real defence expenditures declined by 7 per cent and the capital portion of the budget declined to a mere 8 per cent.[30] Although the freeze was lifted in 1973–74, inflation ate up increases in the defence budget that averaged 3 per cent per annum. Moreover, these increases were driven more by military expenditures as an attractive instrument of electoral economic policy – "Industrial Regional Benefits" that appeal to politicians of all stripes provided their ridings benefit – than by security considerations.[31] Defence spending did increase in absolute terms, but as a percentage of gross domestic product (GDP) it declined, while, in accordance with OECD data that suggest that declining defence expenditure is one of the correlates of growth in GDP, Canadian GDP increased overall.[32] Beset with slow economic growth and deficits from entitlement spending, from 1984 on Brian Mulroney's Conservative government maintained Canada's active involvement in Western collective defence, replacing equipment as necessary while restraining defence expenditures. As a result, Canada, in a prescient validation of its grand strategy, was said to have already cashed in its "peace dividend" well before the Cold War had ended.

REINVENTING WALMART: OVERCOMING THE LIMITS OF SPENDING "JUST ENOUGH"

In the wake of the first Gulf War, Canada (which was ill-prepared to contribute) turned its attention to achieving higher levels of interoperability with allied, especially American forces.[33] It was a useful, inexpensive, certainly stylish approach with "the best" at a reasonable price. The high tempo of UN and NATO operations came at a time when budgets were again under pressure. Saddled with a $40-billion deficit, in the *1994 White Paper on Defence* the government of Prime Minister Jean Chrétien sought to reduce the number of civilian employees in the Department of National Defence by 25 per cent and headquarters by 50 per cent. In the aftermath of the Somalia inquiry, the government had little difficulty rallying popular support for sharp cuts to military spending. By 1997–98, defence had been cut by 28 per cent; by 2001–02 it was still 13 per cent lower than in 1993–94. Between 1993–94 and 1998–99, defence funding had been reduced by 30 per cent in real terms, falling from $12 billion to $9.38 billion. However, defence got away fairly unscathed compared to just about every other federal direct spending program, but other federal spending also recovered quicker and steeper than defence.[34]

JETTISONING WALMART FOR SAKS

But money was not the only concern facing the Canadian military. By the mid-1990s the CAF was facing an existential crisis. During the Cold War, the armed forces had served at least two functions: deterrence and peacekeeping (as a preventive measure to avoid the superpowers from going to war). In the post–Cold War era, by contrast, the CAF's purpose was no longer obvious. That changed with the Dayton Accords in 1995 and the subsequent appointment, in 1996, of Lloyd Axworthy as Canada's minister of foreign affairs. The articulation of Canadian foreign policy principles into a reasonably cogent human security "doctrine" – women, children, landmines, and democracy – reinvigorated Canada's energetic commitment to human rights.[35] It resonated with Canadians: staunchly internationalist in orientation, feeling more confident than ever about Canada's standing in the world – despite decades of government divestment from its armed forces. While the doctrine's moral and humanitarian objectives were admirable, hard vital national interests related to the country's security, prosperity, and stability were not at stake; *ergo*, the underlying logic of the doctrine could be divorced from military power. In keeping with Canadian defence policy, Ottawa could continue to benefit from discretion as to when, where and how it would apply the doctrine. In this sense, the Axworthy doctrine was consistent with the Walmart approach to grand strategy: it afforded Ottawa participation in domestically popular undertakings that looked good, but that could be had at low cost.[36] The international engagement preserved by the Axworthy doctrine prodded the Canadian government to reinvest in its armed forces. At the same time, the high tempo of UN and NATO operations in the 1990s and commitment to a war in Afghanistan made Ottawa realize that just showing up would no longer suffice and doing so was proving increasingly dangerous absent sufficient quality and quantity. Having shifted from peacekeeper to putative stabilizer, "just enough" would no longer do.

Premonitions that the cuts of the 1990s would leave the country "without armed forces"[37] proved premature. In 2005, the Defence Policy Statement (DPS) committed the government to expand the Canadian Armed Forces (CAF), transform its capabilities and increase the defence budget. That same year, the federal budget entitled *Delivering on Commitments* reinvested in means by increasing defence spending by $13 billion over five years.[38] A subsequent commitment by the Conservative Harper government went $5.3 billion further. As a result, the first decade of the twenty-first century witnessed a marked renaissance in Canada's military posture: defence spending grew from about 1.1–1.2 per cent of GDP to 1.5 per cent of GDP by 2011, the highest level it had attained since the mid-1990s.[39] Those figures do not account for the supplementary appropriations for the Afghanistan mission that, by 2011, reached $11.3 billion, $9 billion of which accrued directly to National Defence. Aggregate defence spending was up by 51.8 per cent between 2001 and 2010, and grew from $13 billion annually in 2000 to more than $19 billion by 2012. By 2011, Canada was the thirteenth top spender on defence globally and the sixth biggest contributor to Afghanistan among the twenty-eight NATO countries. Although the Canadian forces constituted only 4 per cent of the combined allied force (and not much more in total expenditure),[40] unlike some contributors, such as Germany, it did not put "caveats" on its participation and undertook a much-appreciated and costly combat role.

Increased defence spending was not merely making up for previous reductions; it also reflected Canada's continued overseas military engagements. These operations also had an impact on civil-military relations. They served to equalize what Eliot Cohen has called the "unequal dialogue" between civilian leaders, who hold the final decision-making power, and their senior military advisors[41] – a dialogue which in Canada tilted heavily in favour of civilians. Successive

Canadian governments have had an image of the military as an instrument of alliance politics rather than national security; consequently, civilians assigned military leadership a marginal role in the formulation of defence policy.[42] This sharply circumscribed the military's influence over civil-military relations.

By the late 1990s, the combination of previous budget cuts and the high tempo of overseas operations persuaded the senior military leadership that it had to be more proactive. Aided by retired officers, academics, and public intellectuals, pro-military interests mounted a sustained campaign to build public support for the CAF, convince Canadians that their military was in disarray because the advice of senior officers was ignored, and persuade politicians that a large-scale increase in defence spending was needed to save Canada's supposedly free-falling international stature.[43] In other words, the military could appeal to the political leadership's continuing desire to maintain an expeditionary posture by arguing that the CAF had been so depleted that its ability to deliver the expected political payoffs was now in jeopardy.

Rick Hillier's 2005 appointment as chief of the defence staff signalled a greater willingness to heed professional military advice. To distinguish himself from his predecessor, newly elected Prime Minister Paul Martin was intent on tuning up the image of the Canadian Armed Forces, not for the sake of the CAF per se, but hypothesizing that a robust defence portfolio now stood to reap political payoff at home and abroad.[44] But the prime minister may have got more than he bargained for in Hillier who broke with the convention of the "silent soldier" as he set out to loosen the strictures of control by politicians and senior civilian defence bureaucrats who had reigned over CAF policy and finances since 1973.[45] In his attempt to reshape public perception of the military, Hillier not only cast himself as the public defender of the CAF's interests but also as the country's top defence expert, an image he cultivated through media interviews. He offered unsolicited policy suggestions, advocating for more robust funding. He took the even more unprecedented step of explicitly criticizing government policy and had a public spat with Minister of National Defence Gordon O'Connor that culminated in O'Connor's resignation. The change in civil-military relations was palpable: "Previously, it was held that a CDS who failed to abide by the defence minister's decisions and dictates was unqualified to head the Canadian military. Now the mood was that a defence minister who failed to heed the advice of the CDS was unworthy of the office."[46] Straddling a Liberal and a Conservative government, Hillier's image of "his" Canadian military was one of kinetic expeditionary force projection that would offer the government a wider array of choices for discretionary deployments, an image that would count where it mattered most: in Washington.[47]

Although Hillier's efforts, combined with the world-class performance and great sacrifices of the men and women of the CAF in Afghanistan (and in Libya in 2011) dramatically enhanced the image and support for the CAF among Canadians as a national institution of which to be proud, this did not translate into widespread and robust public support for continued and costly expeditionary operations and the increases in defence spending required to sustain such undertakings. Canadians found the cost of such a force and such missions even more disquieting, especially during an economic downturn when they were pleading for fiscal stimulus at home. Between 2010 and 2015, Canada's defence budget will have shrunk from 1.4 per cent of GDP to 1.08 per cent – a far cry from the goal of 2 per cent envisioned as recently as the 2008 update to the Canada First Defence Strategy. A revisionist "Canada First" defence policy would henceforth reprise a more traditional meaning: maintain an expeditionary strategic culture tempered by fiscal expediency.

This return to a "not-so-grand" Canadian grand strategy is driven by politicians and bureaucrats who are reasserting the traditional inequality in the civil-military dialogue in Canada when it comes to defence decision making. As one analyst observed, if the military is asking for a "Cadillac and you actually need a Corolla," then the system needs someone who "has the authority to ask why do you need this Cadillac?"[48] The Harper government proceeded to curb the military's role in the acquisition of weapons systems and, reminiscent of previous governments, drawn out the timeline for others. This appears to persist under the newly elected Liberal government. Even if one acknowledges that the premium Saks version of the CAF's shopping list had only recently been encouraged by the government and that few "Cadillacs" were actually purchased, evidently the political and civilian leadership is no longer deferring to the military's professional expertise and are instead exercising their prerogative to ask the hard questions that come with ultimate authority and responsibility for the public purse.

BETWEEN EASY- AND FREE-RIDING:
THE LESSONS OF THE CANADIAN EXPERIENCE

Though never known as a source of grand strategic thinking, the lessons of the Canadian experience when it comes to defence policy resonate in the contemporary comparative context. Throughout the West, the protracted, costly, and ambiguous Afghanistan mission and the economic downturn have prompted a reassessment of defence expenditures demanded by overseas interventionism as an element of so-called grand strategy. Even in the world's greatest military power, the United States, budgetary pressures and war-weariness have already reduced defence spending, especially on the army, with more to come. Thus Canada's Walmart approach, which never received due recognition for prowess in strategic thinking, may not play too badly in today's Washington. Barry Posen recently derided America's post–Cold War grand strategy of "liberal hegemony" as "unnecessary, counterproductive, costly, and wasteful" and suggests a more restrained approach to US military strategy.[49] Similarly, President Barack Obama told the 2014 West Point graduating class:

> Since the Second World War, some of our most costly mistakes came not from our restraint, but from our willingness to rush into military adventures without thinking through the consequences ... Just because we have the best hammer does not mean that every problem is a nail. And because the costs associated with military action are so high, you should expect every civilian leader – and especially your Commander-in-Chief – to be clear about how that awesome power should be used. The United States will use military force, unilaterally if necessary, when our core interests demand it – when our people are threatened, when our livelihoods are at stake, when the security of our allies is in danger ... On the other hand, when issues of global concern do not pose a direct threat to the United States, when such issues are at stake – when crises arise that stir our conscience or push the world in a more dangerous direction but do not directly threaten us – then the threshold for military action must be higher.[50]

Criticism notwithstanding, Obama has employed military force, both latent and applied. Yet, consistent with the theme of restraint, the administration explicitly sought to avoid "boots on the ground" and did not throttle reductions in defence expenditure.

Canada has again joined the United States in recent operations but, along with the United States and other allies, appears intent on continuing to restrain defence spending. Does this mean that Ottawa is making disciples to follow its bargain grand strategy? Hopefully not, for the red line between "easy riding" and "free-riding" can be a thin one. As the unpredictability of the international security environment shows, it is in Canada's interest both to avoid excessive US entrenchment as well as a race to the bottom among allied defence capabilities and expenditures. NATO, conceived of not as a military alliance but as a forum to overcome precisely these types of collective-action problems, is Canada's means to that end. Though weary and mindful of some of its power slipping away, the West will nonetheless face new challenges from non-traditional sources and countries who will stir up disorder in certain regions that may threaten the interests of countries focused on prosperity. As such, Canada still has national interests to assert, and its prevailing calculus on defence spending would have to shift beyond thrift, possibly quite significantly, if the synergies and economies of scale that NATO provides no longer worked to Canada's advantage.

Which raises an interesting question (that is beyond the scope of this chapter): To what extent are states locked into their shopping patterns? That is, what endogenous and exogenous variables determine a state's behaviour in this regard? This is an important question. Walmart may offer utility and discount prices, but there is something to be said for the quality and style that buttresses internationalism and collaborative solution-seeking, especially when, notwithstanding the current widespread reassessment of military expenditures, there is no reason to believe that the utility of armed force per se is on the wane. Under President Obama, the United States has been moving from an emphasis on the ability to fight big wars, which led to the quagmires of Iraq and Afghanistan, to more precise, limited, targeted operations using drones and special operations, including targeted strikes against known terrorist leaders.[51]

Fiscal realities are a major driver of foreign and defence policy, especially when states, such as Canada, enjoy the externalities of sharing a border with the major, friendly, military power. Money will dictate what Canada can and cannot do. The change in government in 2015 notwithstanding, the newly elected Liberal government's mantra of fiscal restraint and modest deficits to fund increased infrastructure and program spending foreshadows prevailing and possibly mounting restraint on defence spending. The chapter's Walmart thesis thus looks to stand the test of time. The challenge for Canada is to draw upon the realism of its traditional low-budget approach to defence expenditures as well as the lessons of the post–Cold War, post-9/11 Afghanistan experience: regardless of how little you spend on defence or limited your contributions, armed forces need the right equipment to succeed at what is asked of them. Just showing up is not enough if you do not have the proper kit to get the job done. As in motorcycling so, too, in realist international security relations: easy riding is not joyriding. NATO members would, therefore, be well-advised to steer clear of both Saks and Walmart when it comes to defence spending. So as not to succumb to the fallacy of composition, collectively, they will want to shift their business to Sears: a down-scale retailer that affords the ability to achieve utility and savings in defence policy, just not at rock-bottom prices and with more style and flair.

NOTES

1 An earlier, longer version of this chapter appeared in *Armed Forces & Society* 41, no. 3 (July 2015): 541–62.
2 David Perry, *Doing Less with Less: Canadian Defence Transformation and Renewal*, Vimy Paper (Ottawa: Conference of Defence Associations Institute, 2014), 3.
3 James Cudmore, "Budget 2014: Military Wings Clipped Again," CBC News, 11 February 2014, http://www.cbc.ca/news/politics/budget-2014-military-wings-clipped-again-1.2532827.
4 Steven Chase, "Ottawa to Curb Military's Role in Procurement after Costly Delays," *Globe and Mail*, 5 February 2014, http://www.theglobeandmail.com/news/politics/ottawa-to-curb-militarys-role-in-procurement-after-costly-delays/article16703809/.
5 For example, see David G. Haglund, *The North Atlantic Triangle Revisited: Canadian Grand Strategy at Century's End* (Toronto: Canadian Institute of International Affairs, 2000); Hugh Segal, "A Grand Strategy for a Small Country," *Canadian Military Journal* 4, no. 3 (Autumn 2003): 3–6; David Pratt, *Is there a Grand Strategy in Canadian Foreign Policy? The 2007 Ross Ellis Memorial Lectures in Military and Strategic Studies* (Calgary,

AB: Canadian Foreign and Defence Affairs Institute, 2008); Charles
F. Doran and David Pratt, "The Need for a Canadian Grand Strategy"
in *Canada's National Security in the Post 9-11 World: Strategy, Interests and
Threats*, ed. David S. McDonough (Toronto: University of Toronto Press,
2012), 25–44; J.L. Granatstein, *Can Canada Have a Grand Strategy?* (Calgary, AB: Canadian Foreign and Defence Affairs Institute, 2011); and
Matthew Trudgen, "A Canadian Approach: Canada's Cold War Grand
Strategy, 1945–1989," *Journal of Military and Strategic Studies* 34, no.
3 & 4 (2012).

6 Andrew Richter, "Forty Years of Neglect, Indifference and Apathy: The
Relentless Decline of Canada's Armed Forces," in *Handbook of Canadian
Foreign Policy*, eds. Patrick James, Nelson Michaud, and Marc O'Reilly
(Lanham, MD: Lexington Books, 2006), 51–82; Roy Rempel, *Dreamland:
How Canada's Foreign Policy Has Undermined Sovereignty* (Montreal: McGill-
Queen's University Press, Policy Study Series, 2006); Andrew Cohen, *While
Canada Slept: How We Lost Our Place in the World* (Toronto: McClelland &
Stewart, 2003).

7 Ferry de Kerckove and George Petrolekas, *The Strategic Outlook for Canada:
The Search for Leadership 2014*, Vimy Paper (Ottawa: Canadian Defence
Associations Institute, 2014), 1.

8 For example, see Frank Harvey, *North Korea, Ballistic Missile Defence and
Canada-US Defence Cooperation* (Calgary, AB: Canadian Defence and Foreign Affairs Institute, 2013).

9 As quoted in Trudgen, "A Canadian Approach," 3.

10 John Fund, "Is Canada Now More American than America?" *National
Review*, 5 September 2014, http://www.nationalreview.com/
article/387201/canada-now-more-american-america-john-fund.

11 Richard Reeves and Pete Rodigue, "Has the American Dream Moved
to Canada?," *Social Mobility Notes* (blog) (Washington, DC: Brookings
Institution, 1 July 2014), http://www.brookings.edu/blogs/social-mobil-
ity-memos/posts/2014/07/01-has-american-dream-moved-to-canada-
reeves.

12 Randall Schweller, "Bandwagoning for Profit: Bringing the Revisionist
State Back in," *International Security* 19, no. 1 (1994): 72–107.

13 David J. Bercuson and J.L. Granatstein, "From Paardeberg to Panjwai:
Canadian National Interests in Expeditionary Operations," in *Canada's
National Security in the Post–9/11 World*, ed. David S. McDonough (Toronto:
University of Toronto Press, 2012), 193.

14 Joel J. Sokolsky, "A Seat at the Table: Canada and Its Allies," *Armed Forces
& Security* 16, no. 1 (1989): 11–35; Justin Massie, "Alliance Value and

Status Enhancement: Disproportionate Military Commitments to the War in Afghanistan," paper presented at the 23rd World Congress of Political Science, International Political Science Association, Montreal, 22 July 2014.

15 Bercuson and Granatstein, "From Paardeberg to Panjwai," 193–4.

16 James Eayrs, "Military Policy and Middle Power: The Canadian Experience," in *Canada's Role as a Middle Power*, ed. J. King Gordon (Toronto: Canadian Institute of International Affairs, 1965), 84.

17 Ken Booth, *Navies and Foreign Policy* (London: Croon Helm, 1977).

18 Philippe Lagassé and Paul Robinson, *Reviving Realism in the Canadian Defence Debate*, Martello Paper no. 34 (Kingston, ON: Queen's Centre for International Relations, 2008).

19 David Haglund and Stéphane Roussel, "The Contradictions of Canadian Strategic Culture: 'Imperial' Commitments within a 'Democratic Alliance,'" paper presented at the Biennial Meeting of the Association of Canadian Studies in the United States, Portland, OR, November 2002.

20 Joseph T. Jockel and Joel J. Sokolsky, "Canada and NATO: Keeping Ottawa In, Expenses Down, Criticism Out ... and the Country Secure," *International Journal* 64, no. 2 (2009): 315–36.

21 Eayrs, "Military Policy and Middle Power," 84.

22 Department of National Defence, "Defence in the 70s: White Paper on Defence," Ottawa: Information Canada, 1971, in *Canada's National Defence Volume I – Defence Policy*, ed. Douglas L. Bland (Kingston, ON: Queen's University School of Policy Studies, 1997), 121–82.

23 Sean M. Maloney, *Canada and U.N. Peacekeeping: Cold War by Other Means* (St. Catharines, ON: Vanwell, 2002).

24 David Last, "Almost a Legacy: Canada's Contribution to Peacekeeping," in *Canadian Military Experience*, ed. Bernd Horn (St. Catharines, ON: Vanwell, 2002), 367–92.

25 Carsten Holbraad, *Middle Powers in International Relations* (New York: St. Martin's Press, 1984); and Margaret P. Karns and Karen A. Mingst, "International Organizations and Foreign Policy: Influence and Instrumentality," in *New Directions in the Study of Foreign Policy*, ed. Charles F. Hermann et al. (Boston: Allen and Unwin, 1987), 462–3.

26 Sandra Whitworth, "Militarized Masculinities and the Politics of Peacekeeping: The Canadian Case," in *Critical Security Studies in World Politics*, ed. Ken Booth (Boulder, CO: Lynn Rienner Publishers, 2005), 102.

27 Peter Kasurak, *A National Force: The Evolution of Canada's Army, 1950–2000* (Vancouver: UBC Press, 2013), 53–74.

28 Royal Commission on Government Organization [Glassco Commission] (Ottawa, Queen's Printers, 1963); Paul T. Hellyer, *Damn the Torpedoes: My Fight to Unify the Canadian Forces* (Toronto: McClelland and Stewart, 1990).

29 David P. Burke, "Canadian Armed Forces: Unification Revisited," paper presented to the International Studies Association, Anaheim, CA, March 1986, 2.

30 J. Craig Stone and Binyam Solomon, "Canadian Defence Policy and Spending," *Defence and Peace Economics* 16, no. 3 (2005): 152.

31 John M. Treddenick, "The Arms Race and Military Keynesianism," *Canadian Public Policy* 11, no. 1 (1985): 77–92.

32 David Alan Aschauer, "Is Public Expenditure Productive?" *Journal of Monetary Economics* 23, no. 2 (1989): 177–200.

33 Department of National Defence, *Shaping the Future of Canadian Defence: A Strategy for 2020*, June 1999, 10, http://www.cds.forces.gc.ca/str/index-eng.asp.

34 Stone and Solomon, "Canadian Defence Policy," 151.

35 Lloyd Axworthy and Sarah Taylor, "A Ban for All Seasons: The Landmines Convention and Its Implications for Canadian Diplomacy," *International Journal* 53, no. 2 (1998): 183–96.

36 Joseph T. Jockel and Joel J. Sokolsky, "Lloyd Axworthy's Legacy: Human Security and the Rescue of Canadian Defence Policy," *International Journal* 56 (Winter 2000–01): 1–18.

37 Douglas L. Bland, *Canada without Armed Forces?* (Kingston, ON: Queen's University School of Policy Studies, 2004).

38 Don Macnamara, "Happiness Is – A Rising Defence Budget?" *Institute for Research on Public Policy, Special Commentary* (The Institute for Research on Public Policy, 25 February 2005).

39 Stockholm International Peace Research Institute, 2012.

40 International Institute for Strategic Studies (IISS), *The Military Balance*, 2002–11. London, 2012.

41 Eliot A. Cohen, *Supreme Command: Soldiers, Statesmen, and Leadership in Wartime* (New York: The Free Press, 2002), 209.

42 Douglas L. Bland, *The Administration of Defence Policy in Canada, 1947–1985* (Kingston, ON: Ronald P. Frye, 1987), 95–124; and Lagassé and Robinson, *Reviving Realism.*

43 Philippe Lagassé, "Matching Ends and Means in Canadian Defence," in *Canada among Nations 2004: Setting Priorities Straight*, ed. David Carment

et al. (Montreal: McGill-Queen's University Press, 2005), 73–92; Bland, *Canada without Armed Forces*; Conference of Defence Associations (CDA), *A Nation at Risk: The Decline of the Canadian Forces* (Ottawa: Conference of Defence Associations, 2002); Senate Committee on National Security and Defence (SCONDSAD), *For an Extra $130 Bucks ... Update on Canada's Military Financial Crisis* (Ottawa: Library of Parliament, 2002).

44 Janice Gross Stein and Eugene Lang, *The Unexpected War: Canada in Kandahar* (Toronto: Viking Canada, 2007), 109–51.

45 Philippe Lagassé and Joel J. Sokolsky, "A Larger 'Footprint' in Ottawa: General Hillier and Canada's Shifting Civil-Military Relations," *Canadian Foreign Policy* 15, no. 2 (2009): 16–40.

46 Ibid., 29.

47 Joel J. Sokolsky. *The 'Away Game': Canada–United States Security Relations Outside North America.* Working Paper Series no. 2004-09 (Montreal: IRPP, 2004).

48 As quoted in Chase, "Ottawa to Curb Military's Role."

49 Barry R. Posen, *Restraint: A New Foundation for U.S. Grand Strategy* (Ithaca, NY: Cornell University Press, 2014), xi–xii.

50 United States, White House. Remarks by the President at the United States Military Academy Commencement Ceremony, 28 May 2014, http://www.whitehouse.gov/the-press-office/2014/05/28/remarks-president-united-states-military-academy-commencement-ceremony.

51 Andrew Bacevich, *Breach of Trust: How Americans Failed Their Soldiers and Their Country* (New York: Metropolitan Books, 2013).

CONCLUSION

Summary and Implications:
The Will to War[1]

H. CHRISTIAN BREEDE

Are we going to war? This is the question that – in general terms – this book has sought to answer. Based on the discussion in the preceding chapters, covering motives, the impact of austerity, the connection between the soldier and the citizen, regional security issues, and the challenges of measuring success, our answer is clearly nuanced. The answer is no, large-scale war is unlikely, given that motives, fiscal realities, and the domestic political risks are not aligned at present to set the conditions for ambitious military interventions going forward. Our answer is also yes, because allied interventions can mitigate some of the aforementioned risks. Moreover, there are security realities and relationships that will compel Canada to intervene, even if in a token way. First and foremost, the authors argue that interventions or wars of choice – to borrow a somewhat polemical phrase – will not be entered into lightly. This book, thus, examined the conditions under which decisions leading to the use of force are made.

Collectively, the chapters show that side payments matter. This will be discussed in the first section of this chapter. In game theory, a side payment is made to a player who is otherwise at a marked disadvantage should they choose a given strategy; a form of compensation to the player for choosing a strategy with a less-than-desirable outcome. The chapters highlight that the path to war was rarely linear or obvious. States enter into a conflict often for reasons other than what was declared and those reasons tend to change over time.

Canada's experience in Afghanistan is but one example where the reasons for intervention shifted three times over the course of the mission; first framed as support to an alliance member, then shifting to a fight against terrorism, and finally adapting to the necessity of nation building.[2]

The second theme that runs across many of the chapters is about the connection between soldiers and society. To go back to the example of Afghanistan, the Canadian experience shows that the connection between soldiers and citizens remained strong as the frequent "Red Friday" rallies of the mid-2000s illustrated. That connection was even made symbolic with the renamed section of one of Canada's major highways as the "Highway of Heroes." However, this connection was expressed through not only the impact of casualties upon the domestic audience, but also in the way in which austerity – the state-level need to do more with less – has become an increasingly important concern in decisions leading to the use of force. In short, the answer to the question of going to war is as much as it is about the domestic political climate as it is about the international security environment. Even if foreign policy rarely plays a role in Canadian public opinion, the domestic environment matters.

In order to demonstrate the importance of the domestic environment, the second part of this chapter will be devoted to exploring some of the mechanisms that connect citizens and soldiers and show how those either empower or restrain the choice to go to war. It will show that wars of choice, such as those entered into the past decade and half, are unlikely to be repeated on the same scale, even though other forms of intervention may still occur.

THE INDIRECT PATH TO WAR

Although written with the expressed intent to explain the unpredictable behaviour of alliance members, *American Allies in Times of War* by Stéfanie von Hlatky presented three strategies that an alliance member state could follow when deciding on the use of force. These strategies can be applied outside of the formal alliance construct and can be used to explain the decision to go war by any state, particularly "secondary powers" like Canada. Strategies of leveraging, hedging, and compensating were identified by von Hlatky to explain why member states behave the way they do – and why their unpredictable actions are in fact based on a very rational calculus.[3] Other scholars, notably Justin Massie, argue that countries like Canada engage in wars based on prestige concerns. He uses the example of Canada in Afghanistan, arguing that Canada participated, not so much because it felt it had to compensate, but rather, to be seen in a favourable light by its allies, notably the United States.[4]

Whether states enter into war for reasons of prestige, a need to compensate, a desire to leverage, or by seeking to hedge against uncertainty, the overall impact is that states go to war for reasons other than threat response. The reasons for going to war are often not clear or direct. With this in mind, several chapters in this book suggest that conflict in the future will continue to be guided by these strategies and that countries such as Canada, which are relatively small, developed, and prosperous, will likely face more situations where these strategies will be seen as optimal. Canada participated in Afghanistan as a side payment to compensate for other foreign policy decisions *and* to gain prestige for policies that would otherwise have harmed the reputation and perception of Canada among its allies. The concept of the side payment also explains the motives for foreign interventions by countries other than Canada and the US.

Christian Leuprecht and Joel J. Sokolsky make this point clearly and with wit as they argue that Canada is pursuing a policy of "just enough" and that this policy is rather consistent in terms of Canada's overall defence policy track record. Put in the context of shopping, Canada buys defence policy at Walmart (select brand names at a steep discount) while the United States shops at Saks (latest brand names sold at a premium). Leuprecht and Sokolsky posit that future policy-makers look to the analogy of Sears, suggesting that a consistent policy of "just enough" will prove to be too little in the long run. Sometimes, they argue, you need to buy some brand names at full price to remain effective and influential, but this can still be done in a frugal way. Indeed, money matters.

Jan von der Felsen's chapter clearly articulates the mechanisms of European intervention in Africa as distinct from those in Canada or even the United States. Put simply, the geographical proximity of Africa to Europe gives instability in Africa increased urgency to European allies. However, even the major European powers of France and Germany are primarily focused on indirect, capacity-building efforts rather than the commitment of troops in the field to actively fight the various insurgent groups within the continent. As a form of hedging, the strategies chosen by European countries toward Africa are seeking to employ the minimum resources to stave off a need to deploy larger and more robust forces in the future. Europeans are engaging in Africa in an indirect and frugal manner.

Rachel Lea Heide's chapter shows that it is likely that Canadians will witness an increase in disaster-assistance interventions, in which armed forces are deployed to help deliver aid and provide some limited security during the distribution of that aid. These types of missions are important and Canada can make (and has made in the past) a real contribution as part of a broader relief effort, but these missions are conducted in a generally permissive environment where the threat is considered low and military forces are generally welcomed. This permissiveness works at home too. As the threat is low, the policy of intervention is a relatively easy sell.

In his chapter, Bob Martyn reinforces the idea of this indirect route to war, suggesting that these decisions are made complex by competing interests and events. He examined the possible triggers for future intervention and for Martyn, the answer is either economic concerns or the completely unforeseeable events that will surprise policy-makers in the future. Setting those "unknown unknowns" aside, the economic interests are – for Martyn – the trigger that could lead us to war. Short of that, altruism or a sense of commitment to a global society will be insufficient to justify costly deployments in the future. That being said, warns Martyn, this does not mean that Canada's future soldiers will have an easy time of it; rather, future engagements will likely remain violent, complex, and risky.

Ali Dizboni and Peter Gizewski's chapter, although arguing that Western and in particular Canadian willingness to engage militarily in the Middle East will not fundamentally change, concedes that the form of such engagement will. Indeed, the image – seared into Canadian minds over the past decade and a half – of Canadian soldiers in LAV IIIs and Leopard tanks rolling through deserts is one that is unlikely to be seen again for some time to come. Rather, engagement will take the form of airstrikes and special operations forces. These capabilities are cheaper in terms of money, blood, and political risk. Canada will still engage, but only in specific ways. However, as with any attempt at forecasting, changing conditions will lead to different responses.

Based on these contributions, decisions will be made taking into account many different factors, making the side payment analogy a useful analytical device. For example, Canada does not share the sense of urgency with regard to African crises, as Europeans do. Canada, therefore, is likely to seek further compensation and leveraging strategies to respond to African instability and to maintain good relations with Europeans. By contrast, continued instability in Haiti could see renewed Canadian attention for the same reasons Europe is engaged in Africa. In that context, European states may use side payments as a way to contribute. Strategies of leveraging, hedging, and compensation, if successful, lead to improved prestige for the country in question and more latitude in the decision-making process. This serves to illustrate that the path to war will be an indirect one for wars of choice in the immediate future.

THE CONNECTION BETWEEN
THE CIVILIAN AND THE SOLDIER

The various ways in which soldiers and the societies they purport to protect interact has been an enduring puzzle for political scientists, sociologists, and policy-makers. A soldier, the manifestation of a state's ability to impose its will by force, is also a member of the state in which he or she resides. Soldiers are trained to kill, through the effective use of lethal weapons as well as through organizational training such as tactics and the operational art. These skills create a cohort of society that is capable of extensive coercive force that, unconstrained by the discipline to adhere to government policy, could easily be turned against the state itself. A military coup (or the "military veto" as it is colloquially known) is the manifestation of that threat.

Furthermore, at an individual level, the soldier and the civilian have very different identities that can threaten to create differing values as well. Where soldiers value obedience, a willingness to take the life of others, as well as the acceptance of "unlimited liability" (in that soldiers are expected to sacrifice their own lives if necessary as part of the terms of their employment), civilians value individuality, freedom of choice and equality, and are actively discouraged from having a willingness to take the life of another. For civilians there is no such expectation to risk their own lives for the sake of their employment.[5] At both the collective and individual levels then, soldiers and civilians are at opposite ends of the spectrum. How that tension is mediated matters and that mediation will either effectively manage the different identities of soldiers and civilians or it will exacerbate them, creating communities within the broader society that could erode the overall cohesion of the state over time. The quality of the connection between civilians and its soldiers is critical to the decision to go to war – but is often taken for granted.[6]

Further highlighting the importance of the connection between the soldier and the civilian are the chapters by Peter Tikuisis and Christopher Barron. Although both take different approaches, and in some cases draw different conclusions, both contributors have rightly identified a key factor in the choice to go to war: the impact of casualties. For Barron, the proliferation and evolution of improvised explosive devices (IEDs) witnessed in the past decade and half indicates that opponents understand the importance of the connection between the soldier and the state and they see that connection as a weakness. The IED has marginal tactical impact on the battlefield, but – like other such weapons of the past – has immense strategic impact back home. The IED and more importantly the image of the IED, conveyed back home through the soldiers' testimony and social media sows doubt in the domestic audience and constrains further action.

Although Tikuisis has identified that casualties in war are decreasing over time and that technology is making the individual soldier more capable in comparison to historical counterparts, this trend will also make the modern soldier increasingly hard to replace and – normative concerns aside – an increasingly scarce resource to be used sparingly and carefully. Interestingly, a decrease in the lethality of the modern battlefield may not in fact lead to an increased willingness to go to war; rather, the increased costs of this decrease in lethality may be the prohibitive factor. War is getting expensive. By way of example, the state of the art in high-performance fighter aircraft technology in the 1940s was the P-51 Mustang, which cost just under $50,000 per unit (in 1945 dollars). The equivalent today, the F/A-18E Super Hornet, is roughly $65 million (according to Boeing's own numbers from their website). Even when adjusted for inflation (into 2014 dollars), the Mustang would have cost around $650,000 per unit or 1 per cent the cost of a modern warplane (to say nothing of the emerging fifth-generation aircraft like the F-35).

Aaron Ettinger's contribution on the contractors' role in modern war highlights the fiscal pressure on the conduct of war and another aspect of the distinction between the soldier and the civilian. Although his work focused primarily on the loss of capability by an over-reliance on contractor support, Ettinger also suggests that failing to account for contractor casualties as part of the 9/11 Wars "obscure[s] the human cost of war."[7] In what he calls "social control," the civilian's ability to hold their elected officials to account depends upon their ability to fully understand the costs and benefits of a given policy. If the true costs are hidden, the ability to control policy is constrained. By moving capabilities out of the all-volunteer force to the private sector, not only is the capability lost but the impact upon society is reduced when people (no longer soldiers) are killed. What is interesting to note with Ettinger's contribution is that, although increased contractor support can empower the foreign policy executive to engage in more wars of choice, the marginal cost savings of using contractors in place of professional soldiers will likely constrain, rather than empower. This will likely result in a net reluctance to engage in wars of choice, where existential threats to the state are neither clear nor present.

WHY THE CONNECTION MATTERS: PAST AND FUTURE

To further understand the connection between civilian and soldier, one inevitably turns to Prussian military thinker and soldier Carl von Clausewitz. In his book *On War*, he presents a trinity that has enduring relevance.[8] Clausewitz places the military as a vertex between government and the people[9] and he (along with other classic theorists) have suggested that a strain in the connection between the military on the one hand and the government and the people on the other, can enable wars to be pursued that may not be in the overall national interest of the state in question.[10]

The trinity presented by Clausewitz in his classic remains relevant today and speaks to the theme of soldier-civilian connection that has been a constant theme in the study of civil-military relations[11] and which is present in this book. The trinity suggests that as the connections between the soldier and the civilian are strained, the government is further empowered to employ the military in missions that may have little salience with the public. To put things in context, a

Figure 11.1
Population and service in the United States over time

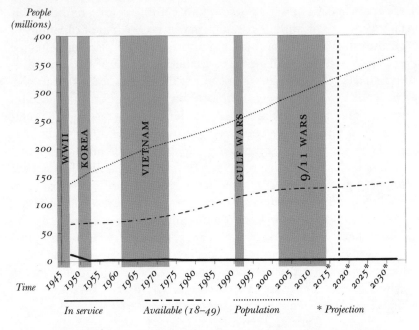

Sources: Data compiled by author. Population data from www.populationpyramid.net, accessed 18 August 2015. Size of service data from the US Department of Defense, through www.infoplease.com, accessed 19 August 2015. Forecasts are based on holding 2012 service ratios constant as population forecasts grow.

useful exercise is to examine the proportion of the population that has actually served in the military since the Second World War.

I will compare Canada and the United States to illustrate. The number of people of age – in this case, aged 18–49 – were gathered for both Canada and the United States in five-year intervals beginning in 1945 to coincide with the close of the Second World War (figure 11.1). At the same time, the sizes of the active component of both the Canadian and American militaries were measured across that same time scale. Finally, the overall populations of both Canada and the United States were captured as well.

Figure 11.1 traces the population growth from 1945 through today then projects these numbers out to 2030. Overlaid upon this graph are the major conflicts in which the United States participated. The graph clearly shows a divergence that is active at two levels. The first level of divergence is between the overall population

Figure 11.2
Population and service in Canada over time

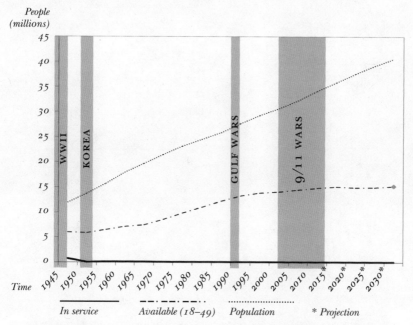

Sources: Data compiled by author. Population data from www.populationpyramid.
net, accessed 19 August 2015. Size of service data from http://www.
thecanadianencyclopedia.ca/en/article/armed-forces/, accessed 19 August 2015.
Forecasts are based on holding 2012 service ratios constant as population forecasts.

and the population of those available to serve (defined as those
between the ages of 18 and 49 for this study). The second level of
divergence is between these first two trends and the overall trend in
the size of the active component of the US military over that same
time period. As can be seen in the graph, not only has the population of those available to serve declined, so too has the size of
the active component. In effect, the trends are moving in opposite
directions. All things being equal, one would expect parallel growth
patterns between all three. Divergent growth patterns indicate that
not only are fewer people in absolute terms serving in the military,
but those who serve make up a steadily shrinking proportion of the
overall population.

A similar pattern emerges when the focus shifts to Canada. Figure 11.2 shows a youth population that is shrinking in comparison
to the overall population trend, along with a smaller and smaller

Figure 11.3

ABCA and major NATO allies service ratios

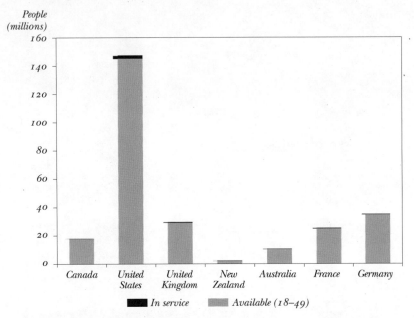

Sources: Data compiled by author. Service ratio derived from demographic information from www.populationpyramid.net and 2012 figures for regular and reserve component members of the militaries drawn from https://www.cia.gov/library/publications/the-world-factbook/, accessed 19 August 2015.

proportion of the population serving in the active component. In both Canada and the United States, fewer and fewer citizens are serving in the active components of the military. More importantly, with the trends projected out to 2030 and holding the percentage of the available population serving in uniform constant at 2010 levels, the size of the militaries in both countries continues to decline until 2025, where in both Canada and the United States, both militaries see a small increase in growth.

Even if the numbers are adjusted to account for the reserve components in both countries, the proportion of those who serve is incredibly small. Figure 11.3 presents another way to view this data and presents for added comparison other states such as the ABCA allies (American, British, Canadian, Australian, and New Zealand) along with the two other major NATO allies: France and Germany.

The United States, among all the ABCA and major NATO allies, has the highest proportion of those aged 18–49 serving in the military

Figure 11.4
BRIC Service Ratios

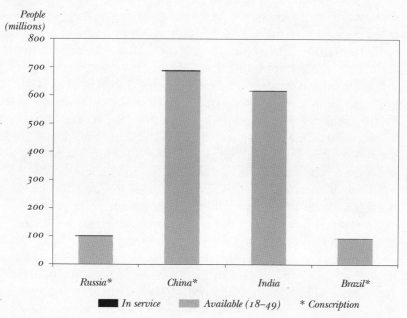

People (millions)

Russia*   China*   India   Brazil*

■ *In service*   ▨ *Available (18–49)*   * *Conscription*

Sources: Data compiled by author. Service ratio derived from demographic information from www.populationpyramid.net and 2012 figures for regular and reserve component members of the militaries drawn from https://www.cia.gov/library/publications/the-world-factbook/, accessed 19 August 2015.

(including active, National Guard, and reserve). In the United States, fully 1.5 per cent of the available population serves in some component of the military. The United Kingdom and France are second and third respectively while in Canada, only .5 per cent of the available population serve. What these numbers show is that although participation in the military in Canada and the United States has declined, overall participation at present is consistent with other major allies. The service ratios in Canada and the United States are consistent with other ABCA and NATO countries. Even when factoring in major, non-Western states, such as Brazil, Russia, India, and China, service ratios are no different, with ratios anywhere from 1.8 per cent of those aged 19–49 (in Russia) to a low of 0.2 per cent (in India). Figure 11.4 presents the service ratios for the BRIC states of Brazil, Russia, India, and China. Also notable is that conscription is not used in any of the states presented in figure 11.4 and Russia, China, and Brazil still have a policy of conscription, but this does not seem to have a discernable impact upon the service ratios. Although Russia enjoys the highest service ratio of all countries examined, if conscription is held as the key variable, it only adds 0.3 per cent above and beyond the state with highest, non-conscription service ratio (the United States at 1.5 per cent). Conscription, it would seem, does not positively affect service ratios.

So why does it matter if only between 0.5 and 1.5 per cent of a given available population serves? How does this threaten the connection soldiers feel to their fellow civilians? One reason, discussed above, is that if few serve, there is a risk that those that do will form their own community, at the expense of broader social cohesion. To put it crassly: it is about who gets killed.

To put it succinctly, if casualties are kept low and the impacts confined to the immediate military community, policy-makers are empowered. Conversely, if the impact of casualties is felt broadly, either because of high casualties or strong civilian-soldier ties, the policy-makers are checked by domestic political pressure to keep wars short, and only engage in them when clear, national interests are at stake. In sum, a conscript force should be more casualty-averse and an all-volunteer force should be more resilient to casualties.

Interestingly, the data shows that as fewer serve, wars themselves become less deadly for soldiers as fewer soldiers are dying in battle.[12] Take for example the United States. In the First World War, total war dead amounted to just under 3 per cent of those who served. Although that number jumped to almost 3.5 per cent for the Second World War, it declined for Korea and Vietnam to less than 2 per cent and further declined for the 9/11 Wars to two-tenths of a per cent. To further reinforce this, during Canada's twelve-year commitment to Afghanistan, more than 40,000 soldiers served there at one point or another, and deaths related to the mission amount to just under one-half of a per cent.

It is a cruel twist of logic to see this as a bad thing. Science and technology have improved to the point that weapons are more accurate, protection is improved, and the health sciences can now save lives in ways unheard of only fifty years ago. However, as fewer casualties result from combat, decision makers will find it easier to exercise a military option. If few serve and casualties are fewer still, what constrains policy-makers?

The media – the classic fourth estate – has long been held as the check on executive power. By making information available to citizens, it keeps policy-makers keenly aware that they are being monitored and the public will not tolerate policy that does not benefit the state. Political careers are dependent upon the votes of the electorate in democracies and the fear of open rebellion in non-democratic states. As media has transformed from the town crier who reached a few people in the village square to the Internet that reaches millions around the world, policy-makers should be feeling more constrained than ever. Are they? Has the media tightened the Clausewitzian trinity of government, civilian, and military?

Of the many images of the 9/11 Wars, the embedded reporter is certainly one of the most memorable. The images of well-known television reporters, wearing helmets and Kevlar vests, interviewing soldiers in the back of an armoured vehicle on the front lines during the opening days of the Iraq War marked a new phase in war reporting. Images of soldiers on the front lines and in combat were being sent to living rooms back home. The media's access to military operations was unprecedented. Surely, casualties under this much scrutiny would ensure that such wars were short and only engaged for most dire of reasons. However, this clearly has not been the case.

Recent literature, such as that by James Nathan and Charles Tien, has confirmed earlier assertions that civilians are not *casualty*-averse but rather *failure*-averse. Nathan and Tien provide a comprehensive review of the literature on this topic and confirm the contention that popular wars are successful wars.[13] If the war is perceived as successful, the population deems the human costs acceptable. However, in wars in which success is in doubt, suddenly, the casualties begin to have an impact on the support for the war and the public begins to pressure the policy-makers to change course and get out of the war.

The question of success is in and of itself a challenge to answer. Recent research on this topic suggests that success is made up of coherence (in terms of polices across all organs of government as well as the degree to which that policy is implemented on the ground) as well as perception (of that policy's merit at home). Policies that are incoherent or beset by divisions within government and which are poorly perceived at home cannot be assessed as successful.[14] Drawing on the experiences of Denmark during the 9/11 Wars, Stig Hjarvard and Nete Noergaard Kristensen find that where such coherence was present, the media tended to frame the war positively. In this sense, the fourth estate, rather than serving as a check on military intervention, became an empowering force, shaping public attitudes toward the war that encouraged continued participation in it.[15]

However, Hjarvard and Noergaard Kristensen include a caveat to their findings. They caution that this empowering feature may be unique to small countries where policy-makers and the media are closely connected to begin with.[16] The media remains a dynamic shaper of opinion, some of which may not be in line with the policies emanating from the government of the day. But again, this role is not so simple and clear-cut. Douglas Kriner and Francis Shen recently reported that although citizens generally tolerate casualties so long as government policy is coherent (in line with Hjarvard and Noergaard Kristensen's, as well as Nathan and Tien's works), the location of the casualties matters. In two different studies, Kriner and Shen found that although the public is generally accepting of casualties, if those casualties are local (within their own community), their support for the war decreases.[17]

This adds weight to the concern over dwindling service ratios discussed above. As fewer and fewer serve, the loss of connection is not in the aggregate, but rather in the specific. Having less than 1 per cent of your eligible population in uniform not only ensures aggregate loss of connection but it also keeps specific connections small and remote. A few communities within a state – where only a 0.5 per cent serve – will feel the brunt of casualties while the rest of the state will go unaffected, save the sad acknowledgement of a new statistic.

The media is another component, which in the language of the trinity, *can* further connect the three vertices of government, public, and military. The media *can* act like a binding force. As the science and technology of media advances, however, the media's role as a binding force *will* strengthen the connection for what was considered local now has wider and wider reach. The service ratios will have less impact as the various communities are being increasingly connected through new media technologies. Casualties and the political risk they pose are no longer a sufficient deterrent to the employment of force abroad for reasons other than direct national interest. Even with the advent of digital media and the increased availability of information, casualties – on their own – still fail to fully connect civilians with the soldiers. Yet another mechanism is at work that is strengthening the civilian-soldier connection, one that in the past decade worked in concert with the shift away from conscription discussed above to empower pursuit of wars of choice, and one which is now no longer present: money.

THE CASH CONNECTION

In the late 1990s and early 2000s, both the United States and Canada enjoyed strong economies and federal budget surpluses. In short, both governments were flush with cash. This enabled the payment for the pursuit of foreign policies to come without having to turn to the citizens through borrowing and taxation. The United States and Canada could go to war and domestic life at home would change little and therefore the impact upon the political decision makers would be minimized. In both Canada and the United States, since the 9/11 Wars began in 2001, the conflicts were funded through indebting the country. Taxes in fact decreased and little mention was made of domestic borrowing. This was another shift, with the first being the adoption of a volunteer force and the second, the adoption of debt financing rather than financing through domestic lending and taxation.

Reliable and consistent historical data for Canada on how wars are paid for is hard to find, however, thanks to a recent Congressional Research Service (CRS) report, such information is now available for the United States and the findings are revelatory.[18] The US experience is a good example of how the funding of war has changed alongside the force generation mechanisms. Table 11.1 summarizes the CRS data for the US role in the major wars of the twentieth century and aside from the staggering cost of the Second World War, which accounted for approximately 36 per cent of US gross domestic product (GDP) in 1945, Korea, Vietnam, and the 9/11 Wars were all much smaller proportions of GDP. Since the Second World War, the American economy has grown seventy-five times as large (from $200 billion in 1944 to over $15 trillion in 2011). With this in mind, the 9/11 Wars represent just over 1 per cent of US GDP. In absolute terms, the Second World War cost three-and-a-half times what the 9/11 Wars have cost *so far*.[19] Although a substantially smaller proportion of the overall GDP, the cost is just over a third in real terms. The 9/11 Wars cost ten times what the 1991 Persian Gulf War cost and one-and-a-half times the ten-year war in Vietnam.[20]

The key feature of this data however is not in the absolute costs or the relative size of the costs compared to the GDP of the time, but in how the wars were paid for. In the Second World War, taxes were

Table 11.1

Costs and sources of revenue for American wars

	Cost (2008 $, millions)	GDP % (peak year)	Funding source
WWI	253	13.6 (1919)	Bonds,[1] taxes, borrowing
WWII	4,104	35.8 (1945)	Bonds,[1] taxes
Korea	320	4.2 (1952)	Taxes
Vietnam	686	2.3 (1968)	Taxes
9/11 Wars	859	1.2 (2008)	Borrowing

1 Bond is a debt owed to domestic lenders.

Source: Stephen Daggett, "RS22926 – Costs of Major U.S. Wars," *Congressional Research Service* (2010), http://www.crs.gov.

raised and applied to a broader swath of American society as taxes were now garnished directly from the employers' payroll. Not only that, but a savings instrument was introduced – the famous "war bond" – that encouraged people to invest in the government, which was form of domestic lending. Between one-third and one-half of the war's total cost was covered by taxes and the rest was paid for by war bonds.[21] Although a much smaller cost, the Vietnam War was paid for primarily through an increase in taxes as well.

The 9/11 Wars, however, have been paid for through the assumption of debt. Taxes were not raised and with the exception of the poorly publicized "patriot bonds," no investment instruments were introduced to pay for the 9/11 Wars.[22] Not only has the overall tax rate dropped over the last fifteen years but so too have the overall tax exemptions and deductions.[23] Americans today are, in effect, not financially paying for the war in any direct, immediate way.

That the 9/11 Wars are being waged not only by a volunteer military but are also being financed through the incurrence of massive amounts of debt simply reinforces the lack of connection present today between the population, its government and its military. A 2011 report by Elise Foley suggests that the wars have already cost nearly $4 trillion and that interest payments on the debt that results from this price tag are in the hundreds of billions of dollars. The report indicates that the war added an additional $1.5 trillion to the American national debt.[24]

Adam Smith, in his classic work *The Wealth of Nations,* suggests that wars financed through taxation would be completed quickly and undertaken with discretion.[25] Interestingly, Smith explicitly rejects the financing of war through the incurrence of debt or the expenditure of a "war chest."[26] By taxing the people in order to finance a war, all the people feel the impact of the war upon their daily lives and the feedback – especially if the war is seen as wasteful or inconsistent with some national interest – will constrain decision makers.

CONCLUSION

A volunteer force (which represents a minuscule proportion of the overall population) combined with the assumption of debt (rather than generating revenue through taxation and domestic lending) enabled the United States and other countries like Canada and the United Kingdom to engage in protracted missions where the direct national interest was unclear. Recalling the trinity presented above, the civilians, already removed from the military by the employment of volunteers, was distanced from the government when they did not have to pay directly for the war through taxation or lending. This combination, however, is fleeting and since the 2008 financial crisis and global recession that followed, the surpluses have been replaced with massive deficits and the ability to incur further debt to pay for such interventions is now gone. The credit cards are maxed out.

A major condition for future interventions will be the generation of revenue through higher taxes and that will quickly reconnect the citizens with their government and directly constrain foreign policy of that nature. It is for this reason that large-scale interventions will remain unlikely unless direct national interests are threatened. Fiscal realities today and the fragile state of the global economy have given new importance to this condition for war. Indeed, money is having a direct impact on readiness and the willingness of countries to respond security issues overseas. The restraint is coming from domestic considerations, not from the perceived salience of the actual issue overseas.

We contend that going to war will depend heavily upon domestic consideration, especially fiscal realities. Despite the low (and decreasing) proportion of citizens serving as soldiers, the connection between soldiers and civilians remains a constraining factor, especially in democracies. Countries like Canada will likely not be engaged in wars like those fought in Afghanistan again for quite some time and the United States, although operating with a different logic, will likely face increased domestic constraints as well to do something when direct, national interests are questionable.

NOTES

1 An early version of this paper was presented at the annual International Society of Military Sciences conference held at the Royal Military College of Canada in Kingston, Ontario, on 25 October, 2012. It has, however, been significantly revised since and the support and insights provided by the *Future Trends* workshop held at Queen's University in April 2014 has been invaluable.

2 Jean-Christophe Boucher, "Selling Afghanistan: A Discourse Analysis of Canada's Military Intervention 2001–2008," *International Journal* 64, no. 3 (September 2009): 717–34.

3 Stéfanie von Hlatky, *American Allies in Times of War* (Oxford: Oxford University Press, 2013), 24.

4 Justin Massie, "Canada's War for Prestige in Afghanistan: A Realist Paradox?" *International Journal* 68, no. 2 (June 2013): 280.

5 Bonnie M. Vest, "Citizen, Soldier, or Citizen-Soldier? Negotiating Identity in the US National Guard," *Armed Forces & Society* 39, no. 4 (October 2013): 603.

6 Stephen M. Walt, "The Top Five Reasons America is Addicted to War" *Foreign Policy*, 4 April 2011, http://www.foreignpolicy.com/posts/2011/04/03/top_five_reasons_we_keep_fighting_all_these_wars; Thomas E. Ricks, "Toss Out the All-Volunteer Military," *Washington Post*, 19 April 2012, http://www.washingtonpost.com/opinions/its-time-to-toss-the-all-volunteer-military/2012/04/19/gIQAwFVTT_story.html.

7 Aaron Ettinger's chapter in this volume.

8 Peter Paret, "7. Clausewitz," in *Makers of Modern Strategy: From Machiavelli to the Nuclear Age*, ed. P. Paret (Princeton, NJ: Princeton University Press, 1986), 189.

9 Carl von Clausewitz *On War*, eds. and trans. Peter Paret and Michael Howard (Princeton, NJ: Princeton University Press, 1984), 89.

10 Ibid., 589.

11 See Samuel Huntington, *The Soldier and the State: The Theory and Politics of Civil-Military Relations* (Boston: Harvard University Press, 1957) as well as more recent articles in *Armed Forces & Society*.

12 See Peter Tikuisis's chapter in this volume as an example.

13 James A. Nathan and Charles Tien, "Casualties and Threats: Conditions of Support for War," *Defence & Security Analysis* 26, no. 3 (2010): 291–2.

14 H. Christian Breede, "Defining Success: Canada in Afghanistan 2006–2011," *The American Review of Canadian Studies* 44, no. 4. (December 2014): 483–504

15 Stig Hjarvard and Nete Noergaard Kristensen, "When Media of a Small Nation Argue for War," *Media, War & Conflict* 7, no. 1 (2014): 66–7.

16 Ibid., 66.

17 Douglas L. Kriner and Francis X. Shen, "How Citizens Respond to Combat Casualties: The Differential Impact of Local Casualties on Support for the War in Afghanistan," *Public Opinion Quarterly* 76, no. 4 (2012): 767; see also Douglas L. Kriner and Francis X. Shen, "Responding to War on Capitol Hill: Battlefield Casualties, Congressional Response, and Public Support for the War in Iraq," *American Journal of Political Science* 58, no.1 (2014), 157–74.

18 Similar data has yet to be compiled for ABCA, NATO, or BRIC states and this development is beyond the scope of this project.

19 It should be noted, however, that consensus on the costs thus far for the 9/11 Wars has not been reached. A recent report by Brown University's Watson Institute for International Studies suggests that the 9/11 Wars are actually costing Americans some $3.7 trillion. The reports suggests the official costs estimates do not account for ongoing entitlements to veterans and – most importantly – over a trillion dollars' worth of interest payments. See Watson Institute for International and Public Affairs, "Costs of War," http://www.costsofwar.org. See also Daniel Trotta, "Cost of War at Least $3.7 Trillion and Counting," *Reuters*, 29 June 2011, http://www.reuters.com; and Elise Foley, "Cost of War in Iraq, Afghanistan and Pakistan to Reach $3.7 Trillion," *The Huffington Post*, 29 August 2011, http://www.huffingtonpost.com/2011/06/29/cost-of-war-iraq-afghanistan_n_887084.html.

20 Stephen Daggett, "RS22926-Costs of Major U.S. Wars," *Congressional Research Service* (2010), http://www.crs.gov.

21 Christopher J. Tassava, "The American Economy during World War II," *EH.net* (2010) http://eh.net/encyclopedia/the-american-economy-during-world-war-ii/.

22 John T. Bennett, "Panetta: Paying for Iraq War on Credit Was a 'Mistake,'" *US News and World Report*, 13 June 2012, http://www.usnews.com/news. See also Robert D. Hormats, *The Price of Liberty: Paying for Americas Wars* (New York: Times Books, 2007).

23 This data was compiled through Wolfram Alpha, using the input of "US Tax Rate 1920–2012," http://www.wolframalpha.com.

24 Foley, "Cost of War."

25 Edward Meade Earl, "8. Adam Smith, Alexander Hamilton, Friedrich List: The Economic Foundations of Military Power," in *Makers of Modern Strategy: From Machiavelli to the Nuclear Age*, ed. P. Paret (Princeton, NJ: Princeton University Press, 1986), 222.

26 Ibid.

Contributors

CHRISTOPHER BARRON is a colonel in the United States Army, currently serving as the district commander for the United States Army Corps of Engineers in New England. Prior to this appointment, he was the United States Army War College Visiting Defence Fellow at Queen's University. He has deployed experience in Haiti, Iraq, Somalia, Macedonia, Bosnia, and Germany.

H. CHRISTIAN BREEDE is a major in the Canadian Armed Forces and an assistant professor of political science at the Royal Military College of Canada (RMCC). Concurrent with this appointment, Major Breede is also a Visiting Defence Fellow at the Centre for International and Defence Policy at Queen's University. He has deployed experience in Haiti and Afghanistan.

PAUL DICKSON is a defence scientist and strategic analyst with Defence Research and Development Canada's (DRDC) Centre for Operational Research and Analysis (CORA). Dr Dickson holds a PhD in military history and was awarded a Canadian Forces Medallion for Distinguished Service for his service in Afghanistan.

ALI DIZBONI is an assistant professor of political science at the Royal Military College of Canada. His research is focused on cultural issues of international security. He holds an MSc and a PhD in political science from Université de Montréal.

AARON ETTINGER is an assistant professor of political science at the University of Waterloo. His research is focused on the political economy of war. Specifically, he is focused on the role that private military corporations play in terms of national and international security. He holds a PhD in political studies from Queen's University.

PETER GIZEWSKI is a strategic analyst for Defence Research and Development Canada's Centre for Operational Research and Analysis. He is working on projects related to international security, specifically how the future security environment can shape military operations. He pursued his doctoral studies in international relations at Columbia University.

RACHEL LEA HEIDE is a defence scientist and strategic analyst at Defence Research and Development Canada's Centre for Operational Research and Analysis (DRDC CORA). Foci include humanitarian assistance, futures scanning, concept development, war-gaming, and terrorism and counterterrorism. Dr Heide is also an air force historian, specializing in the period from 1916 to 1946.

HEATHER HRYCHUK is a defence scientist and strategic analyst with Defence Research and Development Canada's (DRDC) Centre for Operational Research and Analysis (CORA). She holds a master's in war studies from the Royal Military College of Canada and a combined honours degree in law and political science from Carleton University.

CHRISTIAN LEUPRECHT is a professor of political science at the Royal Military College of Canada (RMCC) and fellow at the Queen's Centre for International and Defence Policy.

BOB MARTYN earned a PhD in military history from Queen's University and pursued post-doctoral research on intelligence at Carleton University and terrorism at the College of William & Mary. He is affiliated with both the Centre for International and Defence Policy and the Canadian Institute for Military and Veteran Health Research. His previous military experience includes deployments spanning a year with the UN in Cyprus, two NATO missions in Bosnia and Kosovo, and ten months in Afghanistan with multinational Special Operations forces.

ASA MCKERCHER is the L.R. Wilson Assistant Professor of History at McMaster University and completed a PhD in international history at Cambridge. His research focuses on Anglo-American-Canadian foreign and defence policy post-1945, and his articles have appeared in a variety of fora including *Diplomatic History, International History Review, Cold War History,* and *Journal of Transatlantic Studies.*

ANTON MINKOV is a defence scientist and strategic analyst with Defence Research and Development Canada's (DRDC) Centre for Operational Research and Analysis (CORA). Dr Minkov holds a PhD in Islamic history from McGill University and has written extensively on the Soviet experience in Afghanistan. In 2012, he received the NATO Scientific Achievement Award for developing transition metrics for Afghanistan.

JOEL J. SOKOLSKY is a professor of political science at RMCC and was the Killam Visiting Professor of Canadian Studies at Bridgewater State University in 2013–14.

PETER TIKUISIS is a senior defence scientist in the Socio-Cognitive Systems section at Defence Research and Development Canada (DRDC) in Toronto, Ontario, and holds an adjunct research professorship at the Norman Paterson School of International Affairs at Carleton University. His work includes the science and technology to enhance warfighter protection and performance, operational research and analysis, and terrorism and state fragility. He holds a PhD in mechanical engineering from the University of Toronto.

JAN VON DER FELSEN is a lieutenant colonel in the German Air Force, assigned as Visiting Defence Fellow to the Queen's University Centre for International and Defence Policy. During his military career he was assigned to operational and commanding positions related to air defence, as well as staff positions in national and international headquarters.

STÉFANIE VON HLATKY is an assistant professor in the Department of Political Studies at Queen's University and director of the Centre for International and Defence Policy. Her first book, *American Allies in Times of War: The Great Asymmetry,* was published by Oxford University Press in 2013. She obtained her PhD in political science from the Université de Montreal where she was also executive director for the Centre for International Peace and Security Studies.

Index

References to tables are denoted by the letter *t.*

184, 229, 207; minority and
coalition governments, 6; role of
media in, 224, 225
France: Franco-German brigade
(Mali, 2014), 168; intervention
in Mali, 106, 159, 171; Operation
Sérval, 106, 166; Paris attacks
(2015), 181; relations with EU,
160, 168; strategy in Africa, 165–
6, 168. *See also* Libya, war in
Friedman, Thomas, 100
Fuller, J.F.C., 24
Fund, John, 195

Gadhafi, Moammar, 8, 162, 163,
190n11
Gauck, Joachim, 167
genocide: and R2P, 108; in Sudan,
47, 105
Germany: Bundeswehr, 167, 169;
co-operation with UN, 167–70; fall
of Berlin Wall, 96; Franco-German
brigade (Mali, 2014), 168; as
international actor, 167–9; role in
Africa, 167–9; wars of unification,
22, 24
Gizewski, Peter, 13, 32, 216
grand strategy: American, 206;
Canadian, 194–6, 200–2, 205
Guinea-Bissau, 43, 52, 164
Gulf War: cost of, 227; Operation
Desert Storm, 12, 60, 85.
See also Hussein, Saddam; RMA
(Revolution in Military Affairs)

Haiti, 43, 51–2, 84, 96, 217;
Operation Uphold Democracy, 84
Hart, Basil Lidell, 23
Harper, Stephen, 4, 190n16, 193–4,
203, 205. *See also* Canada
Heide, Rachael Lea, 13, 191, 216
Hezbollah, 59
Highway of Heroes, 214. *See also*
Canada

Hillier, Rick, 204–5
Hjarvard, Stig, 225–6
Hollande, François, 160, 166
Horowitz, Michael, 7
Hrychuk, Heather, 13
human security, 9, 43, 45, 182, 186,
202
humanitarian assistance, 47–52, 186
Huntington, Samuel, 99
Hussein, Saddam, 8, 12, 27. *See also*
Gulf War
hybrid-warfare, 81. *See also* Russia;
Ukraine

IED (improvised explosive device):
American casualties, 56; American
strategy against, 62; Canadian
casualties, 98; cause of traumatic
brain injury, 56; counter-
IED strategy, 56, 61; explosive
ordinance disposal (EOD), 63,
65, 67; impact on public opinion,
56, 59, 88; Joint IED Defeat
Organization (JIEDDO), 64;
monetary cost of, 65–6; mine-
resistant ambush-protected
(MRAP) program, 63–5, 67,
75n38, 77n57; use in 9/11 Wars,
56–7, 59–62, 64, 65–70; use in
Vietnam War, 56, 59
Ignatieff, Michael, 108
international relations theory:
liberal internationalism, 29;
neo-classical realism, 6, 11, 194;
realism, 99, 190n11, 195, 208
Iran: and NATO, 147–8, 162;
nuclear program, 181, 186;
regional interests, 148; relations
with Afghanistan, 147, 148;
Stuxnet attack against, 31, 121
Iraq, 4, 180–1, 183. *See also* Iraq War
Iraq War: financial costs associated
with, 64, 75n39, 76n42, 109,
227; lessons learned from,